P9-BIW-594

Cadogan's Crimea

Cadogan's Crimea

Illustrated
by
General the Hon. Sir George Cadogan K.C.B.
Written
by
Lt. Col. Somerset J. Gough Calthorpe

Atheneum
New York 1980

Text first published under the title
"Letters from Headquarters" by a Staff Officer
by John Murray Ltd. 1856
Second edition 1857
Third edition 1858

This abridged and illustrated edition
published in 1980 by Atheneum Publishers

Copyright © 1979 by Editor Books Ltd.

All rights reserved.

Library of Congress catalog number: 79-88574
International Standard Book Number: 0-689-11022-7

First American edition

Editor: William Luscombe
Designer: Bryan Austin Associates Ltd.
Filmset, reproduced and printed by
Ebenezer Baylis and Son Ltd.
The Trinity Press, Worcester and London
Bound by Webb Son & Co. Ltd.

CAMROSE LUTHERAN COLLEGE
LIBRARY

DK
215
C332 / 30,813

Contents

*Minor changes only have been made to the spelling
of the text and punctuation. The spelling of
Omar Pasha, Inkerman, Sebastopol, etc. have been
reproduced as in the 1856 edition of this book.*

FOREWORD

by

The Earl Cadogan

MY ancestor, General the Hon. Sir George Cadogan, K.C.B. was undoutedly a most unusual and gifted man, especially in his ability as an artist. Between the years of 1854-1855 he served as a colonel in the Eastern campaign and, while on active duty in the Crimea, recorded his impressions in exquisitely executed water-colours. As fresh and alive today as the day they were painted, these pictures, reproduced in this book, capture with acute awareness the tragedy and suffering of war, yet, they also depict observations of scenes, activities and happenings during the interludes in the fighting; festivities, impressions of personalities and even some of the wives who invariably accompanied the armies in those days. The paintings represent an authentic and extraordinary eyewitness account of both the appalling and humorous aspects of life during the Crimean War.

Some years ago, when on a visit to Italy, the late Mr. Hardy Boer was shown these beautiful water-colours which were kept in an album and treasured by my family. The pictures left an indelible impression. Efforts were later made to find a suitable text to marry with the illustrations and it was during this research that *Letters from Headquarters* by a Staff Officer came to light.

The text of this book is based on letters sent home, almost daily, by a fellow officer, Lt. Col. S.J.G. Calthorpe, who recorded in writing the scenes my ancestor painted. On his return to England, Lt. Col. Calthorpe, who was Lord Raglan's nephew and aide-de-camp, decided to publish these letters in book form because he realised how much calumny and abuse were unjustly heaped upon Lord Raglan's head, the man whose judgement in matters of warfare he greatly respected.

It is a tribute to Hardy Boer's determination and drive that, 125 years after the event, the combination of the written word and quite outstanding pictures have now been published by Mr. Christopher Sinclair-Stevenson of Hamish Hamilton Ltd. who shared his enthusiasm for the project. The result is a volume that provides students of military history and others with a fascinating record of a much talked of and criticised episode which to this day is captivating, if not nostalgic.

I wish the book the success it so richly deserves.

Cadogan

London, 1979

CHAPTER 1

Start of the Expedition

WE left the Dockyard Stairs, Woolwich, on April 8th, 1854, at 9 a.m. the band of the Royal Artillery playing us off to the tune of 'Cheer, boys, cheer !' We took the hint literally, and cheer followed cheer from the troops on board as the steamer got into the stream ; we were answered from the shore by the dockyard workmen and the crews of all the vessels near. It was curious to watch the countenances of the soldiers ; some faces so full of hope, and glowing with excitement ; others so sad and dejected that one wondered how they could cheer so lustily. Here you had a young soldier already talking of how he would 'thrash the Rooshians' ; there you saw a veteran with some Indian medals on his breast, vainly endeavouring to suppress the tears that would come into his eyes as he gazed on his wife and little one standing on the wharf, and bidding him farewell, perhaps for the last time. However, all feeling must give way to duty ; in a quarter of an hour everyone was doing something to get things into order. We are somewhat crowded on board : here is the cargo : — two general officers, 10 staff do., three regimental do., 13 medical do. ; a company of 120 men of the — regiment ; 46 officers' horses, one cow, 12 sheep, four pigs, and baggage and food for the same.

Almost three weeks later we steamed into the Bosphorus at 6.30 a.m. on April 24th, following calls at Gibraltar and Malta. On the 23rd we weighed anchor at 6 a.m., and steamed up the Dardanelles; passed the castles of Europe and Asia about 8 a m., and arrived off Gallipoli soon after 10 a.m. On the morning of the 25th we landed early at Scutari. Everything appeared in the greatest confusion ; nobody knew where anybody was to be found, and all and each were looking out for themselves, so that new-comers fared badly.

Spirits and liquors of all sorts were very cheap, and the consequence was that the amount of drunkenness was frightful. The other night 2400 men (!) were reported drunk at watch-setting, and we have not above 14,000 men here altogether.

Two battalions of the Guards, viz. the Grenadiers and the Fusileers, arrived early on April 27th ; the same morning there was a grand review of all the English troops for the inspection of the Seraskier Pasha (Commander-in-Chief). We had about 11,000 men on parade, under the command of Sir De Lacy Evans ; the troops looked very well, although not quite so clean as in England. The Seraskier Pasha came attended by a numerous but very ragged staff : such dirty, untidy-looking

Left: A group of officers in various uniforms near the refreshment tent. In the group are Count Pettitti, chief of the Sardinian Staff, General Windham and Sir Colin Campbell.

fellows, and so badly mounted. The Pasha himself is a very fat man, with a bad expression of countenance, and sits like a sack on his horse. He expressed himself much delighted with the appearance of the troops; but it is also reported that one of our interpreters overheard him say to an attendant, "That the English were very fine to look at, but he dared say they would run away!"

This morning, as we were crossing the Bosphorus to Pera, we saw a salute fired from all the men-of-war; and as we were passing under the stern of the steam-frigate *Terrible*, someone proposed that we should go on board and see the effects of the Russian shot on her at the bombardment of Odessa. Accordingly we went up her side, and were received with that civility that one always meets with from the officers of the Royal Navy. We found that the salute we had just before seen fired was in honour of Lord Raglan, who had arrived in the *Emu* steam-transport, having left the *Caradoc* at Malta, that she might go to Trieste to meet the Duke of Cambridge, who is coming by Vienna.

May 24th, being Her Majesty's birthday, there was a grand review of all the troops. At midday Lord Raglan and an immense Staff came on the ground: then followed three cheers from the troops, but all the bands playing in different keys 'God save the Queen' spoilt the fine effect it would otherwise have had. There were about 16,000 men on parade; and as they marched past no one could help being struck with their appearance. There were some French officers there who had never before seen English troops on parade; they were perfectly astonished, and one of them said to me, "The Guards march as if they were walls advancing." In the evening I went up to the camp of the Guards, where much fun was going on; dancing and singing. They had also erected a sort of monument made of wood, and covered it with evergreens and variegated lamps, which when lit up had really a very handsome effect.

Sir George Brown left on May 30th with his Staff for Varna, and his division followed him yesterday, consisting of seven battalions of infantry, one troop of horse artillery, and three troops of the 8th Hussars. All the sailing transports were towed by steamers. The distance from Constantinople to Varna by sea is about 140 miles. In a few days the Duke of Cambridge's division, consisting of the brigade of Guards and Highlanders, will go up; and after them the 2nd Division, under Sir De Lacy Evans. The whole of the infantry has, I believe, arrived, with the exception of one battalion. The 8th Hussars and the 17th Lancers are the only cavalry regiments yet come, but the transports with cavalry on board are arriving daily. It is very bad policy of the government sending out the cavalry and artillery in sailing transports: many horses die on the voyage, and almost all arrive in bad condition, and are not fit for service for some time after they are landed. Some of the horse-transports have been 60 and 70 days coming out. Far better to keep the horses in England till they have steamers available that would bring them out in 10 or 12 days: in so short a time the horses would not lose their condition, and would therefore be fit for active service the moment they arrived in the East. The commissariat are now getting on with their purchase of baggage animals, and during the last three weeks they have bought some 3000, and I believe many more are collected at Varna.

Yet, if you were to believe the English newspapers, everything we have is not to be compared to the French. Somehow or other, I don't know how it is, but the reporters of the English journals have made themselves very unpopular. They appear to try and find fault whenever they can, and throw as much blame and contempt on the English authorities as if their object was to bring the British army into disrepute with our allies. Altogether they write in a bad spirit, and in a manner calculated to occasion much discontent and grumbling among the troops, and therefore tending to injure the discipline of the army. A few days ago two reporters of newspapers went to Headquarters, and asked for an order on the commissariat for tents and animals to carry their baggage, rations for themselves and their servants, etc.; and when told that no provision could be made for them, appeared to think they were very hardly used, and grumbled not a little, and one, as he was going away, talked about the 'respect due to the press'! In the French army no reporters are tolerated and, though that may be rather too strong a measure, some sort of constraint might be kept on these gentlemen, so that they should not send home the complaints of every discontented man, and keep people in England in constant agitation and anxiety by their reports of *official mismanagement*, which are really oftentimes purely imaginary.

The whole of the 1st Division (Duke of Cambridge's) embarked on June 13th, and steamed away for Varna soon after midday.

I went on board the *Megaera* steam troopship 48 hours later to see the Russian prisoners. There were 12 officers and 202 privates, all belonging to the Russian artillery. I believe they were taken by one of our ships off the coast of Circassia. The officers looked very dirty and grim; the men badly clothed, but fine-looking fellows generally. They get exactly the same food as our sailors, but no grog! at which, I understand, they rather grumble. Lord Raglan went up to Varna today in the *Caradoc*, accompanied by some of his Staff and returned within two days and took up his residence at Lord Stratford's, as he has not been very well. Despatches have arrived from Silistria: the Russians continue their attack, and are daily increasing their trenches, but there is reason to believe the Turks will be able to hold out against them till we come to their assistance.

On the 20th Lord Raglan left Pera for good in the *Caradoc*, and steamed up the Bosphorus soon after 6 p.m. and arrived in Varna Bay on the afternoon of the 21st. He was received by Lord George Paulet and Lord Edward Russell (Captains of the *Bellerophon* and *Vengeance* line-of-battle ships), and went on shore in the barge of the former. Lord Raglan's Headquarters, like those he had at Scutari, are of very humble appearance; they are in a small house at the back part of the town, near the gate leading to the Shumla road.

Varna looks well from the sea; it is prettily situated on the north side of the bay, with high wooded hills behind it. The town itself is like all the rest of the Turkish towns, with its ill-paved streets and tumbledown houses, and, as usual, smells of every sort of abomination. It is all day swarming with troops, English, French, and Turkish. One great drawback to the town is the want of water, and what little there is, is very indifferent. There is a well in the house where I am quartered, but the water comes up green! — it is not bad, though far from agreeable. The fleas are just as plentiful here as at Scutari, and the rats too, only, if anything, larger, — great big grey fellows, that make me shudder to think of. There is a great deal of drunkenness here, I am sorry to say; unfortunately spirits are very cheap, and, I believe, of bad quality. The consequence is, that insubordination is not uncommon. The French have had to make two examples of men who refused to obey some order given them, and, when made prisoners, resisted, and struck a non-commissioned officer; they were both shot. The health of the troops at the present moment is good; but there are a great many cases of diarrhoea.

Just after the rain came on one day I overtook a Turkish officer, riding a very handsome little Arab, and, whilst admiring the horse, I observed that the officer's person was enveloped in a regular Mackintosh coat. It instantly occurred to me that a Turk possessing such a civilised garment must certainly speak a civilised language. I went up to him and found he spoke French; and after a few moments' conversation he told me he was secretary to Omer Pasha, and was then on his road to join him.

On July 1st, the 1st Division marched from their camp near Varna (eight miles on the Devna road), and encamped close to the old ground of the Light Division at Aladyn. The Light Division has moved on to some high ground above Devna, not far from the cavalry camp. Yesterday the 2nd Division marched from Varna to some ground 13 miles from here, between Aladyn and Devna.

Omer Pasha arrived last night in his carriage. General Bosquet's division of the French army, near 12,000 men, came in today; they have marched all the way from Gallipoli, a distance of 250 miles. Marshal St. Arnaud promised Lord Raglan two months ago that this division should arrive at Varna on June 15th and 16th. They are consequently three weeks out of their reckoning;—you see the French sometimes make mistakes as well as ourselves.

On the 5th, there was a grand review of the French army on the heights to the north of Varna for Omer's inspection. Lord Raglan and his Staff were present, as well as the Duke of Cambridge, Admirals Dundas and Lyons, and a large number of English officers, both military and naval. There were nearly 27,000 men on parade, all infantry, except two batteries of artillery, and one regiment of four squadrons of the Chasseurs d'Afrique. The whole had a fine effect as they marched past; on coming opposite the Generals, the commanding officer of each battalion threw up his sword and called out *"Vive l'Angleterre! Vive la Turquie! Vive l'Empereur!"* which was responded to by the troops according to their humour; some made a great noise and others said nothing; poor Turkey came off second best, as one rarely heard any cheer from the soldiers for her. Lord Raglan rode a beautiful white Arab stallion that had been presented to him a short time ago by Omer Pasha. After the review there was a grand luncheon at Prince Napoleon's encampment.

On the following day Omer Pasha inspected some of the English troops, but, as he had already seen the Light Division and some of the light cavalry on his way from Shumla to Varna, it was only thought necessary to show him the 1st Division at Aladyn, a regiment of heavy cavalry, and some of the artillery at Devna. Lord Raglan and his Staff rode out to Aladyn, and arrived there at eight a.m., and shortly after Marshal St. Arnaud and Omer Pasha came in their carriages. The Guards and Highlanders looked splendid, and marched past as only the Guards and Highlanders can. After some simple manoeuvres, the troops, taking the time from the Duke of Cambridge, gave three cheers for the Marshal and three for Omer. They were both charmed with this, and Omer Pasha (who, it seems, knows how to pay compliments) said to Lord Raglan, "It is well known that the Emperor of Russia is mad, but he cannot be mad enough to fight against troops like those!"

12

The monument at Camp Scutari made of wood and covered with evergreens and variegated lamps, which was lit up for the Guards to celebrate Queen Victoria's birthday on May 24th, 1854.

On our way to Devna we met a Maltese who informed us that he had just been robbed by two Turks of 1700 piastres, and he pointed out a thicket where he said one of them was hid. P— — and I rode to the spot and dragged out a scoundrel-looking fellow, and gave him over to some of Lord Raglan's escort, who conducted him to the nearest picket of the Guards, and the following day he was sent in to Varna, and, I believe, is to be comfortably hanged.

It is interesting to assess the personalities of the different Generals. To begin with the head. Lord Raglan, it is needless to say, is much liked by all, but, by those brought often into contact with him, perfectly beloved. I never met a man who had so completely the power of pleasing whomever he chose. It is wonderful how hard he works, and I believe his influence is great with Marshal St. Arnaud and Omer Pasha. H.R.H. the Duke of Cambridge is most deservedly popular for his great good nature, independently of his military qualities. Sir George Brown, although not so popular as some others, is respected more perhaps than any, as being a thorough soldier; his fault may be that he carries discipline a little too far, but anyone must admit that it is an error on the right side. Lord De Ros, the Quartermaster-General, works like a slave; he is certainly rather eccentric, both in his habits and dress, but these are forgotten in his many estimable and amiable qualities. General Estcourt, the Adjutant-General, is very much liked by all who know him; he is one of the most gentlemanlike persons I ever met. I think him perhaps too lenient for an Adjutant-General, whose duties require a stern and rather severe man, and this General Estcourt certainly is not. Don't misunderstand me: I throw no blame on him, only I think his nature too kind and too forgiving for one who is to carry out the discipline of the army. Of the two Generals of cavalry, I fear I cannot say they are popular, although both are thought by some to be good soldiers; but as I know so little in their favour, I had best leave them alone. Active service shall decide. Both have violent and imperious tempers, so if they don't clash ' 'tis passing strange.'

Some officers have been sent up to Kustendij on the Black Sea, about 100 miles north of Varna, to see if a good landing could be made there, and also if the Lake of Karasu, between the sea and the Danube, is navigable. I do not mean to say that it is in the least intended that the army should go there; but only in the event of any large body of our troops being ordered to move across the Danube into Wallachia, it would be one way of keeping them supplied with stores, etc., and advantageous, as it would save so much land-carriage. There would always be great difficulty in marching any large force from here to Silistria into any part of the Dobrudscha on account of the want of water. The better route would be by Shumla and Rustchuk, and so on to Bucharest. However, all this is speculation, and I do not believe anything is settled by the allied Commanders-in-Chief. I suspect they are waiting for instructions from home.

Lord Raglan received despatches from Omer Pasha, giving an account of an affair between his troops and the Russians. It appears that on July 10th a column of Behrim Pasha's division made the passage of the Danube at Rustchuk, and crossed over to Giurgevo, where they were met by a large force of Russians. The main body of the Turks was led by Lieutenant Burke, R.E. (whom I had met at Silistria); he was shot dead at the head of his men, after having killed five of the enemy with his own hand. There was also Lieutenant Meynell, of the 75th Regiment, on leave; he too led a portion of the Turkish troops and was killed. Then Captain Arnold, of the 3rd Madras Light Infantry, who had only arrived at Rustchuk the evening before, fell when leading on the Turks. All this is very unfortunate, but we have the satisfaction of knowing that, owing chiefly to the example of these gallant officers, our allies the Turks were victorious, and held their ground, whilst the Russians had to retire. The Turks are said to have lost 500 killed and 800 wounded; the Russians 1500 killed and wounded; probably 500 more they carried off.

Two Austrian officers arrived on July 11th at Varna, on a mission from General Hess and the Austrian Government, to confer with the allied Generals. They had a long conference with Marshal St. Arnaud and Lord Raglan, but left, I understand, an impression on the minds of both the allied Generals unfavourable to Austria, as they do not approve of the position the Austrians propose taking in the ensuing war. Some of the French go as far as to say that these officers were sent more to see in what sort of state the French and English armies were, and whether preparations for immediate moving were going on.

On the morning of July 19th Lord Raglan sent one of his aides-de-camp to Devna for Sir George Brown. It appears that orders have arrived from home that an expedition is to take place without loss of time against the Crimea; the great point of attack to be Sevastopol. It has therefore been settled that certain officers shall be sent from each of the allied armies, to cruise along the coast of the Crimea, to ascertain the best place for landing the invading army. This afternoon Sir George Brown and one of his Staff arrived in Varna, and they embark tomorrow morning.

On Sunday last (16th), the day on which the order from home for the expedition was received, Lord Raglan also heard that another division of infantry is to be sent out under command of Sir George Cathcart; it is to consist of six battalions of the Line. There are also two more regiments of cavalry under orders, viz. the 4th Light Dragoons and 2nd Dragoons (Greys), besides two batteries of artillery.

I understand that there are several officers of high rank, French and English, and of both services, who strongly object to the proposed invasion of the Crimea, as being far too late in the year for so large an undertaking. I believe those most strongly against it are Marshal St. Arnaud, Admiral Dundas, and Lord De Ros. On the other hand, there are many strong advocates for its being done, on the score that it would be impossible for the army to remain where it is for the winter, on account of Bulgaria being so unhealthy, and it is said that the climate of the Crimea is particularly good. They say that at any rate a landing might be made, and Sevastopol itself not besieged till next spring. I do not think that would do, for the Russians would make it during the winter just as strong by land as it is at the present time by sea. It has lately been discovered that the soil in the neighbourhood of Sevastopol is of a very rocky nature, and mixed with sand, consequently it will only be with great labour that entrenchments of any strength can be opened, and therefore the siege would in all probability be much protracted beyond the usual time necessary for the reduction of a fortified place. Two siege trains have arrived, consisting of 60 heavy pieces of ordnance, and 20 $5\frac{1}{2}$-inch mortars, and a third is expected shortly. The 44th Regiment is employed making gabions and fascines, and I understand the whole of the brigade of Guards are to begin making them to-morrow. The health of the army is not so good as it was; there are many cases of cholera. The French have had it very badly. I was told yesterday by one of Marshal St. Arnaud's aides-de-camp (Duc de Grammont) that they had lost, in one of their battalions of the 5th Infantry of the Line, over 200 men. This was at Gallipoli. They have many men in hospital with cholera here.

The French have marched two of their divisions (General Canrobert's and General Forey's) towards the Dobrudscha; and this morning two battalions of Zouaves embarked from Varna for Kustendij, on the Black Sea, and about 60 miles further north. These are to disembark, and make a junction with troops going by land, a few miles from the sea, at a small place, the name of which I forget. They are then to advance on Karasu, where it is reported there is a small Russian force. The ostensible reason for this movement of the French is to make a diversion and mislead the Russians, and try and make them believe that we are not going to the Crimea. However, it matters little, as of course the newspapers will do all in their power to inform the enemy of any movement likely to take place. Oh, the blessings of a free press! Another reason given for Marshal St. Arnaud's sending these troops is, that he wants it to be said that the French army was the first to be in the field and the first to meet the enemy. I think this all humbug, especially as we could move the whole of our force now with greater ease than the French. I believe his real reason is, that he thinks it likely to stay the prevalence of cholera. The Marshal wanted Lord Raglan to do the same, but he very wisely declined to march any troops into the Dobrudscha, which is notoriously the most unhealthy portion of the Danubian provinces. All our divisions have had orders sent them to change their camping-ground in consequence of the cholera.

I saw Horace Vernet the other day. As I had met him when I was in Algeria, we had some conversation together. He has been sent out by the French Government to paint historical pictures of the war. Rather premature I think. He is somewhat alarmed at the cholera, having felt two slight attacks already. I doubt his staying here much longer, but he has now gone with General Yusuf and his Bashis. He showed me a capital drawing of the famous female Bashi-Bazouk, *Fatima Hanoum*. You never saw anything half so repulsive as this horrid old hag. I had the pleasure of seeing her the other day, surrounded by some fifty followers: it is said she has great influence over these gentry, as they think this dirty old piece of goods a prophetess. There is no accounting for taste, or the wonderful fancies people take.

The preparations for the grand expedition are going on rapidly, and it is said everything will be ready by August 15th. The Turkish fleet cast anchor yesterday in the bay. It consists of one immense three-decker, the *Mahmoudie*, of 136 guns, and over 4000 tons; said to be the largest ship in the world; no doubt the clumsiest. Then there are six liners of from 70 to 100 guns each, two large steam-frigates, and five brigs of war. Admiral Slade is second in command, and carries his flag on one of the largest two-deckers. There is now a proposal that the Turkish fleet, with 10,000 of their troops on board, should make a demonstration at Kaffa (Theodosia) on the day previous to the landing of the allied forces in the Crimea, to take off the attention of the Russian troops in the neighbourhood of Sevastopol from the north side, where it is proposed for us to land. Sir Edmund Lyons and Sir George Brown have been down at Constantinople for the last ten days, making the necessary arrangements for the transport of the army across the Black Sea. They have bought five steam-tugs, and a great number of large lighter-boats for the landing of artillery and horses, etc.

The French, during the last month, viz. from July 14th to August 5th inclusive, admitted into their hospitals at Varna *alone* 1287 cases of cholera. Of these, 705 died, and 563 remained under treatment on August 6th: 100 of whom were convalescent, and 19 discharged for duty. On August 7th, 257 men more were admitted into hospital, and they lost 112, which left 693 under treatment. The news came from our principal medical officer in Varna. Yesterday, August 8th, they broke up their cholera hospital, and had the patients dispersed into the different hospital camps which have been formed in the immediate neighbourhood of the town. They have four large ones for cholera only. In one camp, about two miles from the town, there are 700 men laid up with cholera. But all this is nothing as compared with their losses in the Dobrudscha. It is said that General Canrobert's division has lost no less than 1700 men since the 24th of last month and that they have near 3000 sick. General Forey's division has lost between 400 and 500 men dead, and has brought back 2500 sick! I am told that, on the second evening after the expedition had got into the Dobrudscha, they arrived at the Lake of Karam; and here the troops were encamped during the night, and died like rotten sheep, and literally fell upon one another! The next morning, when General Canrobert saw what had happened, that is, that there were between 200 and 300 men dead and dying, he ordered the retreat back to Varna, first having the dead buried in the lake. It is currently reported and very generally believed by the French soldiers, that many of their comrades were buried before they were actually dead! although doubtless they would have died in the course of a few hours. Still, what a horrible idea, that the sick and dying should be hurried into eternity in so awful a manner!

The two battalions of Zouaves returned by sea, the same manner as they went, embarking at Kustendij, but disembarking near Baldjick instead of Varna, on account of the dreadful way in which the cholera is raging among them. In their short voyage back, only 14 hours, they threw overboard near 300 corpses. So great was their state of panic and confusion, that the bodies were neither shotted, nor sewn up in canvas or hammocks, as is usual. There is consequently a report afloat, that all along the coast, from 10 to 30 miles from here, the shore is strewed with the corpses of these unfortunate French soldiers. All these horrid details were given me by an officer of rank in the Etat Major, and, high as the numbers may seem, I fear there is no exaggeration in them. Altogether this expedition has cost the French,

General Bosquet's division of the French army, near 12,000 men, passing through the Grenadier Guards camp on arrival at Varna. They had marched all the way from Gallipoli, a distance of 250 miles.

and put hors-de-combat, from 8000 to 10,000 men! When Marshal St. Arnaud heard of the dreadful losses his army had sustained, it is said he went to Lord Raglan and tried to get him to put off, for this year, the expedition against the Crimea, but his Lordship answered, that was not a sufficient reason, much as he deplored the shocking mortality among the French.

The Bashis, I understand, are returning, having quite disgusted General Yusuf, who says he will have nothing more to do with them. It appears they fell in with some Cossacks, and, after great demonstrations of preparing to charge and attack, ran away, leaving one of their officers (a Frenchman) to be killed by the Cossacks. Yet General Beatson is going to 'make them a most useful body of troops'.

Lord Raglan went up to Baldjick Bay on Thursday last, on a visit to Admiral Dundas, and stayed on board his flag-ship, the *Britannia*, 120 guns, till the following day. On the evening of Thursday, Sir Edmund Lyons and Sir George Brown, in the *Agamemnon*, joined the fleet, from Constantinople, and then there was a grand Council of War on board the *Britannia* immediately after their arrival. It appears that the 'powers that be' are divided in their opinions as regards the practicability of invading the Crimea, on account of the sickness in the French army and navy. However, these objections have been overruled, and it is now thought that we shall embark on August 25th. The following are said to be the opinions of the Chiefs:—Lord Raglan, Sir George Brown, Sir Edmund Lyons, and Admiral Bruat *for* the expedition; Marshal St. Arnaud, Admirals Dundas and Hamelin *against* it. About three weeks ago, when it was first decided that an expedition should sail for the Crimea, the French declared they would certainly be ready by the 8th of this month. Lord Raglan said he thought the 14th (today) the earliest period at which he could be prepared. A few days ago the Marshal sent to say that he must have ten days longer, and that their arrangements could not be completed till the 20th instant. Yesterday it was officially reported to Lord Raglan that everything was ready for the embarkation of the English troops.

On Thursday night a most destructive fire broke out in Varna, which destroyed in a few hours a third of the town, extending over nearly nine acres of ground. It began in a French spirit-shop, and, as the whole of the lower part of the town is built of wood, it was impossible to put it out. Marshal St. Arnaud was present, and displayed great coolnesss and judgment in the manner in which he directed the troops employed. For some time it was thought that we must have all been blown up, as the great powder magazine was surrounded by burning houses. The sailors sent on shore from the English men-of-war in Varna Bay worked in a manner that excited the admiration of everyone.

The newspapers, especially *The Times*, continue to give us some wonderful information. A month ago, according to that publication, the English and French had a force of 25,000 men at Rustchuk, and by the last post I see we are all gone to Kustendij, and also that Prince Napoleon is staying with Omer Pasha, and other such little bits of news, which, although not *quite* correct, still are very amusing.

The number of deaths from cholera in the English army in Bulgaria amounts to 606, but I am glad to say that it is rapidly diminishing; there are, comparatively speaking, but few fresh cases of cholera, although the hospitals are still full of men who have been suffering from it, and many of whom it is to be feared will die of debility. Once one gets thoroughly weak, it seems impossible in this climate to regain strength. Some of the cavalry regiments have been suffering very considerably, and in the 5th Dragoon Guards four officers have died of it. It is rather strange that, although camped with other regiments infected with the disease, the 8th Hussars have not as yet had a fatal case, although they have lost eight men from fever and other causes. We have also heard that it has broken out among our troops in the Bosphorus. The 1st battalion Rifle Brigade had 150 men taken ill out of four companies, and in 24 hours eight were dead. The French navy still suffer much, it is said that the flag-ship, the *Ville de Paris*, has lost 140 men, and the *Montebello* 230 men! The health of their army is nevertheless improving. In our navy the cholera has almost disappeared. In the *Britannia*, Admiral Dundas's flag-ship, they have lost 120 men. There have been also some cases in the different transports lying in Varna, but fewer than one would suppose.

On August 17th Lord Raglan received a despatch from Colonel Simmons, the English Commissioner attached to the Headquarters of the Turkish army, informing him of the arrival of the Turkish troops under Omer Pasha at Bucharest, and of the rejoicings of the inhabitants thereon. He also said, that from deserters and prisoners it appears that the Russians are in full retreat for the Pruth, and that the impression was, that the allied armies had marched from Varna to the Danube.

Omer Pasha supposes that the Russians, during their retreat from Silistria, must have lost upwards of 16,000 men from sickness. This is perhaps an exaggeration. Moreover, he has so bad an opinion of the Bashi-Bazouks, that he would not allow them to cross the Danube, as they would only bring disgrace on his army by the robberies and atrocities they were certain to commit.

On the evening of August 25th, Sir J. Burgoyne arrived quite unexpectedly. He is to be attached to the army without any actual appointment, as, from being senior to Sir George Brown (who is second in command), he would be cutting him out. He has come chiefly to give his counsel on the best mode of attacking Sevastopol, and is not in any way to interfere with General Tylden, who commands the Royal Engineers, but merely to give his valuable advice and opinion on engineering matters. On August 29th, the whole of the 1st Division and 2nd battalion Rifle Brigade embarked on board seven steamers. There was no end to the work going on in the bay—embarking cavalry, infantry, artillery, stores, and indeed every sort of thing that forms in any way a part or necessity of an invading force.

A despatch came to Headquarters from Captain Drummond, H.M.S. *Retribution*, who had been for some days off Odessa, that he had received information that 40,000 men had left the neighbourhood of that place about a fortnight ago for the Crimea, and that it was stated that the Russian army in the Crimea had been augmented to the number of 140,000 men! All the 'chiefs' laugh at this; the number is too great to be true; and therefore probably the whole is false.

Sunday last 80 staff horses were embarked on board the *Ganges*. The sea was very rough, and it took us some time getting alongside, and then no little difficulty in putting the slings on to already frightened horses. I never saw anything like the pluck of the blue-jackets: they hauled about the horses in a manner that no groom or batman dare do. One horse would not allow the slings to be put under him, and kept on lashing out with one hind-leg in a most furious manner (it was too rough for him to kick with both, as he would have fallen). This beast was delaying the embarkation of the other horses, so one sailor called out to his messmate, "Jack, next time he kicks, lay hold of his leg," which Jack very coolly did, and, to our utter astonishment, the horse stood perfectly still, and only snorted: in another second he was swinging in the air, half-way up the ship's side. The horse, I suppose, was so surprised at this uncommon freedom on the part of 'Jack', that he fancied he had found his match, and surrendered accordingly.

The French (I was told by one of their officers high on the Staff) have lost nearly 7000 men dead of cholera and fever, and have at this moment from 12,000 to 15,000 men in their various hospitals. This number of sick men require upwards of 4000 effective men as extra hospital orderlies, camp guards, and cooks, etc., so that their army is probably 25,000 men less than on its leaving France. The English have lost under 700 men altogether, and we have at the present time in our various hospitals 1900 men under medical treatment; but I am glad to say many of these are but slight cases. For instance, a week ago, we had 2400 men in hospital, and since that period 500 have returned to their duty.

On the evening of September 4th we went on board ship, and early the following morning left Varna Bay and steamed up to Baldjick. Lord Raglan and his personal Staff on board the *Caradoc* lay close to the flag-ship *Britannia*.

Marshal St. Arnaud and the greater part of the French fleet went to sea at daylight on the 5th, and also the Turkish, as the Marshal, though a wretched sailor, was most anxious for a move. We have been waiting in Baldjick Bay until the whole of the allied flotilla is assembled, which it now nearly is. It was a fine sight watching the different great steamers and transports getting into their places. This occupied our attention the whole day, which was fortunately magnificent. The old Admiral appears to amuse himself by signalling every ship in his fleet, giving them orders, etc., and then a minute after cancelling them.

Soon after daybreak on September 9th the *Agamemnon*, *Sampson*, and *Primauguet* joined the *Caradoc*. These vessels started away from the fleets and steered straight for Cape Chersonese, just south of Sevastopol. The expedition still kept on its course for the rendezvous off Cape Tarkan. The French and Turkish fleets are to beat up there as soon and as best they can. During the day there was another long discussion on board the *Caradoc*, without anything being settled. The truth is, that the French army and navy don't hit it off; the former are said to be 'Imperialists' and the latter 'Legitimists', consequently there is a constant jealousy going on between the two. The army complains that the navy throws impediments in their way, and the navy says the army asks impossibilities. The upshot of all this is, that it is very difficult for our Commander to get anything definitively arranged: but, fortunately, Lord Raglan and Sir Edmund Lyons both being good diplomatists, they manage to keep things in their right places.

At a quarter to 5 a.m. next day we first caught sight of Sevastopol, or rather the fortifications, which looked like a small white spot on the horizon: it was not yet day and we were five miles off; 20 minutes later we were within two and a half miles; and, as day broke, the town with its beautiful harbour appeared before us, each moment getting more distinct, and every house and window lighting up with the morning sun. It reminded one of a scene at a diorama, as it got clearer and clearer. Sir Edmund did not think it prudent to go any nearer, as, if they fired and hit the *Caradoc*, as they did the *Fury*, we might possibly go down; for the *Caradoc* is built of iron, and therefore, if struck by a heavy shot, a whole plate might

*Tartar children at Aitodou near
the pass of Korales —*

*Great difficulty in unearthing the above young ladies who
could not be persuaded they were not looked upon in the light
of luncheon, but by baiting a stick with a shilling,
Her majestys effigy had the desired effect, and we ultimately
became very intimate —*

probably be knocked out, which would have been very awkward. We remained for upwards of half an hour gazing at the scene before us, with an interest deeply excited by the thought that there lay the prize for which we were to fight, the great object of the ensuing campaign. The fortifications looked of immense strength, and appeared to bristle with guns. Our being there did not apparently cause any commotion, although probably the early hours prevented people from being about in any numbers. We counted 12 large ships of war in the great harbour, but we could distinctly see the masts of many more in the inner harbour and Dockyard Creek. All this time the *Sampson* and *Primauguet* were within half a mile of us, and the great *Agamemnon* three miles off, so as not to frighten the Russians, I suppose. About 6 a.m. we turned round, and steamed S.E. to Cape Chersonese, on the extremity of which is the lighthouse before alluded to.

The coast from Sevastopol to the cape is generally a low cliff, with a beach; the former varies in height from three to 15 feet; the ground rises gradually, but to no height, and appeared undulating, not unlike low downs. It was proposed by one or more of the Generals, that a landing should be effected here, as the natural harbours north of the cape appeared admirably adapted for the purpose, as doubtless they were. But this was at once put aside, as being far too near Sevastopol, and it might have risked an action before the troops could be all landed. This, of course, is to be avoided if possible.

There were two or three camps nearer the town, but apparently for few men; I should say 5000 quite the outside. On our turning northwards, as we passed again near the town, we observed a vessel getting up its steam, but otherwise our appearance did not seem to cause them any uneasiness. Steamed N.N.E. on to the Belbec river, nearing the land all the time. The mouth of the Belbec presented the same objections as Cape Chersonese, on account of its proximity to Sevastopol: indeed, it is probably within range of some earthen batteries on the heights of the northern side of the harbour. About half a mile beyond this there was a small camp of infantry, not more than one battalion—possibly 1000 men. We next arrived off the Katcha river, which appeared in many respects well adapted as a landing-place. This was the spot originally chosen by the reconnaissance made by Sir George Brown two months ago. The naval men, both English and French, objected to it, as the bay was far too small for our enormous flotilla. No doubt they are perfectly right; if the ships are in the least crowded there will be endless confusion. We then steamed on to the Alma river, 18 miles by the coast from Sevastopol. We found on both banks largish camps: the one on the southern side appeared to be chiefly artillery; the other, on the northern side, infantry—perhaps 6000 men, but two and three miles inland we could see several other camps, quite as large as these nearer ones. There are high cliffs all the way from Sevastopol to the Alma river, say of 80 to 100 feet, except at the mouths of the Belbec and Katcha rivers, when on either side of both rivers the ground gradually slopes down to the sea-shore. At the Alma river we stood in quite close to the land, within half a mile, and two small boats were sent from the *Caradoc* to take soundings. They went within a quarter of a mile of the shore, and found five fathom water,—deep enough for anything. Seeing some sort of commotion going on in the Russian artillery camp, it was thought better to sheer off, especially as we were within easy range, and had nothing wherewith to return the compliment, should they fire at us.

From the river Alma, all the way to Eupatoria, about 25 to 30 miles, the coast is quite low, and anywhere practicable for landing. The only doubt is about water. From all accounts there appears to be a great want of it all along this part of the coast. It was finally decided that the landing should be made about seven miles north of the little stream dignified by the name of the river Bulgânak; the English to land on the strip of land between the sea and Kalamita salt lake; the French just south of them, at a place which signifies in English 'Old Fort', from an old ruined tower which the Tartars are pleased to call a fort. The allied commanders were very anxious to go in close and have a good view of Eupatoria, but a Tartar spy on board informed us that there was a battery of guns to the north of the tower. However, as it was thought necessary to go near and view the place, Russian colours were hoisted on the *Caradoc*, and we stood in as if we were friends. The good people of the town did not seem to know what to make of us, and collected in considerable numbers on the esplanade to look at their visitor. There appeared to be a battery, but no guns in it. The town itself looked clean, though dull; a good many ladies were walking about, and some few soldiers; these were said to be only invalids. It was decided that the town should be taken, if only as a base to fall back upon in case of emergency. Soon after 4 p.m. we steamed away from the rendezvous of Cape Tarkan. We had a lovely day, and it was one of the most interesting and exciting I ever passed in my life.

We arrived on the morning of September 11th about 7 a.m. at the place of rendezvous, 50 miles due west of Cape Tarkan. The whole of the immense flotilla was at anchor in 17 fathom water, and wonderful it was; such a forest of masts, yet quite out of sight of land: it was very calm, hundreds of boats were going about; one fancied that one was inside some great port, and wondered where the land could be. At midday the Admiral made signal to 'weigh anchor', and by 2 p.m. the whole fleet was in motion, with the exception of the *Caradoc*, which remained to be coaled from a vessel that had arrived for that purpose. The *Caradoc* caught up the fleet by 8 p.m. There was every appearance of thunder this evening, and the naval men were somewhat anxious as to this fine weather lasting.

Early on September 12th we made the land (Cape Tarkan), and continued in sight of it the rest of the day. The French and Turkish fleets were observed 15 miles west of us; so the Admiral sent two of our largest steam frigates to render them assistance. At 9 a.m. we 'lay to', to give time to our allies to come up. Later in the day we steamed slowly on, but cast anchor at 7 p.m., in order that the French and Turkish fleets might join us during the night. It rained in torrents for some hours in the earlier part of the night, but afterwards cleared up fine and bright.

We weighed anchor at 2 a.m. next morning, and did not arrive at our destination in Eupatoria Bay till 1 p.m.—the distance only 18 miles. This delay was caused by the confusion into which the flotilla had fallen, constantly anchoring, etc. At 2 p.m. there was a Council of War as to how Eupatoria was to be summoned. After considerable delay it was decided that the *Caradoc* should go close in with a flag of truce. Accordingly the *Caradoc*, attended by the *Sampson* and *Firebrand*, steamed to within a quarter of a mile of the town, having a white flag at the fore. The *Tribune* screw steam frigate was anchored 'broadside on', cleared for action; captain and crew longing for the place to make resistance, that they might have the honour of opening the expedition. When the *Caradoc* got within a quarter of a

French troops passing through an avenue of trees on their way to take up battle positions.

mile a boat put off from her, containing Colonel Steele, the military secretary, and Colonel Trochu, chief of Marshal St. Arnaud's personal Staff, Mr. Calvert to interpret, and Captain Derriman to steer the boat. In the bows of the boat was a white pillow-case by way of a flag of truce. An immense crowd came down to the jetty stairs, and begged them not to land, as they would be put in quarantine. The talking and confusion were such that it was impossible to hear a word said by the officer who had come down to meet them; it was therefore decided that they should go to the quarantine, where they were joined by the governor, an old Major of the Russian army, who informed them that he had only 200 invalid soldiers quartered in the town, and that all the principal inhabitants had left a month ago; also that all the stores had been moved into the interior some time back. He said, of course he could make no resistance, and consequently it was quite at our disposal, adding the inhabitants were very badly off for food, and the Tartar population almost starving. Shortly after the boat returned to the *Caradoc,* and after some consultation it was decided that the town should not be occupied till after the landing of the army, when it is to have a battalion of French, some Turks, and some marines from our men-of-war. We are to land at daybreak tomorrow; and I trust that by the evening the allied armies may have a firm footing on the soil of the Crimea.

CHAPTER 2

Battle of Alma

ON the morning of September 14th, 1854, at 3 a.m., we weighed anchor, and from then till 8 a.m. the transports, etc. were getting into their proper places. There was some confusion in consequence of the French taking up one of our buoys as they left, so in that manner they threw us out by half a mile, which caused much crowding. The French were the first to land. Soon after 7 a.m. they sent a boat on shore with half a dozen men, who erected a flag-staff and hoisted the French colours. Their first flat of troops landed at 8.45 a.m. about two miles south of us. Sir G. Brown and General Airey and their Staffs were the first English on shore; half a minute afterwards a boatload of the 7th Fusileers landed. It was then 9.50 a.m. By 10 a.m. the French had upwards of 6000 men landed, and we about 70. Our being so slow was entirely the fault of Admiral Dundas; for he did not even act up to the programme, drawn out previously on board the *Agamemnon*, which he had signed and promulgated to the fleet. Instead of approaching near the shore, as agreed upon, he anchored upwards of four miles off, with seven ships of the line, two large frigates, and several war-steamers. Consequently, Sir Edmund Lyons and Lord Raglan* did not think it prudent to commence landing the English troops with the few boats they had then at their disposal, and therefore waited a considerable time for the arrival of those belonging to the men-of-war with Admiral Dundas: it was not until the approach of one of the *Britannia*'s boats, followed by others, that the signal for landing the army was given from the *Agamemnon*. Some boats, indeed, did not appear for several hours after the time fixed; all caused by Admiral Dundas's want of co-operation. He has been from the first against the expedition, and, it is said, predicted all sorts of disasters, and, now that he sees everything is likely to go well, he appears to do all in his power to thwart and annoy Sir Edmund Lyons and Lord Raglan. After this most unnecessary delay the landing went on very rapidly; all worked with a will, and the manner in which the naval officers and sailors assisted was beyond all praise. The enemy never made the least resistance to the landing; indeed we saw no troops, except some half-dozen Cossacks, who galloped up to the cliffs and then off again as fast as they came. Strange that they should have attempted nothing, for, although

---

* Lord Raglan left the *Caradoc* early in the morning, and joined Sir Edmund Lyons on board his flag-ship, the *Agamemnon* to witness the landing of the army. The annoyance of both these chiefs was great at the tardiness of Admiral Dundas, as it, to a great degree, frustrated the plans they had decided upon, and delayed the carefully-detailed arrangements they had drawn out for the speedy disembarkation of the troops.

they could not have prevented it, as we were covered by the heavy guns from the fleets, still they might have annoyed us very much and caused great confusion. By 3 p.m. the Light, 1st, and 2nd Divisions were almost all landed — about 14,00 men and 12 guns. Soon after this, Lord Raglan and his Staff came on shore and rode up to the advanced posts of the army. The 2nd battalion of the Rifles had been pushed on to a village five miles inland, called Tagailii: here they had established themselves in capital quarters, and, as it was situated on rather higher ground than any in the neighbourhood, it was well adapted as an advanced post. From it one overlooked the country in front for some miles, every here and there could be distinguished Cossack videttes; but they took good care not to come within range of our rifles. Another advantage this village had, viz. plenty of good water, and it has not yet been found elsewhere.

Lord Raglan rode round the whole of the outposts, and did not return until quite dark, past 8 p.m. Wherever he went today the troops cheered him, and indeed all seemed animated with the most enthusiastic spirits. By night we had landed 23,700 men and 19 guns, with their horses, etc., complete. The French by the same time *said* they had landed 22,000 infantry and 53 guns (but without horses).

I am sorry to say the cholera is still with the armies. We lost on the voyage about 70 men in the infantry dead, and 200 bad cases are left on board. In the cavalry the proportion is greater — 22 deaths, and 104 bad cases left. The French have suffered much more severely; but that is not to be wondered at, as their men are so dreadfully crowded on board their line-of-battle ships. The *Montebello* and *Ville de Paris* each brought 1500 soldiers; the *Valmy*, I hear (it sounds almost impossible), 2400 soldiers! the *Henri Quatre* the same! their other liners in like proportion. I understand they will disembark 1100 men fewer than they embarked at Varna.

By night nearly the whole of the cavalry (1100 horses) were disembarked. Lord Raglan took up his quarters during the day on some rising ground near the landing-place. His camp is a very modest affair, consisting of one small marquee for himself, a bell-tent for stores, and a bell-tent which acts as a sort of military office. His personal Staff have each what are called dog-kennel tents, being about the size of those canine residences. *Violà tout*. Marshal St. Arnaud, on the contrary, has everything on a grand scale. He has a large marquee comfortably fitted up in two apartments, for his bed and sitting room, also an immense Algerine tent as a dining-room, and all his Staff and attendance are equally well off in proportion to their respective ranks.

Lord Raglan rode all round the outposts again, and was very much annoyed to find that during last night the Zouaves had been into the village of Tagailii and robbed the inhabitants of everything. Our men of the Rifles, who were quartered there, interfered as much as possible, but without coming to actual blows it was impossible to stop them. The commanding officer of the Rifles turned out his men, placed sentries all round the village, and made every Zouave put down whatever he had taken; when they had all gone, some of our sentries were surrounded by heaps of fowls, geese, and turkeys, etc. I understand that 12 men of the Zouaves have already been taken prisoners by the Cossacks in one of their expeditions.

This day, the 18th, has been passed in preparations for the march, for we leave here tomorrow morning and advance towards Sevastopol. The French take the right and the English the left.

On the morning of the 19th we marched from Kalamita Bay, or Old Fort, which-ever one pleases to call it, in fact from the scene of the disembarkation of the allied armies. Such was the confusion in consequence of the want of transport that great delay was occasioned, and it was three hours before the army was in motion. The Commissary-General had been misled by some Tartars as to the number of arabas that could be procured. I should say that at least 700 carts would have been required to have carried the proper baggage for the army, whereas not one-third of that number were forthcoming. Then, in consequence of this want of transport, all the tents of the army, with the exception of some hospital marquees, had to be returned on board ship, or rather down to the beach. This took a long time and occasioned the troops employed much labour and fatigue. One of the brigades of the 4th Division, under General Torrens, and the 4th Light Dragoons, were left to

English troops arriving at a Tartar village. Most of the Tartars soon fraternised when they realised that payment was promptly made for any provisions purchased.

clear the beach of the stores, etc., and to embark the sick, of which I am sorry to say there were no inconsiderable number. All this delayed the movement of the troops, and they actually did not start till near 9 a.m. The Turks, in column (about 6000 men), under Suleiman Pasha, were on the extreme right next to the sea; then the four divisions of the French army, General Bosquet on the right next the Turks, then General Canrobert's division in the centre, and Prince Napoleon's division on the left of their army, with General Forey's division covering their rear. Sir De Lacy Evans's (2nd) division had its right resting on the French left, and Sir Richard England's (3rd) division in his rear in support. Sir George Brown's (Light) division formed the left of the English front, and the Duke of Cambridge's (1st) division in his rear in support. Covering the front of our infantry was a regiment of cavalry (13th Light Dragoons) in skirmishing order, and another regiment of cavalry (11th Hussars) in support, with a troop of horse artillery. Some way to our left were the other two regiments of the brigade of light cavalry (the 8th Hussars and 17th Lancers), four squadrons in all: these protected our flank, whilst a mile in rear came Sir George Cathcart with General Goldie's brigade of the 4th Division (the other brigade being, as I before stated, left to clear the beach). The baggage and commissariat of the two armies were drawn more to the rear of the centre of the ground taken up by the troops.

The day was excessively hot, and many men fell out from exhaustion. There were frequent halts during the march, to allow the stragglers to join their regiments again. No ground could be found better adapted for the movement of troops than that we marched over; the only want was water, and from this the troops suffered much. The army arrived at the Bulganak river by 2 p.m. when everyone rushed forward to drink. The distance marched by the majority of our troops was 10 miles, though some had to come much farther. The river, as it is called, proved only to be a small stream, but still the water was good, and consequently most acceptable to our thirsty men and horses. On arriving here a good number of Cossacks were observed on the brow of the hill, at a distance of half a mile. Lord Raglan, being desirous of ascertaining if the enemy were in force beyond, ordered Lord Cardigan forward with the two regiments of light cavalry in advance, to drive the Cossacks off and endeavour to ascertain if any number were in support. Accordingly the cavalry moved on at a trot, and soon came up to where the Cossacks had been, and from there they discovered a large body of cavalry on some rising ground a mile off, there being a sort of valley between them. On this being communicated to Lord Raglan, he ordered up the Light and 2nd Divisions, and sent for the other two regiments of light cavalry, which were on the flank of the army. In the meantime Lord Cardigan had advanced down into the hollow, and thrown out a troop in skirmishing order. The Russians did the same, and the skirmishers on both sides commenced firing at one another. This went on for 20 minutes, and during the whole of that time I do not believe a man or horse on either side was touched. So much for firing on horseback! An officer of the 11th told me afterwards that he had seen a Cossack get off his horse and lead him to the rear; but that was not much to boast of. During this time the 8th Hussars and 17th Lancers came up and remained at a short distance to the left rear of the other two regiments of cavalry. Also the Light and 2nd Divisions had got up just to the brow of the hill, but hardly forward enough for the enemy to see their strength.

Lord Raglan was particularly anxious *not* to bring on a general action, and therefore would not allow the cavalry to attack; indeed, it would have been madness to have done so, as the enemy had five times our strength. The cavalry were consequently ordered to retire by alternate squadrons, which they did as quietly and as orderly as if at a field-day on Hounslow Heath. The enemy advanced slowly, with his skirmishers in front and firing. These movements on both sides went on for some 10 minutes, when what appeared to be a squadron of cavalry came down from the left of the Russians towards our cavalry. When half-way down the hill they halted, and the squadron opened in the centre, wheeled back right and left, and discovered a battery of guns. One of these was instantly fired—the first gun of the campaign. The movement was beautifully done, and did great credit to Russian drill. Lord Raglan ordered our artillery to reply, but, finding that the troop of horse artillery attached to the cavalry of 6-pounders did not reach with good effect, he ordered up the troop of horse artillery and battery attached to the Light Division, both of which had 9-pounders. These opened with considerable effect, and the Russians 'limbered up' and retired in a hurry. The whole affair was the prettiest thing I ever saw, so exactly as one had done dozens of times at Chobham and elsewhere. If one had not seen the cannon-balls coming along at the rate of a thousand miles an hour, and bounding like cricket-balls, one would really have thought it only a little cavalry review.

The Russians fired 16 shot; we fired altogether 44 shot and shell. Our casualties were four men wounded (two amputations) and five horses killed, all of the cavalry. We had no means of ascertaining at the time the loss of the enemy, except by seeing the bodies of several horses lying about; but we have since heard that they lost 25 men killed and wounded. The enemy's cavalry consisted of the 12th (Saxe Weimar) Hussars, and two regiments of Don Cossacks, regulars; the artillery was Cossack artillery, and, as far as their practice was concerned, was certainly good. Their guns were only 6-pounders. The French army was rather more than a mile to our right, and consequently had nothing to do with the affair, and could only look on. Lord Raglan sent Colonel Lagondie (one of the French officers attached to his personal Staff) to Prince Napoleon, to request him to take ground to his left, so as to decrease the interval between the two armies. Colonel Lagondie took and delivered the message to the Prince, but never returned. It appeared afterwards that on his way back he saw what he thought was Lord Raglan and his Staff on an eminence, and rode up to them; being very short-sighted, he never discovered, until quite close, that the horsemen were Russian cavalry on picket. It is needless to say that he was made prisoner. What a prize for the Russians! The first officer taken in the war, and he a Colonel on the Staff. I have been thus minute in giving the details of this trifling affair, because it was the opening of the campaign, and for that reason alone worthy of especial remark.

That night the army bivouacked on the low hills south of the Bulganak river. Lord Raglan occupied a ruined post-house, which had been burnt that morning by the Cossacks. His Staff passed the night outside the house. It was a strange sight seeing the hundreds of watch and bivouac fires; and from the immense extent of ground they appeared to cover, would mislead anyone as to the number of men on the ground. The morning of the 20th broke bright and clear; and soon after 6 a.m. the army was under arms and on the move, marching in an oblique direction towards the sea; for from the nature of the ground, we had, on the latter part of the preceding day, got a mile or two too much inland.

The advance was made in an oblique line, even after we had closed in with the French, the divisions of General Bosquet and Suleiman Pasha being nearly two miles in advance of the left of the English. About 11 a.m. we came within sight of the heights of Alma. The army was then halted, and the allied Generals advanced to the front of our skirmishers, and reconnoitred the enemy's position. Even at this distance we could see that it was a position of immense strength; and what appeared at first sight as dark patches of underwood on the side of the hills, proved to be masses of infantry when examined with a telescope. The plan of attack was then finally settled as follows:—The division of General Bosquet, supported by the division of Turks, were to endeavour to cross the river Alma at its mouth, and, under the protection of the guns from our ships-of-war, to gain the heights, and in that manner turn the Russian left. This done, the two other divisions of the French army were to force the river, and the English the same; but it was clearly understood that the English were not to advance to the attack until the French had gained the heights nearest the sea, and turned the Russian left. The relative positions of our divisions were the same as yesterday, except that the 4th Division, under Sir George Cathcart, marched more in the rear of the 1st, thus forming as it were a deeper side; so that the baggage, etc., which was in rear of the centre of the allied army, was more completely protected against any sudden attack the enemy might make on our flank. After a halt of 20 minutes the advance was sounded, and the troops moved on with an eagerness not observable before, for they saw before them their enemy.

Cholera ravaged the armies constantly. A typical morning scene showing the sick being taken to high ground—in the evening, the dead would be taken down the hill.

30

It may here, however, be as well to give some idea of the position held by the enemy. The river Alma is a winding stream, and at this time of year of no great depth. Here and there are pools, but generally speaking the water was not more than knee-deep. Its banks are very steep, varying in height from four to 10 feet, and on both sides are either copses or vineyards, and occasionally groves of trees of larger size, of which the common poplar is most frequently met with. On the northern side (our side) of the river, the enemy had cut down and removed all trees and brushwood that could in any manner make cover for our men during the attack. There were two villages on that side of the river; one about a mile from the sea (Malamak), opposite the centre of the French army; and the other (Bourlick) two miles higher up, and just in front of our right. Both of these villages were small, not exceeding 50 houses each, but still giving admirable cover for the riflemen of the enemy. On the south side of the river, extending from the sea nearly to the village of Bourlick, is a range of heights, at places almost perpendicular, resembling cliffs varying from 300 to 500 feet above the sea. On the top the ground is level, and not unlike what we had been marching over for the last two days; at a distance of half a mile from this edge, and about two miles from the sea, was an unfinished stone tower, probably intended as a telegraph station. Round this the enemy had constructed a low parapet, in which they had placed some field guns: this was again protected by large masses of infantry. Such was the position in front of our allies, and so strong was it by nature, that the Russians had not thought it necessary to strengthen it further than I have stated, except indeed by having large numbers of infantry on the south side of the river, thrown out as skirmishers.

I fear from my description the reader will hardly understand the nature of the ground occupied by the enemy: I must therefore refer to the accompanying map, which, although rough, will, I hope, show more clearly than my explanation the difficult ground which the British troops had to attack. About 1 p.m., Marshal St. Arnaud gave the order to his troops to advance. We also were approaching the enemy, but slowly, as Lord Raglan did not wish them to be inactive under fire a moment longer than was necessary. The French advance into the river was received by the Russian skirmishers with a well-directed fire, and many of our allies fell to rise no more. However, they went steadily on, and crossed at a rapid pace, driving the enemy up the steep heights before them. Some confusion was occasioned here among the French by the inequality of the ground, and the difficulty of getting up the steep bank of the Alma. Nevertheless, they by degrees formed up on the opposite side, and then commenced climbing the heights in front of them. This delay had given time for the Russian skirmishers to regain the plateau, so that, as the French advanced, the enemy poured upon them a most destructive fire, which they were almost unable to answer.

But to return to the British. Lord Raglan had placed himself in front of the troops with his Staff, and by this time the latter had grown to three times its proper number: that is to say, every officer of the commissariat or medical department who had a quadruped chose to join the Headquarters Staff, as probably the best position for seeing the battle. I should think there could not have been less than 50 or 60 mounted officers. This great number began to be an inconvenience, as it perpetually obstructed the view, and they crowded round the Commander-in-Chief in a manner that in any other service would have been thought highly impertinent,

Plan of the Battle
of Alma
Fought on the
20th Sept. 1854.

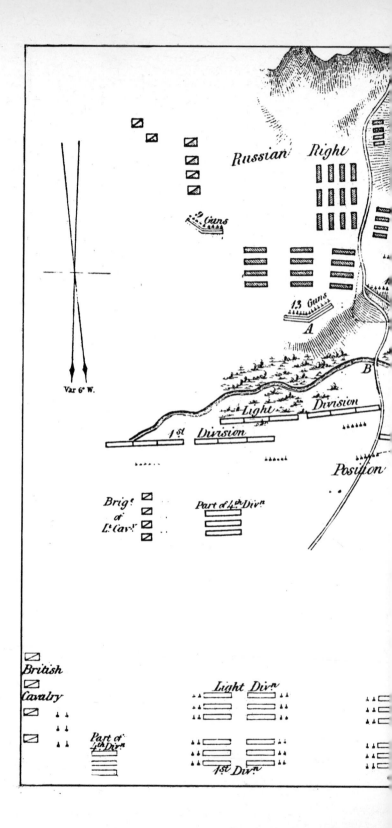

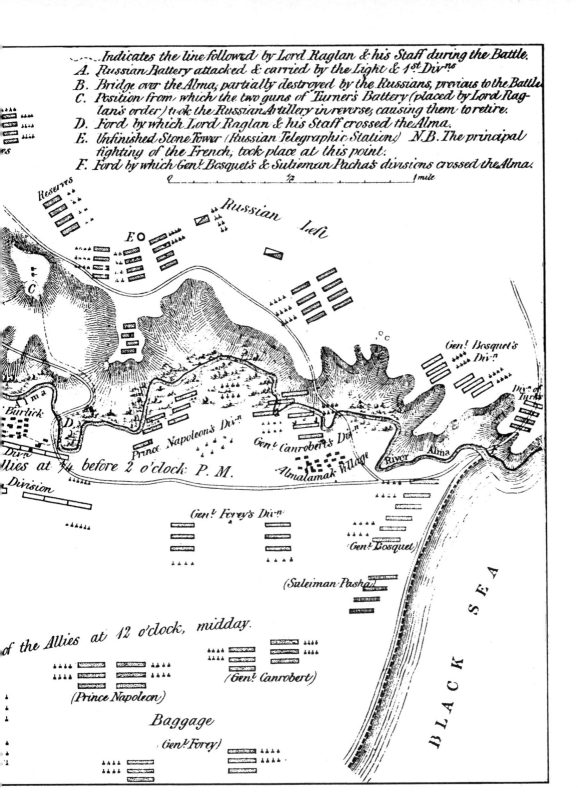

_ _ _ _ Indicates the line followed by Lord Raglan & his Staff during the Battle.
A. Russian Battery attacked & carried by the Light & 1st Divns
B. Bridge over the Alma, partially destroyed by the Russians, previous to the Battle.
C. Position from which the two guns of Turner's Battery (placed by Lord Rag-
  lan's order) took the Russian Artillery in reverse, causing them to retire.
D. Ford by which Lord Raglan & his Staff crossed the Alma.
E. Unfinished Stone Tower (Russian Telegraphic Station) N.B. The principal
  fighting of the French, took place at this point.
F. Ford by which Genl Bosquet's & Suleiman Pacha's divisions crossed the Alma.

Reserves

E O

C

Russian Left

Genl Bosquet's Divn

Divn of Turks

Burliok

D

Prince Napoleon's Divn

Genl Canrobert's Divn

Almatamak Village

River Alma

...lies at ¾ before 2 o'clock. P.M.

Division

Genl Forey's Divn

(Genl Bosquet)

(Suleiman Pasha)

BLACK SEA

of the Allies at 12 o'clock, midday.

(Genl Canrobert)

(Prince Napoleon)

Baggage
(Genl Forey)

and resented accordingly. Someone suggested to Lord Raglan that it would be as well to hint that those gentlemen not actually serving on the Staff had better move off. However, Lord Raglan, with his usual good-nature, said, "Let them stay;" and then added, "You know, directly we get under fire, those not obliged to remain will depart, you may rely upon it." Lord Raglan was quite right. In two minutes the first shot against us was fired by the enemy. I looked at my watch; it was exactly 1.30 p.m. The shot, which was evidently fired at the Staff (the only body of horse-men in sight and the most advanced), fell short and bounded over us with a whiz that made many duck their heads. You should have seen the hangers-on scattered in all directions. There was no more crowding round Lord Raglan!

Lord Raglan, immediately after the first shot, ordered Sir George Brown to deploy his division into line, and then let the men lie down; he also sent the same directions to Sir De Lacy Evans. This was done, and during the time thus occupied the Russians poured an unceasing torment of round shot and shell at them, but as yet without doing much harm. The enemy's skirmishers also kept up a sharp fire against our rifles, who replied to them with equal vigour, but not, I fear, with equal success, as the Russian sharpshooters were behind walls and trees, etc., whereas our men had no cover of any sort or kind. Two batteries of artillery attached to the 2nd Division opened on the Russians, but they had hardly sufficient range to be of much service. Some rockets were also thrown, which we afterwards heard caused the enemy some confusion. The Russians kept a certain number of guns firing at the Staff, and, as for some time Lord Raglan remained on the road, the shot came bounding along half a dozen at a time: anything but pleasant. We were very fortunate, for no one was hit. Two horses were killed, and the shot that struck the last almost touched Lord Raglan's back. He took no more notice of the firing than if he had been at a review; all his thoughts were turned to the French, for he had expected before this to have heard from Marshal St. Arnaud that he had successfully turned the Russian left. He accordingly despatched Commandant Vico to see how they were going on. Vico had not been gone a moment when a French staff-officer came galloping up (I think from Prince Napoleon), begging Lord Raglan to advance, and adding, *Nous sommes massacrés!* Lord Raglan thought it no use remaining inactive any longer, although he had heard nothing from the Marshal. We were losing men every moment from the heavy fire of the enemy, and the troops had now been lying down for nearly 20 minutes. He consequently ordered the whole line to advance. A minute more and the men were on their feet, and the two divisions, Light and 2nd, advanced towards the river. The 1st and 3rd Divisions were then deployed into line and took up the ground in rear of the Light and 2nd Divisions respectively, and in support. Directly Lord Raglan saw them in motion he turned to his Staff and said, "Now we will cross," and, himself taking the lead, he trotted on to the right of the burning village. Here there was a moment's pause as to how we should get over the river: someone suggested a road to the left; down this we went, and found ourselves under as heavy a fire from small arms as I should ever wish to be. There were several burning hayricks close to us, and to see the way in which the bullets knocked out the sparks was wonderful. I know nothing so disagreeable as the singing sound of a Minié bullet; it is quite different from a round ball, which whistles softly as it passes.

We now came to the bank of the river, which here makes a sudden bend; there was a drop of about three feet into the water, for, although this was evidently a regular ford from the road running down to it, and another a little lower down on the opposite side, the enemy had cut the bank away, though in a very ineffectual manner. It was no use waiting to be shot on the bank, so—more from fear, I believe, than courage—I stuck my spurs into my horse and jumped into the river, and to my intense disgust down he went, and I got wet up to my middle; however, he was up again in a moment. My first impression was that he had been shot; it turned out to be a hole the enemy had dug so as to break up the ford; my ducking was of use, for everybody avoided the place where I had been, and no one else met with my misfortune. Just going into the river we were under cover from the Russian riflemen, as there was a high bank by the waterside which protected us. Directly we got into the river, and were crossing to the road on the opposite side, a very heavy enfilading fire was poured upon us, both from cannon and small arms. In the river two of the Staff were shot down; but Lord Raglan, whose presence of mind never left him for a moment, turned to one of his aides-de-camp and said, "Ah! if they can enfilade us here, we can certainly enfilade them on the rising ground beyond. Order up Turner's battery!" He then went on, following the road, which turned away to the right. In a minute more we were among the French skirmishers, who looked not a little astonished to see the English Commander-in-Chief so far in advance. A sudden bend of the road again to the left brought us under the most infernal fire from some of the guns posted, as I before mentioned, in front of our line. We were in a sort of lane with high hedges on both sides, and the round shot came down it in a manner I shall never forget. What appeared to save us was that almost invariably the Russians fired too high, as all the shot went just over our heads. I say all, though more than one horse was killed in this lane, but I think always from ricochet shot. We were not long in this lane, or none would have been left to tell the tale; for presently to our right we came upon a bit of open ground, which gradually rose higher and higher to some 70 or 80 feet. Here there was a sort of landing-place, and from it could be seen the whole of the Russian guns almost in line with us. Lord Raglan at once perceived the immense importance of getting guns up here, where they could enfilade all the Russian artillery. One, two, three aides-de-camp were sent to know why Turner's battery did not arrive.

During all the time I have been recording the movements of the general Staff, the Light and 2nd Divisions had been advancing. Sir George Brown took his division into action, with his right resting on the road, and with a certain interval between him and the left of the 2nd Division. The Light advanced in admirable order; but in crossing the Alma, the banks of which were very rugged and steep, they got into some sort of confusion, and during the whole time the Russian riflemen kept up a most murderous fire upon them from behind the walls of a vineyard which was just the other side; nevertheless these brave men moved on regardless of the severe loss they were every moment sustaining. The 2nd Division advanced at the same time as the Light, but, in consequence of the burning village of Bourlick being in their immediate front, they were not able to advance in one line. One brigade, under General Pennefather, marched on the left of the village, and then crossed the river, leaving the bridge to their left; whilst the greater portion of the other brigade, under General Adams, went down the road to the right of the village and forded the river just below where Lord Raglan immediately after took his station. The 2nd

Division had in front of them a cloud of infantry skirmishers, who caused them very heavy loss in crossing the Alma. They were also under the direct fire of the 18 guns placed in line across the valley; one of these guns they afterwards captured.

The Light Division crossed the river rather sooner than the 2nd; they then got into the vineyard, and as it was impossible to form-up into regular order, from the natural obstacles of the ground, without a halt of some minutes, Sir George Brown urged on his men, and so they advanced, driving the Russian skirmishers and rifle-men before them at the point of the bayonet. But their most terrible time was yet to come: directly they got out of the vineyards double the number of guns opened upon them with grape and canister. In spite of the numbers mowed down, the remainder never flinched, but kept up a telling fire upon the Russian gunners. On they went, and after a time actually reached the Russian battery: then commenced a regular hand-to-hand encounter, the Russians defending themselves with great bravery, but our men fighting with that English determination which almost invariably overcomes every obstacle. For a minute a Russian gun was captured by the 23rd Regiment, but immediately after our men were overpowered by numbers. A fresh column of Russian infantry had come up in support of their beaten com-rades; and the English, being reduced to half their former strength, were obliged to relinquish the hold they had gained, and the division was compelled to give way before the overwhelming forces of the enemy. Still, however, although retiring, these brave men never turned their backs on the Russians, but kept up a regular and effective fire; and wherever the enemy attempted crossing bayonets with them they invariably repented their temerity.

It was just at this time that the Brigade of Guards came upon the left of the Light Division, and the brigade of Highlanders again on *their* left. This magnificent division—the flower of the British army—had crossed the river rather higher up than the Light Division, and consequently were on its left. The attention of the enemy being chiefly taken up in repelling the attack of Sir George Brown, the 1st Division had formed-up after crossing the Alma; and although they incurred con-siderable loss in so doing, they nevertheless advanced in most beautiful order—really as if on parade. I never shall forget that sight—one felt so proud of them. Lord Raglan had been looking on all this time, having arrived on the high ground before alluded to just as the Light Division advanced up the hill. When he saw the 1st Division coming up in support, he said, "Look how well the Guards and Highlanders advance!" An aide-de-camp came up at this moment, and reported the arrival of two guns of Turner's battery. Thank God, the guns at last! The delay arose from the fact that in crossing the ford a wheel-horse of one of the guns had been killed by a round shot, which caused great confusion, and completely blocked up the passage of the river for the time being. I believe also several artillerymen were wounded at the same time. At last two guns were got over, but they arrived at the spot where Lord Raglan was without any gunners. However, this was no time for delay, so the officers of General Strangway's Staff dismounted and served the guns themselves. The first shot fired fell too short; it was aimed at the Russian 18-gun battery, which was causing our 2nd Division in its immediate front, and the Light Division and brigade of Guards on its right front, great loss. Our guns were only 9-pounders, and the distance was considerable. The second shot went through a Russian tumbrel, and killed two horses. Those two shots were sufficient: the

Russian General, seeing that he was taken completely in flank, gave orders for his artillery to limber up. This they did admirably, but, during the time, our two guns kept playing on their retiring artillery, causing them great loss; the gunners and two more guns of Turner's battery having arrived, the firing went on rapidly.

But to return to the 1st Division. They were advancing in beautiful order, and marched straight on the Russian battery; when halfway up the hill, the Fusileer Guards were, to a certain extent, thrown into temporary confusion by the left of the Light Division, who were retiring. This momentary check caused them great loss, but, after a minute or two they rallied, and soon rejoined their comrades. It was then that the guns directed by Lord Raglan came into action, and, as I mentioned before, after the second shot the Russian artillery limbered up and began to retreat. Thus the heavy cannonade which the Light Division had been under was at a most important moment arrested and thus spared the Guards. I say the Guards, because the brigade of Highlanders, being more on the left, were almost entirely out of the line of fire, and consequently escaped with comparatively trifling loss. Directly the Russians had withdrawn their guns, three heavy masses of infantry advanced slowly down the hill. It was an anxious moment, for, if they only had courage to charge, their very weight must have swept our thin line before them. I should say these three columns could not have numbered less than 8000 men, for they were three entire regiments, which as yet had not been into action, each regiment nominally consisting of 3000 men; yet such was the imposing air and perfect formation of the British troops opposed to them that they never advanced out of the slowest walk. The 1st Division paused for a moment—it was only to 'lock-up' more closely. Someone said to Lord Raglan, "The Guards are going to retire;" but he knew them better, for he said, "No such thing; they'll carry the battery. It's time for us to go and join them." Leaving directions with Captain Turner to fire upon the Russian columns of infantry advancing down the hill opposite against the 1st Division, he descended into the valley, and rode over it in the direction of the Guards. Before we had got half-way we saw the 1st Division and the Russian columns approaching towards one another, at a distance of 60 yards apart; the brigade of Highlanders having been brought round so as to take the Russian columns in flank, the whole division sent in a withering volley, which perfectly staggered the Russians, literally knocking over every man in their two front ranks. The enemy stopped, fired a random volley, turned, and fled, without another attempt at staying the victorious course of the British troops. The moment the Russians turned, down went the bayonets, and the whole division charged up the hill, dashing through the battery, and capturing a gun which some Russian artillerymen were in the act of carrying off. Cheering as they went, they bayoneted hundreds of the flying enemy. They were followed by the Light Division, which had been re-formed and even assisted the 1st Division in repelling the advance of the Russian masses of infantry. The 2nd Division advanced also, and charged up the valley; they captured a gun and limber complete, besides driving the enemy like sheep before them. All our artillery were now over the river, and came into action on the knolls and high ground at intervals in the valley, the retreating enemy losing hundreds of men.

In the meantime our allies had carried all before them; after a most sanguinary struggle at the unfinished stone tower which I mentioned, they succeeded in driving the enemy off the field. The Russians, beaten everywhere, retreated as fast as possible. Many hundred men threw away their arms and accoutrements to facilitate their flight; and as the Allies advanced, they found the ground strewed with muskets, knapsacks, cartouch-boxes, great-coats, and helmets, long after the killed and wounded had ceased to fall.

On the further heights, about a mile and a half from the Alma, the British troops ceased their pursuit. And then arose such a cheer!—a cheer from 20,000 victorious men!—even some of the poor wounded fellows joined in it. I shall never forget that cheer as long as I live; it was indeed thrilling; I almost pitied the fallen enemy, it must have been so galling to them, as I heard a man of the Guards say to a comrade, "I say, Bill, pleasant for them poor devils (pointing to some wounded Russians) hearing our chaps cheer so." The men were tired, and many almost exhausted for want of water. Lord Raglan rode up and down the line of troops, the men cheering him vociferously. There was such a shaking of hands; one felt very chokey about the throat, and very much inclined to cry, as one wrung the hand of a friend; and "God bless you, old fellow—so glad to see you all right!" and like expressions, were heard on every side between brother officers. It was a touching sight to see the meeting between Lord Raglan and Sir Colin Campbell. The latter was on foot, as his horse had been killed in the earlier part of the action. He went up to his Lordship, and, with tears in his eyes, shook hands, saying it was not the first battle-field they had won together, and that now he had a favour to ask, namely, that as his Highlanders had done so well, he might be allowed to claim the privilege of wearing a Scotch bonnet. To this Lord Raglan gave a smiling assent; and, after a few more words of friendship, they parted to their several duties.

The brigade of light cavalry had taken no part in the battle, having watched the flank of the army. But now they arrived on the left of the Highlanders, having been ordered up some time previous, together with a troop of horse artillery, which advanced somewhat and fired a few rounds into the still retreating Russian columns; but, although at first they did great execution, the enemy were soon out of range, so they were not able to do them more harm. Lord Raglan now ordered the brigade of Guards, 2nd Division, and 4th Division (which had taken no part in the action), up the opposite heights, commanding the road to Sevastopol. The cavalry went in front of the infantry, and from some misconception of orders no prisoners were allowed to be taken. An officer of the 8th Hussars, who was somewhat in advance with his troop, and who had captured some 60 or 70 Russian soldiers, was ordered to let them go again, quite as much to the astonishment of the Russians who had been taken, as of the Hussars who had captured them. The battle was over at 3.40 p.m. by my watch: that is to say, the last cannon-shot was fired at that moment by the Russians, but far out of range. I suppose it had been intended as a defiance to us.

Nothing struck me more during the day than Lord Raglan's wonderful calmness and presence of mind during the whole battle. He rode everywhere, with round shot, shell, and musket-balls flying about him, with an indifference that was really remarkable; never got apparently excited in voice or manner, and might just as well have been riding in Rotten Row in Hyde Park. Shortly after on these heights Lord Raglan met Marshal St. Arnaud, where, after mutual congratulations, Lord Raglan wished very much that some pursuit should be made of the retreating Russian army. He offered our cavalry, and I think two or three batteries of

Pipers of the 42nd Highlanders. On being captured, the Russian General Karganoff said that he admired these 'savages without trousers'.

artillery, but said the infantry had suffered so much that they could not well advance without weakening too much the English force. Marshal St. Arnaud replied that he could send no infantry, and that his artillery had exhausted their ammunition : indeed he appeared to think that quite enough had been done. Lord Raglan saw there was no help for it, and therefore much against his will gave up the pursuit. The French had upwards of 12,000 men who had never been actually engaged, besides the division of Turks (6000 men); whereas we had only the 3rd Division and a portion of the 4th, in all perhaps 7000 men, that had not taken a part in the action; in fact, not more than sufficient for the immediate necessities of the camp. It was a great error on the part of the French, and one of which they repented when it was too late. The enemy had so large a body of cavalry (about 3000 regulars, besides as many more Cossack irregulars), that it would have been madness to have sent our small force alone, consisting of some 900 horses, all of whom were much fagged with the previous days work, besides which, if our cavalry were absent, in the event of any Cossacks appearing in our rear, we should have been obliged to have kept all our infantry under arms, and the troops would have been perpetually harassed. Indeed I am not sure that, except with a large force, much could have been done against the retreating army, for after the first mile or so they got into some order, and placed heavy masses of infantry and artillery in their rear, who had never taken part in the battle—the reserve troops.

On the more distant heights now occupied by the British troops a Russian General named Shokanoff was taken prisoner, and, when Lord Raglan and his Staff came up, he was sitting on one of the gun-limbers of Captain Wodehouse's battery, looking perfectly comfortable. On being questioned, he said that he was a General of one of the reserve brigades, and that he had been thrown from his horse, and being an old man could not get on again without help, and as his men were all then retreating as fast as possible he could obtain no assistance, so he lay down on some straw, where he was taken prisoner by some of our artillerymen. He stated that the Russians had about 42,000 infantry on the ground, about 80 or 90 guns, and 6000 cavalry; that they had come to fight against 'men', not 'devils'; and finished his account by saying that, as he was an old and almost useless man, he hoped the English General would send him to Sevastopol, or allow him to follow his comrades. Lord Raglan replied that was impossible, but that he would be taken great care of, and every respect shown him, and, as the accommodation in camp would not be first-rate, he should go immediately on board ship, and he would send him to the English Admiral, who would receive him with all hospitality. The poor soul said he had never been on board ship in his life, and had a particular aversion to the water. Nevertheless that evening he was sent down to the shore and taken on board the *Agamemnon*, where Sir Edmund Lyons put him up and treated him like a friend.

Going over the field of battle was a dreadful sight, everywhere torn and mangled bodies of brave soldiers, English, French, and Russians, but three of the latter to one of the two former. In some places where the fight had been hotly contended, the dead and dying were lying on one another, and their groans and piteous cries for water were heartrending. Lord Raglan, till a late hour at night, was giving orders and instructions for the accommodation of the wounded. One of his two tents was given up for the use of some wounded and sick officers. The remaining houses in the village of Bourlick were turned into field hospitals, and here might be seen the surgeons hard at work at their terrible but merciful duty, their arms covered with blood, the floors strewed with limbs just amputated, and slippery with gore. The enormous number of wounded quite overpowered the unceasing efforts of the medical officers, who worked all night without rest, and many were quite knocked up, and had to give in for a certain time. The first night between 400 and 500 wounded were brought into the field hospitals, but this was only a third of the British; there were from 900 to 1000 Russians lying about in all directions. The cholera was also at work and swept off many who had taken part in the battle. Poor General Tylden (commanding the Royal Engineers) died of it during the night.

I was up at daybreak on the morning of the 21st, and, filling my flask and a bottle with weak brandy and water, I sallied out to walk over the field of battle. The poor wounded were far more quiet than the previous evening; many doubtless had died during the night, and many were just too exhausted and weak to do more than moan. I found all glad of something to drink, and my little store was soon finished, and then I went back for more. Although it was only just light, numbers of our men were going about among the wounded, giving them drinks of water from their canteens. Many told me they had been doing so all the past night. God bless them for it. It was a horrible scene—death in every shape and form. I particularly observed that those shot through the heart or forehead appeared all to have died with a smile on their faces, generally speaking lying flat on their backs, with the arms spread out and the legs rather apart. Some looked so happy, poor fellows! that one felt comforted, and thought that they, at least, were now where no sorrow is. Those who appeared to have died in the greatest pain were shot through the stomach; these had always their legs and arms bent, and with all the expression of agony on their faces.

One man, whose leg was dreadfully shattered with grape-shot, and to whom I offered some drink (it was the last drop in the bottle), said, "Oh, Sir, if you would give it to that poor chap there, he has been very bad all night; he is shot through the chest; may be a drink would make him easier." I went to the man indicated, and found him hardly conscious; however, he swallowed what I offered him, and gave me a smile of thanks that was worth any amount of trouble to receive. I fear he must soon after have died, as death was stamped on his countenance even then.

In the course of the morning there was a conference between Marshal St. Arnaud and Lord Raglan; the former wished much to advance and follow the enemy. To this Lord Raglan would not listen; he said he had nearly 3000 wounded English and Russians, and that, as we were over three miles from the sea, it was quite impossible to move them all on board ship under two days. The Marshal said he had lost over 1200 men *hors de combat*, and out of that number 1000 wounded had already been moved on board ship, or would be so by the evening. I say, that is what the Marshal *said*; but everybody else said it was a great exaggeration. I know General Forey, who went over the whole of their field of battle, put their loss at between 700 and 800 at the outside; but he also added, that since leaving Kalamita Bay they had lost nearly 300 men dead from cholera; and it was stated by several French officers that this number had been added to the list of killed and wounded at Alma! It appears strange that, if the French had 1200 men *hors de combat*, they should only have three officers killed, which is all the Marshal admits. It is notorious that the French officers always go in front of their men, and consequently are much exposed. The greater portion of the French wounded fell within a mile from the beach; and they also had a number of large waggons, not ambulance waggons, but store waggons, and these they used to carry down the wounded from the heights to the sea-shore; they were then transferred on board ship.

A Russian general officer was brought in and placed in a tent at Headquarters, close to which had been established the field hospital for the Russian wounded. He was dreadfully wounded; shot in the hip and bayoneted in the stomach. He is Major-General Karganoff, and commanded one of the brigades in the battle that were driven back by the Guards. He was a fine-looking old man of some 60 years of age, and suffered much during the earlier part of the day, but towards noon he became easier: mortification had set in, and, although dying, he was in far less pain. Mr. Calvert, attached to Headquarters, and who speaks Russian perfectly, went and talked to him. General Karganoff said that he had one consolation, which was, that he had received his wounds from the Guards, from the Royal English Guards! "Oh!" he said, "with troops like those, you can beat anything." He also said that he admired "the savages without trousers," meaning the Highlanders.

CHAPTER 3

Surrender of Balaklava

WE arrived at Balaklava on September 26th, 1854, having thus secured a base to commence operations against Sevastopol, and land the siege train, etc., for the reduction of that place. The following morning Lord Raglan went early, accompanied by the general officers of his Staff, and had a long consultation at the French Headquarters, which was somewhat in advance of the village of Belbec, on an eminence in rear of the ground taken up by the French troops. The point discussed was, in what manner Sevastopol should be attacked. Here were the Allies only four miles from that town, and yet it was very difficult to say which was the best mode of advancing on the place so as to attack it with a good chance of success, or, in the event of a repulse, to have a safe base on which to retreat. I understand some of the Generals wished for an immediate assault to be made on the forts on the north side, and when in possession of them they were under the impression that Sevastopol would be in our power: but this was thought rather a desperate mode of proceeding. The French had carefully reconnoitred these works (having them in their immediate front), and declared that it was impracticable to attempt to capture them by a *coup-de-main*, and positively refused to do so. The most powerful outwork of Sevastopol, called by us the 'Star Fort', was in the centre of the plateau then before us. Being a regular work of considerable extent, in fact a small fortress or citadel, it would in all probability require a regular siege to reduce it. As it was situated on ground far above the sea, our fleets would not be able to render any assistance. Besides these objections, in the event of breaking ground on the north side there would be great difficulty in landing the necessary stores and the siege-trains, the only place available being the mouth of the river Belbec, which was within range of the guns from the 'Star Fort', besides being at the present moment completely commanded by what is called the 'Wasp' battery—one very difficult to take from its peculiar position. At this place landing could only be effected in fine weather; and even then, if the wind was strong on shore, it would be impracticable, so that we should stand a chance of being cut off from our supplies. There was another drawback to the plan of attacking the north side, which was, that on our left flank was a dense wood extending some miles inland. We should consequently have been obliged to keep large numbers of troops perpetually in it to prevent the enemy from collecting in force under its cover, and so attacking our flank and rear. One other objection to the plan was, that, even in the event of our getting immediate possession of all the works on the north side, it was very questionable whether the south side would be in our power. The batteries that defended the south were equally massive and as well armed as those on the north side, and we should only have the advantage over them of a few feet elevation. In course of time we might batter down the town, possibly only the nearer part; but that would not necessarily compel the enemy to surrender or even abandon the position.

All these objections having been taken into consideration, it was resolved not to sit down before the north side; there was, therefore, no alternative left but to attack the south. Then came the question of how to get there. It was proposed by the French that the army should force its way down the road which leads across the head of the harbour of Sevastopol, and between the two Inkermann lighthouses, and, following that road, gain possession of the plateau beyond, which extended all the way to the sea. To this there was one great objection, viz. that we should be exposed to an awful fire from the ships in harbour whilst crossing its head, and also that the Russians would be made immediately aware of our intentions. Sir John Burgoyne then brought forward a paper proposing that a flank movement should be made by the Allies, that they should move off in an easterly direction, gain the high road from Sevastopol to Batchi-Serai, and then turn south and march on Balaklava, which, taken by surprise, would doubtless fall without much loss into our hands. We should in this manner possess a harbour said to be admirable; or, if that was not found practicable, we had still only to advance and take possession of the bays near Cape Chersonese, which would form good harbours for landing stores, and for the requirements of the army. There was another advantage in this proposition, namely, that the enemy would in all probability be completely misled by the flank movement. They would probably imagine that we were marching on Batchi-Serai, so as to cut off Sevastopol from assistance or supplies. This paper of Sir John Burgoyne's was strongly seconded by Lord Raglan, and, I believe, was also highly approved of by Marshal St. Arnaud and General Bizot (the French *chef du corps du génie*). It was finally settled that the flank movement should be immediately put into execution, and, as the English were on the left, they were to lead the way. The direction to be taken was south-east, along a range of heights that overlook the ruins of Inkermann and the Tchernaya river, until we arrived at the road before mentioned; the army was then to follow the road down the heights into the plains below, and, after crossing the Tchernaya river, advance on Balaklava. Information of the intended movement was sent to the Admirals, that they might co-operate with the land forces in the event of opposition being made by the enemy to our taking possession of any of the harbours before mentioned.

Our cavalry were now ordered in advance through the wood; then followed the artillery of the Light and 1st Divisions along a sort of track — it could hardly be called a road. The artillery was protected on its left flank by the 2nd Battalion of Rifles; behind them came the Light Division and 1st Division in column of regiments; then the 2nd; then the 3rd. These were followed by the French and Turks: the division of Sir George Cathcart as usual protecting the rear. The infantry had very hard work marching through the wood, especially those in front. The road was left entirely for the artillery and the baggage of the armies.

During the time the army was getting into motion, Lord Raglan and his Staff rode on towards Sevastopol to reconnoitre the works. The first glimpse we had of the town from the land was certainly very striking; there appeared a great number of stately buildings, some of large size, probably barracks. Then there were several handsome churches, and many large private houses with green roofs to them. All the buildings were of white stone, and, with the sun on them, quite dazzled one.

After a careful reconnaissance of the town, Lord Raglan followed the road which the artillery had been ordered to take, and, trotting on, placed himself at the head of the column on the line of march. After proceeding for about four miles through the forest, the trees became thinner, and it was evident that we should soon be clear of them. Lord Raglan had been for some time wondering that we had not come upon the cavalry, who had been ordered in advance, and therefore sent two of the officers of his Staff into the wood on our right to try and find them. Two Hussars of the escort and a staff-officer were a hundred yards or so in advance of the Headquarters Staff; these all at once came back, and reported that there were Russian troops on a road just in front of them. General Airey rode forward with his aide-de-camp to see what they were, and, returning in a minute, announced that it was evident we had come upon a Russian convoy or troops on the line of march, as there were numbers of waggons guarded by infantry passing northwards along a road at right angles to the one by which we were marching. Lord Raglan sent again some of his Staff to search for the cavalry, and also to hurry up the 2nd battalion Rifles, who were close by in the wood to the left, and the Light Division in their rear. The horse artillery were ordered to be in readiness to advance immediately the cavalry got up; and Lord Raglan's escort, consisting of a troop of the 8th Hussars, under the command of Captain Chetwode, were thrown out in skirmishing order in front. After a pause of a few moments the vanguard of the cavalry came up, and just at the same moment the Russians got the alarm and began to run; directly it was seen that they were taking to flight, it was very properly supposed that they were not in force, so the cavalry that had arrived were sent in pursuit, and a troop of horse artillery. The guns opened from some rising ground on the fugitives, causing them some loss. One party of Russians rallied for a moment, and gave Captain Chetwode's troops a volley; but as every bullet went over their heads, they must have been too frightened to take the least aim. The Russians abandoned all their waggons, and fled into woods on either side of the road, where many were followed by our men, and killed, or taken prisoners, according to the amount of resistance they displayed. The Scotch Greys, especially, seemed determined to make up for not having been at Alma, by pursuing the enemy with great perseverance into the thickest parts of the wood near the road. This was continued for a distance of two miles along the road, until, coming to a steep hill, which descended into the valley of the upper Belbec, it was thought best to recall the troops. A large quantity of baggage thus fell into our hands; I believe about 70 waggons and carts, out of which were six for small-arm ammunition; these, as being quite useless to us, were ordered by Lord Raglan to be destroyed, and were accordingly blown up by Captain Fortescue of the Royal Artillery, and made a grand explosion that shook the ground for a long distance. It must have had a pleasing effect on our enemies. The rest of the waggons chiefly contained black bread for the troops, of no great value. There were also several carts belonging to officers of the 12th Hussars. We took a few prisoners, amongst whom was a Russian officer, a captain of artillery, who was found seated on a baggage waggon quite drunk. He had a champagne bottle in his hands, which he offered to us, only unfortunately it was empty. I heard that some were lucky enough to find a case of champagne, which was not long in being disposed of.

The troops were allowed to pillage such of the waggons as did not contain anything of use to the commissariat or artillery; and, consequently, in a few moments the ground was strewed with every sort of thing—handsome Hussar uniforms, rich fur cloaks, every kind of under-garment, male and female. Several wigs I saw being offered for sale, amidst the laughter of the men. French books and novels of an improper kind were not unfrequently met with in the baggage of the Russian officers. All these were offered and disposed of to the highest bidder.

In the late afternoon, about 4 p.m., the line of march was continued from the heights of Mackenzie down the road into the plains below; as we advanced into it the country again assumed the same downlike appearance that it had worn previous to our reaching the Belbec river. The heights of Balaklava were to be seen some four miles in our front. At the foot of the hill we were descending, runs the Tchernaya (or Black) river, a stream of some importance, seeing that it supplied the docks of Sevastopol with water, by means of an aqueduct, which, beginning at the village of Tchorgoun, from there was carried, at an elevation some 10 feet above the river, until it reached the town.

The army bivouacked by the Tchernaya, the centre being at a stone bridge called 'Tractir' on the maps; the Light and 1st Divisions crossing it, and occupying some high ground on the southern side; the remainder staying on the north. Lord Raglan and Staff also bivouacked in the open air, close to the river. As none of his Lordship's baggage had arrived, being still in rear of the French and Turks, he was literally worse off than the rest of the army, as neither he nor any of the Head-quarters Staff had rations with them, with which of course everyone else was provided. However, Captain Thomas, of the horse artillery, had found a side of wild boar on one of the captured Russian waggons, and very politely sent Lord Raglan a leg. A fire was lit, and, one of the Hussars of Captain Chetwode's troop acting as cook, the leg was cut into slices, and it was not long before it was in a state to be eaten.

I awoke from the cold the following morning soon after 4 a.m., and groomed my horse to warm myself and him. Chetwode again supplied us with eatables in the shape of tea and sugar, and we got some rations from the commissariat of the 1st Division, so we made a very tolerable breakfast. The army got into motion soon after 7 a.m. and advanced across the plain towards the heights of Balaklava. It was dreadfully hot, and I was shocked to see the number of men that fell out before we had marched three miles. The cholera was raging in the ranks, and many men died during that day. We reached the village of Kadikoi, which is a mile in front of the harbour of Balaklava, at 10.30 a.m. It was quite deserted, and all the houses emptied of everything that could be of any use to us. A portion of the Light Division was then ordered up the heights on the west of the harbour, and a part of the 2nd Division on to those on the east of the harbour; Lord Raglan and his Staff followed the road into the town. The infantry advanced, covered by a cloud of skirmishers, and gained the heights on both sides of the harbour without even seeing the enemy; Lord Raglan, therefore, rode on towards the entrance of the town. The general impression was that it also had been deserted, we were soon undeceived on that point, by a shell that came flying from the old Genoese castle at the mouth of the harbour, right among the Headquarters Staff: it was followed by several more, but they burst without doing any damage further than that Mr. Curzon (assistant military secretary) had his coat torn by a piece of shell, but without being hurt himself. Just at this time several much louder explosions were heard: these came from the *Agamemnon*, which was firing on the castle from outside the harbour. A few minutes later a small white flag was observed flying from the end of a musket, held by a Russian soldier close to the Genoese fort; on this signal of surrender all firing ceased on both sides, and our Rifles were to be seen entering the old castle in triumph. Lord Raglan then entered the town, and was met by the very few remaining inhabitants, who offered us bread and salt as a token of goodwill and friendship.

The commandant informed Lord Raglan that the wives and families of the officers we had taken, and numbers of women and children of the lower classes, had fled into the hills on the northern side on hearing of the advance of the Allies, and that he was fearful that they would fall into the hands of our soldiers before they could reach Sevastopol, and possibly meet with uncivil treatment; he therefore begged Lord Raglan to intervene on their behalf. Lord Raglan immediately sent one of his aides-de-camp, accompanied by Mr. Calvert, chief interpreter, and a Russian officer on parole (son-in-law of the commandant), to cross the harbour, and endeavour to discover these fugitives, and persuade them to return, under the assurance that no harm should come to them. In an hour and a half the officers sent by Lord Raglan returned, bringing with them about 70 women and children, of whom some seven or eight were wives of officers. At first the poor things were dreadfully frightened, but, on seeing that they were treated with the utmost respect and kindness, their confidence returned. Lord Raglan had ordered that a sufficient number of houses should be set apart for them, and sentries placed round, so that they should not be in any way molested or insulted. A great many of them, seeing that the British soldier was not quite the repulsive creature they had fancied, asked to be allowed to return to their own houses, which was granted; but most of the ladies went into a house all together, and were guarded by sentries against intrusion, and rationed by the commissariat. It was Lord Raglan's intention from the first to send away all the women and children directly a steamer was available to take them.

Lord Raglan established his Headquarters at the house of the late commandant of Balaklava: that is to say, he occupied one room in it for himself, and a large room was appropriated as the military secretary's office; the rest of the house he allowed the Russian commandant to retain for himself and family, until their departure from the town. The aides-de-camp and other officers of his Staff camped themselves in a wretched little kitchen-garden attached to the house. The baggage at last arrived, late in the afternoon. A detachment of the Guards was ordered into the town, to garrison it for the time being, and during the afternoon two war-steamers and several sailing transports came into the harbour, so that the calm and peaceful waters were soon animated with numerous boats.

The position of the troops was as follows:—The 1st, 2nd, and Light Divisions, and the brigade of Cavalry, were bivouacked in the plain in front of Balaklava, supported by divisions of the French army. The 3rd and 4th Divisions were pushed on towards Sevastopol, and occupied some high ground three miles North of

Balaklava, together with a large body of French troops. In the evening Lord Raglan had a consultation with General Canrobert, when the latter proposed that the allied armies should change their relative positions, viz. that the English, instead of being on the left, should take the right; this the French urged we ought to allow, as, having obtained possession of Balaklava, we had a harbour in which to land our material, and that therefore they had only left to them the bays of Kamiesch and Kazatch, near Cape Chersonese, for the same purpose, and it would obviously be far more convenient for them to be encamped as near as possible to the spot where their stores, etc., would be landed. For these reasons Lord Raglan was induced to give way, and thus again occupy the most exposed position, while our allies are protected on both flanks.

Many men continued to be taken ill with cholera, brought on, I believe, to a great extent, by the quantity of fruit to be met with in the vicinity of Balaklava. I heard it stated that a French colonel, whose battalion was bivouacked near a vineyard, sent parties of men to gather all the grapes, and had them brought to him, and saw them destroyed, in the hope that by so doing his men would be spared from the cholera.

Marshal St. Arnaud was brought into the town this afternoon in a very weak state, and accommodated with the best house to be found. He is to embark for France immediately, but is so ill that his medical attendants doubt his living to see it again. Although the town is garrisoned by the English, and it had been an agreed thing that the French troops were not to enter it, they nevertheless took advantage of the Marshal being there to bring in a battalion of Chasseurs and some Zouaves by way of a guard over the Marshal's baggage, etc.! and of course began to commit excesses, pillaging and destroying everything they could find. However, it was not allowed to last long, for the English authorities interfered, and before night our troublesome allies were sent out of the town, except a guard of honour at the Marshal's quarters. I must record a little instance of the cool way in which they try to appropriate everything to themselves. During the short time they were in the town, they discovered the four Russian mortars that we took in the old Genoese fort above the harbour, and which had fired on us when we advanced towards the town. These mortars had not as yet been removed. A large body of Chasseurs, under the command of their officers, proceeded to take them down, utterly disregarding the injunctions of the English sentries. Finding expostulation useless, one of our men went and informed Sir Edmund Lyons (Lord Raglan and almost all his Staff were out on the reconnaissance), who, I understand, immediately landed a body of marines from the *Agamemnon*, and then quietly waited till the French, after no little trouble, arrived with the mortars. He then went up to the officer in command, thanked him most politely for the trouble he had taken, and informed him that he had landed some marines to take possession of them. The Frenchman looked astonished, then foolish.

I was sent up to the 3rd and 4th Divisions with some orders to Sir R. England and Sir G. Cathcart. I found the latter at his dinner, which had been twice most disagreeably interrupted by a shell from the Russian batteries in front of the town. Sir George had pitched his tent in a stone-quarry, and it was just in front of it that he

Right: A ford of the Tchernaya.

and his Staff were partaking of their dinner. All at once they heard 'Whiz—whiz-whiz-WHIZ, BANG!' and a shell exploded a few feet from them, to their intense disgust and the discomfiture of their dinner arrangements. On this being repeated a second time, they thought it more prudent to shift their dining-place to a spot less attractive to Russian shot and shell.

Lord Raglan spent part of the 29th making a reconnaissance with Sir J. Burgoyne of the enemy's works in front of Sevastopol, and the more he saw of it, the more he was convinced of the utter impracticability of attacking the town without first reducing the fire of the Russian batteries. From prisoners, deserters, and secret information, it had been already ascertained that there were upwards of 35,000 fighting men in the town and on board the ships of war in the harbour, and large reinforcements were to be expected daily. Today the ground which each army was to take up, for the purpose of besieging the town, was settled between the French and English Generals of Engineers. The troops of the two armies before the place are now divided by a great ravine, which runs up from the end of the Man-of-War Creek, out of the great harbour of Sevastopol, to the English Headquarters, a distance of some three miles. On the 1st of this month 1000 marines were landed at Balaklava from the fleet to occupy the heights in front and above it; thus relieving the like number of men of the 1st Division, who had up to this time done duty there; the remainder of the division being at the front. An invalid battalion has also been formed of all the young and weak soldiers of the army; they do duty as the garrison of Balaklava. The entrance to the town itself is protected by the 93rd Regiment camped about a mile in front of the head of the harbour, at the commencement of the plain. These, together with the cavalry and three batteries of artillery, form the troops for the defence of Balaklava; the whole being under the command of Sir Colin Campbell. For the last three days the greatest exertions have been made in landing the siege-train and the necessary stores for the gigantic operations about to be commenced for the reduction of Sevastopol.

On October 2nd, after a long conference between Lord Raglan and General Canrobert, the latter agreed to place a portion of the French army (under the command of General Bosquet) on the heights overlooking the valley of Balaklava and the Tchernaya river, in this manner covering our rear from any attack of the enemy. Kamiesch Bay is on the extreme left of the French army; they take up the ground from there to the great ravine running from the Man-of-War Creek, a distance of some six miles. On the other side of this ravine rests the extreme left of the English, viz, the 3rd Division; then comes the 4th and then the Light Division. These divisions are all nearly in line as far as the ground will admit, and parallel to the town at a distance of nearly two miles, occupying high ground which commands an extensive view on all sides. Beyond the Light Division come the 1st and 2nd Divisions, occupying the ground from the Karabelnaia ravine in a backward direction along the heights in front of the ruins of Inkermann and the valley of the Tchernaya—the distance of the English positions being nearly four miles. The ridge of heights overlooking the plain in front of Balaklava, and which runs at right angles from those already mentioned to the head of the harbour, is occupied for the most part by French troops—the heights above and in front of Balaklava being defended by the British; the whole front thus defended by the allied armies extending from Kamiesch Bay to Inkermann, and from there again back to

Balaklava, being a distance of upwards of 15 miles! The position is one of great natural strength, but of too considerable extent for the number of troops that defend it—the Allies mustering at the present moment something under 50,000 bayonets. Nevertheless, it is the very best that could be taken up, and when our reinforcements arrive will be, I believe, almost impregnable against any attack from the enemy.

A careful reconnaissance was made of the ground in front of the ruins of Inkermann by General Airey and some other members of the Staff, accompanied by two or three officers from the French Headquarters. It was not very pleasant work, as the Russians kept up a constant fire on us of round shot and shell from three steamers at the upper end of the harbour. Nobody was hit, but the horse of a French staff-officer was wounded severely by the bursting of a shell. On the 4th instant the Russians sent a great many heavy shot and sometimes a shell over the heights in front of the town, right into the camps of the 3rd and 4th Divisions; they did but little harm generally speaking, though one shell fell at the door of a tent, and, bursting, killed one man and wounded three others. An immense quantity of ammunition has been brought up to the front for the siege. Upwards of 100 guns have been landed off the siege-trains and from the ships, with about 300 rounds per gun—pretty well to begin with.

Lord Raglan shifted his Headquarters on October 5th from Balaklava to midway between Balaklava and Sevastopol, at what was a sort of country villa, with large farm-buildings. I was left behind in Balaklava until late in the day, on duty, and had to witness the parting between the poor old Russian commandant and his family. They had up to this day been allowed to live all together in his house, but he was now to be removed down to Constantinople; his family are to be sent tomorrow in a steamer to Yalta, together with some other ladies who have up to this time continued here. It was a painful scene; those poor women weeping so bitterly, as they clung round the old man, whom they could hardly expect to see again; one felt somehow ashamed of oneself in having to witness their grief, and being obliged to hurry the parting, as the boat was waiting to take him away a prisoner.

The French are constructing five small but strong redoubts, and three batteries connected by a lower parapet, along the ridge of heights in the rear of the position and overlooking the plains of Balaklava. They are well able to do this, having received large reinforcements within the last day or two, to the amount of 12,000 men. When these works are finished they are to be occupied by the division of Turks attached to the French army. Some redoubts and batteries have also been marked out by the English for the better protection of Balaklava. Those on the heights above the town, which are being made by the Royal Marines, are advancing rapidly, but we are dreadfully in want of men. Our brigade of Heavy Cavalry has been most unfortunate; in bringing some of them over from Varna last week, we lost, during a gale of wind, 130 horses—a large reduction to our small force. There are great difficulties in the way of our constructing batteries and trenches in the usual manner, as the ground we shall have to work upon is very rocky, the general depth of earth being not more than 18 inches. I understand the ground the French have got is very good soil, so they will have a great advantage over us when we

Overleaf: Morning excercise: Lord Raglan to General Airey; 'Now Airey, let us see if he can jump.'

commence making the trenches. To make up for this want of soil, an enormous number of gabions, fascines, and sandbags will be used, but these take much time and labour to make, and consequently much retard the progress of the siege. I have always thought that we underrated the defences of Sevastopol on the land side. I know, when the first reconnaissance was made by the French and English engineers, they all said that we ought to get into the town in a day or two : but since then, every day brings to light fresh difficulties which must be overcome, so that now the siege is talked of as likely to last some time. I believe we are really to commence breaking ground tonight ; a large trench, of nearly 1200 yards in length, has been marked out by our engineers, at an average distance of 1800 yards from the batteries of the enemy ; this will be the first parallel of the English attack. There is one drawback to much work being done at night just now, which is, that the moon is so bright that it is wonderful how far one can see.

We have received some small reinforcements — between 800 and 1000 infantry, and 1500 artillerymen for the siege. Besides these, upwards of 1200 sailors have been landed from the fleet, and are known as the Naval Brigade ; they are to be employed in the batteries against the town during the siege. They are a magnificent body of men, and are working hard now dragging up ship-guns from Balaklava to the two siege-trains.

We are proceeding with our trenches and batteries, and it is said shall open fire on the enemy's works in the course of three or four days. Up to the present moment not a single round has been fired by us, as it is thought that opening all at once will have a greater effect on the enemy. On the evening of October 7th we broke the first ground, and during the night a small battery was constructed for one of our new Lancaster guns of 95 cwt. This is to fire at a Russian three-decker, said to be the *Twelve Apostles*, which, being anchored broadside on at the end of the Man-of-War Creek, completely sweeps the ravine running up into our lines from the harbour. It is fondly hoped that these new Lancaster shells may set her on fire. Our battery is over 3000 yards from the Russian liner ; but if the report of the long range and accurate fire of these guns be true, the distance is not too great to cripple the ship in question.

A man of the Rifle Brigade made a good shot today ; he was on out-picket, and, seeing a Cossack officer on a *white* horse at a considerable distance, thought he might as well try and knock him over. He accordingly fired, and the man fell from his saddle, the horse trotting away. The distance was said to be upwards of 1300 yards by several officers qualified to judge on the subject. A perhaps equally good shot was made by the Russians from one of their batteries two days ago. A French officer of Engineers was making a reconnaissance of the enemy's works ; the Russians fired at him at a distance of nearly a mile. The round shot took off his leg, and the poor man bled to death before he could be carried to the hospital.

The French broke ground on the evening of the 9th, and had made a trench upwards of 1000 yards long by daylight the next morning ; this parallel is, on an average, at a distance of 1200 yards from the Russian works. The enemy never discovered that they were at work, so they were unmolested, and consequently the trench was admirably constructed ; the soil was well adapted for the purpose ; being a rich loam, it was easily put into any form, and stood at a good angle. Our ground is very different, being (when not rocky) very loose and crumbling, and therefore cannot be made to stand at a proper angle without an extra amount of gabions, fascines, and sandbags. The next evening Lord Raglan rode out about 10 p.m. to see the first parallel constructed. This was marked out a day or two earlier. The ground taken up by the English for their part of the siege extends from the great ravine on our extreme left to the Karabelnaia ravine, which runs up on the right of the Light Division, and between it and the 1st Division. This ground is divided in two by a third ravine, along which passes the Woronzoff road, and is therefore named after it: this ravine runs up between the 4th and Light Divisions. It is also to divide our siege-works—those on the left being called the 'Left attack', and those on the right the 'Right attack'. It was the 1st parallel on the left attack that was commenced on the evening of the 10th instant; it extended right across the ground from the left ravine to the centre, a distance of something over 1200 yards. To construct this 1200 men were sent down as a working party directly after dark. They were protected by three battalions of infantry (about 2000 men). By daylight the following morning (11th) good cover had been obtained, so that the work was continued throughout the day: in this parallel batteries are to be made for 36 guns.

The weather again became warmer, and on the morning of the 11th, being off duty, Mr. Calvert and myself decided to ride over to the monastery of St. George, situated on the edge of a clif above the sea, about four miles from Headquarters and three south of Cape Chersonese. We found the monastery more beautifully situated even than we had been led to expect from the description we had heard. The cliffs are very high, about 400 feet, and of endless variety of colouring. The monastery, as a building, has nothing imposing about it. It consists of several separate houses, where the superior monks formerly resided, and one long building, containing a passage, out of which lead a number of small rooms or cells: in these lodged the ordinary monks. There is also a refectory and a small hospital, but both are in wretched condition. Just below is the chapel, situated on a terrace which has been constructed in the side of the cliff, and which appears almost to hang over the sea, 350 feet below. The chapel externally has nothing to boast of, being a small whitewashed square building, with a copper dome, painted blue with gilt stars; but inside, like all Greek churches, it is covered with ornaments, chiefly pictures of the Virgin and Child in gold and silver plate, with only the face and hands painted. Mr. Calvert, speaking Russian, entered into conversation with one of the monks who had remained; from him we learnt some information. Directly it was known that the Allies had landed in the Crimea, the superior pape (as he is called) of the monastery retired into the interior, taking with him much of the most valuable plate and relics. He was soon followed by many more, but some 10 or 12 have remained, in the hope of saving their chapel. Directly the English took Balaklava one of the monks came to Lord Raglan and begged him to protect the monastery from pillage, which he promised to do.

There is still, I am sorry to say, a great deal of cholera in the army. The casualties from it are daily 12 or 14 deaths, and from 30 to 40 fresh cases brought into hospital. The casualties from the fire of the enemy, since our arrival at Balaklava to the present day (12th), have only been five killed and 12 wounded. I was sent down into the trenches, left attack, in the afternoon, with instructions from Lord Raglan to the Colonel in command. It was anything but pleasant work, as the last 200 yards before one got into the trenches are quite exposed, so, directly I made my appearance, some five round shot were sent at me, and I had to keep my eyes open to get out of their way. It has been observed that if an officer makes his appearance the enemy fires directly, but a private will probably be left alone; they must have good telescopes to be able to make out which is which at that distance. I got into the trenches just before dusk, and found all the men, with the exception of the sentries, lying close under the parapet, as the round shot came through the upper part, which is not yet of sufficient thickness to resist balls. The last quarter of an hour before dusk the Russians always appear determined to give us something to remember them for the night.

Soon after 4 a.m. (13th) I got up and rode down to the trenches to see what work had been done during the night, and also afterwards to visit the out-pickets and try to get a sketch of the ground some way in advance of our trenches. I proceeded to make an eye-sketch of the enemy's batteries, and succeeded in some measure in doing so for some time, when I heard '*ping, ping!*' close to my ears, and found I had been discovered by some Russian sharpshooters on picket, who were now taking very deliberate aim at me. I retreated as fast as possible, and fortunately escaped untouched to my horse, who was well concealed in a hollow. I rode home to break-fast at 8 a.m., very well pleased with my morning's adventure.

The prisoners of St. George's Monastery. The commandant of Balaklava at the time of the capture of that post asked to remain with his family at St. George.

CHAPTER 4

Defences of Sevastopol

AT last we have begun in earnest to bombard Sevastopol. Yesterday morning saw the commencement of our fire on that unfortunate city.

On October 14th, 1854, we received a considerable reinforcement to our army by the arrival of near 4000 Turkish troops. Although not of the best, they nevertheless appear a strong set of men, and will, it is to be hoped, prove themselves of the same stamp as the brave defenders of Silistria. The greater portion of these men are to occupy the forts now in course of construction in front of Balaklava; a position of considerable importance, and where their worth will, in all probability, be tested before long by an attack from the enemy.

Soon after 1 p.m. the Russians opened a tremendous fire against the French trenches and works. This lasted for one hour and three-quarters, during which time they threw no less than 1500 projectiles; without doing much harm. The supposed object of this Russian cannonade was to try the range of their guns, and also to test the effect of their fire on the besiegers. We all expected the same experiment to be tried on our trenches, nor were we disappointed, although it did not take place until the 16th instant. About 10 a.m. the Russians opened all their guns on the English and French works. It gave us an opportunity of ascertaining to a certain extent what fire they could bring against us. It was computed that they fired about 80 guns against the English and 70 against the French. There is reason to believe that there are some 50 mortars of large calibre in rear of their batteries, which will open on us when the bombardment commences. The fire from the enemy lasted about the same time as that on the former occasion.

As an instance of the admirable practice of the Russian artillery, I record that on this day I had to take some orders to Sir George Cathcart. He was walking about a hundred yards in advance of his tent in the open. I rode up to him, and dismounted, and might have been in conversation with him five minutes. We were all at once interrupted by that most disagreeable sound—a shot approaching. We both looked up, but, the sun being in our eyes, could see nothing. Sir George lay down, and I endeavoured to do the same, but my horse began to take alarm, and it was as much as I could do to hold him. There was nothing for it but to wait the result. Almost immediately a tremendous roar and a heavy 'thud' on the ground five yards from us told we were safe. We laughed when it was over, and congratulated ourselves on our escape. My business with Sir George being completed, I took my leave. A few yards back I met General Torrens, who had come out of his tent close by, to see where the shot had fallen. I stayed talking to him for a moment, when he said, "Look out! here comes another;" and before I could turn round another monster ball fell even closer than the first. Good shots, considering we were 3200 yards from the body of the place. The shots fired were solid 56-pounders.

Immediately the Allies landed in the Crimea, the Russian engineers set to work in earnest, and large batteries were constructed on every available spot that could in any way assist the defence of the place. When we first sat down before Sevastopol, we saw thousands of men employed making earthworks, and daily fresh batteries sprang up as if by enchantment. The Russians seemed determined to make up for their past apathy by working day and night. Women and children even were pressed into the service, and helped not a little by bringing up earth in baskets, filling sandbags, and carrying gabions and fascines from place to place as they might be required. The consequence of all these exertions was, that a parapet has been erected almost round the town with numerous heavy batteries. The most formidable is one in front of and round the Malakoff Tower. This battery alone mounts 18 guns; the majority are 56-pounders, the remainder 32-pounders. Between that and the Redan there is (as far as we can see) only a parapet running across a deep ravine, just to connect the two works. The Redan is said to have 16 guns in it, eight on each face (32-pounders). Almost adjoining the Redan is another heavy battery mounting 14 guns (32-pounders). This we have named the 'Barrack' Battery, as there are huge barracks just in its rear. From it there is only a parapet running down the side of the ravine, and which terminates at the head of the Man-of-War Creek.

Besides the foregoing, which are all immediately opposite our works, we have against us one flank of the Bastion du Mât, which mounts some 15 guns (24-pounders), and which fire right across our front, and would almost take our batteries in reverse if they were somewhat more forward. From it a parapet runs back, down the side of the ravine, and meets the one from the Barrack Battery, at the end of the Man-of-War Creek. There are two small batteries in this parapet, which are close together, and indeed may be considered as one; they mount six guns (18 and 24-pounders). They are called the 'Sandsack' Batteries, from the embrasures being constructed of *sacks* of earth, instead of the usual small bags. But perhaps our greatest annoyance arises from a battery, and one which it will be very difficult for our guns to silence from its peculiar position, situated on high ground in rear of the Bastion du Mât, facing towards our attack. This we call the 'Garden' Battery, from its being surrounded by a garden. It has eight very heavy guns (probably 68-pounders). It will be apparent by this that we have (if the foregoing calculations be correct) 81 guns directed against the English trenches, viz. (going from west to east) : —

		Guns
Bastion du Mât		15
Garden Battery		8
Sandsack do.		6
Barrack do.		14
Redan		16
Round-Tower Battery		18
Malakoff		4
	Total	81 guns.

Besides these there are the 20 mortars in rear of the different works.

CAMROSE LUTHERAN COLLEGE
LIBRARY

The Russian works opposite the French are of somewhat different construction to those just mentioned. The only earthworks they have before them are the Bastion du Mât, and a battery in front of the stone tower, which they call the 'Bastion Centrale' from its position. Both these are of a very formidable nature. The Bastion du Mât brings some 20 guns to bear upon the French works, and the other almost as many. They have also on their extreme left the Quarantine Fort, a large casemated battery with two tiers of guns. Fortunately, however, only a certain number of these can be brought to bear upon the French. In all they have near 70 guns and about 20 mortars that can fire against their approaches.

I must now endeavour to give some idea of the batteries constructed by us for the purpose of subduing, if not silencing, these formidable works of the enemy. The English trenches are divided into two attacks—the right and left. In the right is a battery known as 'Gordon's Battery', and in the left another known as 'Chapman's'. They are named after two officers of the Royal Engineers, from whose directions they had been both drawn out and constructed.

In Chapman's Battery are the following pieces of ordnance:—

	Pieces
24-pounder guns	24
8-inch do.	9
8 inch (Lancaster) do.	3
10-inch mortars	5
Total	41 pieces.

These are to fire against the Bastion du Mât, Sandsack, Barrack, and Redan Batteries. In Gordon's Battery are the following pieces of ordnance:—

	Pieces
24-pounder guns	6
8-inch do.	7
8-inch (Lancaster) do.	1
32-pounder do.	7
10-inch mortars	5
Total	26 pieces.

These are to fire against the Garden, Redan, and Malakoff Tower Batteries.

To the right-rear of Gordon's Battery is another, quite detached, and, for its size, a most formidable work. It consists of five guns of 95 cwt. each, one of them a Lancaster; all capable of throwing 68-pound solid shot. These are to fire against the Malakoff Tower and the battery in front of it, and also at any ships in the great harbour within range. Some way to the rear of this is the one-gun (95 cwt. Lancaster) battery. It was the first that we constructed, and, as I before mentioned, was made to fire on a Russian line-of-battle ship anchored in the Man-of-War Creek with her broadside on, so as to sweep the ravine that divides the English and French trenches. We have therefore 73 pieces of ordnance in all, to fire against 81 of the Russians. The French have constructed in their trenches five batteries and a small redoubt on their extreme left, called by them 'Fort Génois'. They have in these batteries 29 guns (varying in calibre from 18 to 32-pounders), 14 howitzers for

Overleaf: Unfinished painting of a group of officers.

C.t Victor La Marmora
nephew of the General and
his naval aidecamp

Cap.tn Lombardini
Staff

Cap.n Avé staff
and secretary
to the king

centregro
Boronico
(of the isles)

major Govone Colt la Rovère Cap.ᵗⁿ Crespi Colonel Pettitti Cap.ᵗⁿ Bariola
The general   chef d Etat major
     Myself

Piola staff

throwing hollow shot and shell (they are not quite equal to our 32-pounder howitzers), and 10 mortars of about eight inches in diameter; altogether 53 pieces. This shows how much lighter their ordnance is than ours.

A little before 6 a.m. on October 7th, Lord Raglan and his Staff arrived at a quarry in advance of the 3rd Division camp. From this spot a good general view is obtained of the English trenches, and, although under fire of the place, the enemy had too much to do to attend to us, and consequently hardly a shot fell in the quarry all day. The Russians appeared to anticipate our opening fire, as directly it was daylight they commenced a heavy cannonade from all their batteries on our works. At 6.40 a.m. our arranged signal of three shells was fired from the centre French battery, and within five minutes the whole line of guns, English and French, were in action. The roaring and whistling of the shot, as they flew through the air on their course of destruction, surpassed anything ever heard before. In a few moments everything was enveloped in smoke, so that we could only sit and guess and hope we were doing well. About an hour after we commenced 'pounding' a breeze sprang up and cleared the smoke away for a short time; we had then an opportunity of seeing what we had done. The first thing observed was the Malakoff Tower quite silent, and the top of it all knocked to pieces. This had been done entirely by the fire from the four heavy guns (68-pounders) in our detached battery on the right of the right attack; in the course of the day it became a complete ruin. Here and there also a gun had been silenced, but, for the most part, no great advantage had been gained by either party. The cannonade continued without ceasing for the next two hours, pretty equal on both sides; if anything, the French appeared to fire somewhat slower, but this was accounted for by the fact that most of their guns were of brass, and consequently cannot bear quick firing after a certain time.

At 8.45 a.m. the great disaster of the day took place, viz. the explosion of the principal French magazine from a Russian shell. It completely destroyed their 4th battery, knocking over five guns, and burying three other pieces of ordnance. They also lost over 100 men killed and wounded. This disaster appeared quite to paralyse the French, whilst it encouraged the Russians, who augmented their fire till they sent four shot to one from our allies. The consequence was that in a short time the enemy completely silenced their 5th battery, containing 12 pieces; it had from the commencement suffered more than any other. The French lost a large number of men in this battery, independently of the explosion. Immediately after General Canrobert sent word to Lord Raglan that it was of no importance, as it was *not* one of their magazines that had blown up, but a new sort of shell which the Russians had thrown into their trenches. General Rose and one of General Canrobert's aides-de-camp brought this monstrous piece of information, and appeared quite astonished when we all said we did not believe such humbug, and that we had not the smallest doubt that it was a magazine. Major Vico was very indignant that we did not give credit to the General's message; however, half an hour later the aide-de-camp came back with an apology from General Canrobert for having misinformed Lord Raglan, and begged to say that he had received the report from the General of the trenches, and that it had since been ascertained that it was their principal magazine which had exploded—all of which we knew perfectly well before. Soon after 1 a.m. General Rose came again to Lord Raglan from General

Canrobert, to say that it was quite impossible for them (the French) to continue their fire, as two batteries on their right were altogether silenced, and the one on their extreme left (Fort Génois) was in a very bad state, and the cannonade from the enemy since the explosion had almost ruined the remainder of their works. The Russians thus succeeded in silencing our allies; but they had done us very little harm, for our artillerymen and sailors worked away as hard as ever, and at the very time the French 'shut up' we had in a great measure silenced the Barrack and Malakoff Batteries. Those that gave us the most annoyance were the Bastion du Mât, the Garden and Redan Batteries. About 1.15 p.m. we heard the first discharge from the allied fleets upon the Russian sea-forts; but we could barely distinguish them after a few moments, as the smoke completely enveloped them in a cloud; so we had no idea of the effect on either side.

Fifteen minutes later a shell from the enemy blew up a magazine in the French battery No. 1 (Fort Génois); fortunately it was not of so much importance as the last. They had some eight or 10 killed, and from 30 to 40 wounded by it. Not five minutes after this a small Russian magazine was blown up inside the town; it did not however stop their fire in the least. But about 3 p.m. a tremendous explosion took place opposite our left attack, apparently just in rear of the Redan Battery. We could see immense beams of wood and what looked like barrels thrown high into the air; the noise was prodigious, the fire for a moment ceased on both sides; our men jumped up on the parapet of the trenches and cheered.

During the day I was sent into the different batteries of our two attacks, and had an opportunity of seeing the way in which the men worked the guns, and also the accuracy of the fire. The first I visited was the one-gun battery, the most distant from the town. This was a heavy Lancaster gun. It is constructed on a new principle for heavy ordnance. Its peculiarity consists in the bore being oval; the ball, or rather shell, is near 18 inches in length, of conical shape, and contains an exploding charge of 12 lbs. of powder. Its range is pretty accurate at 3600 yards, rather over two miles! The object it was firing at, a Russian liner in the Man-of-War Creek, was at a distance of 3400 yards. When the Russians found this out they moved the ship a few yards further on, and in such a way that we could only bring this gun to bear on her stern, and on about three ports of her broadside. None of the shot from the ship could reach the battery with any effect, as, although they fired their heaviest guns at a great elevation, the balls only came bowling up towards us. The practice made by this Lancaster was not as successful as had been anticipated. The greatest care was taken by the two naval officers in command of the battery, which was entirely manned by sailors, in putting in the exact charge and the proper length of fuze, but nevertheless every shot went either a little too much to the right or left, or too high or too low. I think near 30 of these shells were fired before one took effect, but that one was supposed to have exploded in her, and, if it did, must have much discomposed the crew.

I then went into the five-gun battery, on the extreme right of our attacks. It had done good service during the day, although we had more casualties in it than in any other. They were occasioned chiefly by the fire from two steamers in the harbour, that steamed round and round in a circle, and in that manner fired both their broadsides, and from the fact of their keeping always on the move they were very difficult to hit. Nevertheless, in the course of the day, one of them was disabled by our shot, and had to sheer off. It was most amusing to see the sailors who manned the guns in this battery; there were two reliefs of them, and, as soon as one had done its turn of duty, you heard the officer in command say, "Now then, second relief, fall in; you others can go and sky-lark." A nice place in which to sky-lark, with 68-pound shot and 13-inch shell dropping in amongst you every moment! However, the blue-jackets did not mind, and took the permission given them literally; and in a minute ever so many of them had jumped on the parapet to see 'them b—y Rushions;' then some fellow would cry, "Look out, shot!" and down they all jumped, and after the iron messenger had passed over, or exploded, as the case might be, they were all up again, talking at such a rate, and making the drollest remarks, giving their private opinion as to the siege, and how the place ought to be taken.

At 4.30 p.m. the Russians made a sortie on the French extreme left. It consisted of some 200 men, who advanced rapidly in a most gallant manner, drove in the French pickets, and got up to within 50 or 60 yards of their batteries. They were met with so destructive a fire from the guard of the trenches, that they were forced to retire as quickly as they advanced, leaving behind them many killed and wounded. The allied fleets withdrew from before the batteries of the town, and returned to their former anchorage, about 5.30 p.m. Soon after, as it began to get dusk, the firing on both sides sensibly diminished. Lord Raglan then returned to Headquarters, and sent orders to our batteries that they were only to answer the fire from the enemy, gun for gun, during the night. General Canrobert sent to Lord Raglan to say that he hoped without doubt to open fire again on the Russian works the following morning. Nobody, however, believed him!

Thus concluded our first day's bombardment, of which the English may be justly proud. Our engineers, especially, deserve much credit for the efficient manner in which the trenches have been constructed, and the good cover they afford. To our artillery also (naval and military) great praise is due for the admirable fire kept up during the whole day, under disadvantageous circumstances. In other respects the day was lost to the Allies, for during the night the enemy repaired, to a great extent, the damage our fire had done, and indeed succeeded in opening a fresh battery in the garden on the west side of the Man-of-War Creek.

An artillery officer told me he had calculated that the English and Russians had fired during this day upwards of 20,000 shot and shell at one another. In spite of this our losses have not been as severe as would be naturally expected; as far as I can ascertain they were as follows:—In the trenches, six killed and 17 wounded; with the covering parties, 27 killed and 94 wounded; total, 144 casualties.

This morning Lord Raglan received a letter from Sir Edmund Lyons, giving him an account of the performances of the allied fleets yesterday. I have ascertained the following from some naval officers concerned in the matter: it appears that on October 16th a Council of War was held by the Admirals as to the best mode of co-operating with the land forces on the following day. It was then agreed that the attack should be made by the line-of-battle ships of the allied fleets in a semicircle: the French, on the right, to engage the sea-defences on the southern side of the town, aided by two Turkish liners in the centre; while, on the left, the English fleet was to attack the northern forts of Sevastopol.

There is a shoal running from Cape Constantine (which is half a mile north of the fort of that name) in a south-westerly direction for a distance of a mile and a half; this shoal crosses the direct entrance of the harbour, over which there is only eight fathom water. Consequently it is hardly safe for line-of-battle ships to cross, except in the very calmest weather. But there is a passage somewhat nearer the land where the depth of water increases to 13 fathom. It was proposed that the ships should enter by this passage, take up their positions inside the above-mentioned shoal, placing themselves as near as practicable to the enemy's works. The fleets were to go into action and anchor in their respective places as soon after 10 a.m. as possible. For this purpose it was necessary to weigh early, as the majority of the large ships were at some distance; a portion lying off the Katcha river. Accordingly,

A few minutes relaxation from active duty at Headquarters allows for a political discussion on international problems between the artist and the French Duc de Dino and makes a pleasant interlude from the stresses and strains of battle.

soon after 6 a.m. on the morning of the 17th, the French fleet commenced their preparations, but to their astonishment no signs of movement were apparent among the English. Admiral Hamelin, seeing this inactivity continue, proceeded on board the flag-ship, *Britannia*, accompanied by his *Chef d'Etat Major* (Captain of the Fleet), Rear-Admiral Bouet-Villaumez, to ascertain the cause from Admiral Dundas. He found the English Admiral in a state of indecision respecting the forth-coming attack, as he intimated that 'he could not risk his fleet, which was made of wood, against the batteries, which were made of stone.' Such was the explanation given to Admiral Hamelin by the English Naval Commander-in-Chief, for the non-fulfilment of the arrangements which they had both signed and agreed to on the 16th inst. The French Admiral expressed his surprise and annoyance at the extra-ordinary conduct of his colleague, and, without further parley, quitted the cabin and returned to his ship in high dudgeon. Sir Edmund Lyons (who had come on board during the discussion), however, assured the French Captain of the Fleet, who had remained after his chief had left, that he would be answerable for the English ships being in their places, and with this assurance Admiral Bouet-Villaumez departed.

But all this consultation had taken up so much valuable time, and caused such delay that, instead of the fleet going into action by 10 a.m., they did not commence their fire till near 1 p.m. Each sailing line-of-battle ship had a steamer lashed alongside, so they could shift their position without having to rely on their sailing powers. The whole opened with a tremendous roar of artillery; but the Russians replied almost as heavily. Sir Edmund Lyons brought the *Agamemnon* within 700 yards of Fort Constantine, and then opened fire; he was supported by the *Sanspareil*, *Queen* and *Albion*, and, after a time, by the *London*, *Rodney*, and *Bellerophon* also. The enemy fired a great quantity of red-hot shot, which caused our ships considerable annoyance, especially those just mentioned. The *Queen* and *Albion* were both badly on fire, and had to retire for some time out of action. The *Agamemnon* and *London* were also on fire more than once, but without doing them much damage. The *Agamemnon* never changed her position from the moment she came into action, with only three or four feet of water under her keel, till past 5 p.m., when the ships were signalled to come out, and during this time she fired no less than 3500 shot and shell. Fort Constantine was several times silenced and greatly damaged; and it is said Sir Edmund Lyons thought that, if the original plan had been carried out, the fort would have been completely destroyed. The rest of the English fleet were from 1800 to 2200 yards off from the enemy's batteries;* and at that great distance the shot told with but little effect against the stone walls of the forts. The French fleet were for the most part somewhat nearer. Altogether I fear the naval attack was even a greater failure than that by land. I think the Russians have good reason to be proud of this their first successful check against a hitherto victorious enemy. The loss in our fleet was 47 killed, 234 wounded, total 281 casualties; and in the French fleet (as far as I can ascertain), 29 killed, 180 wounded, total 209 casualties.

* As a proof of the distance that some of the British fleet were from the sea-defences of Sevastopol, it may be mentioned that on board the *Britannia* the rear-trucks were removed to give the necessary elevation to the guns!

We are still firing away as hard and loud as ever, and have made considerable impression on the enemy's works. Their fire is much slower and far less accurate than it was. We have had a good many deserters from the town since the commencement of our bombardment on October 17th. These men all represent the state of things to be very bad in Sevastopol. The losses among the troops have been great, and the sailors of the fleet, who have been employed for the most part in the batteries opposed to the English attacks, have suffered dreadfully. Of course it is difficult to know how much to believe from deserters, especially anything connected with numbers, but they all put their losses at from 3000 to 4000. We had no assistance from the French batteries till the 20th, but since then they have improved their fire very much, and are now pounding away with considerable rapidity. They have knocked about the Bastion du Mât, and nearly silenced it; but the Russians appear to be constructing a very formidable earthwork in its rear which, it is to be feared, will cause us much trouble and annoyance. During the night of the 20th and 21st the Russians made a sortie on the right of the French trenches. Our allies were taken by surprise, and consequently the enemy got into one of their batteries and spiked their mortars; the French rallied immediately, driving the Russians back, killing six and taking four wounded men prisoners, one of whom, a young officer, died within 12 hours of his wound.

Yesterday (22nd) Lord Dunkellin was taken prisoner by a party of Cossacks. About 4.30 a.m., he had to go in command of a working party of the Guards down into our right attack, to repair some damage done to part of a battery from the fire at the place. His party arrived at the engineer park after the time ordered, and consequently too late to go with the morning relief; they, therefore, hurried on to overtake the rest. Somehow in the twilight they mistook the ravine and went down a wrong one, when, suddenly coming on a picket and receiving neither challenge nor reply to theirs, it was thought something was wrong, so Lord Dunkellin halted the party and advanced alone. His men waited for a few minutes and then saw the picket moving away; they still remained, but, finding Lord Dunkellin did not return, concluded that he had been made prisoner, and therefore marched back to the camp. No blame is to be attached to the men, as, being a working party, they were unarmed, and therefore could not attack an armed picket, even should it consist but of a third of their number. Lord Dunkellin is the first English officer captured by the enemy; he was a good deal censured for being late, and thus causing the service to be put to inconvenience.

Our attacks have been, and are being, greatly strengthened both with regard to the number and weight of the pieces of ordnance, and the parapets are made higher and thicker. We have four more 68-pounders in position, and several 32-pounders are now put in the battery in place of damaged 24-pounders. We are constructing a battery on a spur running out into the ravine between the English and French trenches, which will fire up the Man-of-War Creek, and it is expected will cause the Russians to move their ships. It will also command a bridge of boats across the creek, which we hope to destroy. This battery is to be armed with two 32-pounders and a 10-inch mortar. The enemy having placed a heavy gun up on the heights of Inkermann, close to the ruins, which would command a portion of our camp, a sandbag battery for two guns was therefore ordered to be constructed in advance of the 2nd Division, to silence it. This battery was finished yesterday

The dead and dying following the assault on the Malakoff. After a prolonged battle, the Russian batteries were silenced.

morning, and two 18-pounders placed in it. They opened on the enemy's gun at the ruins, and very soon made them withdraw it out of our sight and fill up the embrasure; so we shall not probably again be annoyed by it.

Captain Peel, of H.M.S. *Diamond*, has distinguished himself greatly for his marvellous *sang froid* in action. The other day a shell fell close to a gun which he was laying, so he took the shell and lifted it over the parapet; it exploded as it left his hands without doing any damage, whereas, had it burst on the spot where it fell, probably several men would have been wounded, if not killed.* It is reported that on Friday last the Port-Admiral in Sevastopol, Admiral Korniloff, died of his wounds received on the 17th. The deserters say that he had more to do with the defence of Sevastopol on the land side than anyone else, although not in actual command of the batteries. He was very civil to me when I was in Nicholaieff three years ago. He spoke English perfectly, and had been in London for some months during the time the *Vladimir* steam frigate was being built at Blackwall, as the Emperor's yacht for the Black Sea.

* For this act of bravery, in conjunction with others hereafter noticed, Captain Peel received the Victoria Cross.

CHAPTER 5

Captain Nolan and Lord Lucan

IT is with sorrow that I sit down to write, as I have to tell of the deaths of so many brother officers who fell in the action of October 25th, 1854, before Balaklava — for the most part uselessly sacrificed, as the results do not at all make up for our loss. But I should first endeavour to give the reader some sort of idea of the position occupied by the Allies on the morning that the battle took place. Ever since the occupation of Balaklava we have been strengthening the position — already strong by nature, but still quite open to the attack of an enterprising enemy. As I before mentioned, the harbour is almost surrounded by hills of great height, the sides of which rise with perpendicular abruptness from its quiet waters. The hills on the west of the harbour continue in succession until they merge, near the monastery of St. George, into the high plateau before Sevastopol. On the east of the harbour the heights are the commencement of a long range of hills — indeed one may call them mountains — that extend all along the southern coast of the Crimea. Fortunately for the strength of our position, the first hill is almost cut off from the remainder by a deep ravine which runs up from the plain before Balaklava towards the sea, and is only connected by a narrow ridge a few yards in breadth. One of the earliest works done after our arrival was to construct a battery that would sweep this ridge, and thus render it impracticable for anybody of the enemy to force, except at an enormous sacrifice of life. From this point all the way down to the plain a parapet, with occasional small batteries, had been constructed. In these works are several 32-pounder iron howitzers, which for the most part are manned by marine artillery, as the entire heights have up to this time been occupied by 1100 of the Royal Marines from the fleet — as fine a body of men as you could wish to see.

In front of Balaklava, at the distance of rather more than a mile, near the village of Kadikoi, a considerable work has been constructed, armed with several guns of position, but being unconnected with the heights on either side is not of any great strength, as it is liable to be turned on both flanks. In a short time these defects will be remedied, but up to the present moment our men have been overworked; indeed I think it is quite wonderful the amount of labour that they have accomplished during the short time we have been here. To the west from the last-mentioned work (in front of the head of the harbour) are two small batteries on elevated ground on the road to Sevastopol, and after following this for a mile one comes to the base of the great plateau on which the allied armies are encamped. The edge of this plateau forms the northern side of the valley of Balaklava, and continues in a north-easterly direction till it reaches the valley of the Tchernaya, when, turning sharply round to the west, it passes the heights of Inkermann, and terminates at the head of the harbour of Sevastopol. From the southern extremity of this same valley (Balaklava), commencing at the village of Kamara, winds (literally so) a ridge of hills, coming to an abrupt ending in the table-land in the neighbourhood of Mackenzie's Farm. I have already recorded that we have been for some time constructing a series of redoubts across the above-mentioned valley, about two miles north of the town of Balaklava. The most easterly of these works is situated on Canrobert's Hill; it is that of the greatest importance, as from its elevated position it overlooks the village of Kamara, and commands the two nearest of the chain of redoubts. Such are the works constructed for the defence of our base of operations.

Early one morning it was discovered from the most advanced of the Turkish redoubts that large bodies of troops were marching towards Balaklava. Lord Lucan was in the redoubt at the moment, and lost no time in ordering the Cavalry Division under arms; an affair of only a few moments, as the cavalry are always ready to turn out an hour before daylight. Information of this was sent to Sir Colin Campbell and Lord Raglan. In the meantime Barker's Battery (9-pounders) and Maude's troop (6-pounders) of horse artillery were ordered up, supported by the Greys. Our guns opened a smart fire on the enemy, but, the distance being too great, they did not tell with much effect. The Russians replied with several batteries of heavier calibre than ours, and we therefore got rather the worst of it; added to which, for some reason that I have not heard explained, our artillery had only a few rounds per gun, instead of the usual quantity of ammunition.

On receiving the report of the Russian advance, Sir Colin Campbell immediately ordered out all the available troops under his command. The batteries were all manned, and the Royal Marines lined the parapets on the eastern heights of the town. Sir Colin caused the 93rd Highlanders, and a company from the Invalid Battalion (mustering about 100 men), to be placed in line midway between the defences of the place and the line of redoubts, in a position where they could best repulse any attempt on the part of the enemy to advance on the town. Shortly before 8 a.m. Lord Raglan received intelligence from Lord Lucan (commanding the cavalry) that the enemy were advancing in force towards Balaklava. Lord Raglan and his Staff immediately proceeded to the edge of the plateau, where the whole of the valley could be overlooked, as well as the port and town of Balaklava. On arriving at this point we saw strong bodies of troops advancing, some along the valley (mostly cavalry and artillery), and others appearing over the ridge, at the end of which is the village of Kamara. On seeing the force in which the enemy were, Lord Raglan sent an aide-de-camp to order the 1st and 4th Divsions down into the valley, to reinforce the troops under the command of Sir Colin Campbell. Information was also sent to General Canrobert, who immediately ordered the division of General Bosquet to be got under arms, and came himself with his Staff shortly after and joined Lord Raglan.

A few moments after our arrival the Russians established a battery of field artillery close to the village of Kamara, and opened fire on No. 1 redoubt (that on Canrobert's Hill); at the same time a column of infantry (some 1200 men) advanced up to it, the Turkish garrison firing on them in a desultory sort of way with small arms, but without attempting to serve their heavy guns. To our intense disgust, in a few moments we saw a little stream of men issue from the rear of the redoubt, and run down the hill side towards our lines; these were immediately followed by a regular cloud of fugitives, and the Russians entered the fort to find it garrisoned by dead and wounded men. In this work they captured four iron guns of position which we had lent the Turks. A man of the Royal Artillery had been put in charge of these guns, and did his duty well by spiking them when he found they were to be abandoned to the enemy. They were consequently rendered useless for the time. Thus in a few moments we lost, through the confounded cowardice of the Turks, the key of our advanced line of defence. The Russians poured into the work, and very speedily got some field-pieces up to it, and then opened fire on the next redoubt. The garrison of No. 2 redoubt, when they saw the Russians enter No. 1, immediately bethought themselves of flight, instead of attempting to hold it for a moment against the enemy, and, to the indignation of all, we saw these miserables coming out of the work laden with their baggage, etc., and deliberately marching to the rear. The Russians opened on them from the field-guns they had in No. 1 redoubt, and caused them severe loss. Directly the Turks found they were being fired into, they dispersed like a flock of sheep, and ran across the valley, numbers throwing away their arms and accoutrements to facilitate their flight. So much for our Turkish allies. Many were the curses loud and deep heaped on their heads.

During this time the Russians had been advancing, and we now began to guess pretty accurately as to their numbers. They were variously stated at from 20,000 to 30,000 men. Of these about 2000 were artillery, 6000 cavalry, and the remainder infantry. Large parties of the enemy's cavalry, consisting chiefly of the Cossacks of the Don, were let loose on the runaway Turks. The yells of these wild horsemen could be distinctly heard where we were as they galloped after these unhappy Moslems, numbers of whom were killed by their lances. Directly the Turks abandoned No. 2 redoubt, the enemy sent a body of infantry with two or three field-pieces to occupy it and fire into No. 3 redoubt. They also got possession of three more iron guns of position (12-pounders), but which had been spiked by the English artilleryman in charge. A certain number of the Turks of No. 2 redoubt, when they vacated the work, ran over to No. 3, and thus strengthened its garrison. These, after firing a few shots, were seized with a panic, and consequently got into confusion, and, in the course of a few moments, we had the annoyance of seeing No. 3 redoubt evacuated in the same manner as the others, its garrison for the most part running towards Balaklava, though some few ran into No. 4 redoubt. The enemy directly occupied the vacated fort, and thus captured two more of our guns. Sir Colin Cambell, who was with the 93rd Regiment and invalids, managed to check a certain number of the fugitives, and formed them up on each flank of the English troops. Some 300 might have been thus disposed, but the greater number continued on till they arrived inside our works at Balaklava.

The enemy's cavalry now began to advance over the rising ground between Nos. 2 and 3 redoubts, formed up in a heavy column. These divided in two parts, the larger portion remaining in reserve, and the other (a body of Cossacks and Hussars of 500 horses) moved across the valley in the direction of the English and Turkish troops in line, under the command of Sir Colin Campbell. The enemy advanced at a good pace, but in anything but a confident manner, as there was much *tailing* and flying out of the ranks on each side. On they rode, and, when about 600 yards off, the Turks on our flank (without orders) fired a harmless volley, then turned,

and ran as fast as their legs could carry them towards the town, some calling out, "Ship, Johnny, ship!" alluding to the vessels in harbour. The advancing Russians, seeing this cowardly behaviour on the part of our allies, gained fresh courage themselves, and came on with a rush, yelling in a very barbarous manner, and which on badly disciplined troops would probably have had an intimidating effect. The British soldiers, however, only laughed at their yells, and, when they had come a hundred yards nearer, gave them their first volley, which materially checked both their pace and noise. Volley number two then rang out, as clear and compact as at an ordinary field-day. This was enough for the Ruskies; we immediately had the satisfaction of seeing them wheel round to their left, and gallop off towards Canrobert's Hill in great confusion and fear, marking their course by the killed and wounded that dropped from the saddle, and the number of riderless horses galloping about in all directions.

In the meantime the Russians had been collecting their forces on the most commanding ground. A large mass of infantry was posted close to the village of Kamara: some were also hid from our view, between it and Canrobert's Hill; whilst opposite, extending from there to the Tchernaya river, were several battalions of infantry, three or four batteries, and another large body of Cossacks; and on some high ground close to the river, projecting into the valley, was a battery of eight guns, supported by a regiment of infantry. On seeing these preparations on the part of the Russians, Lord Raglan ordered the brigade of Light Cavalry to take post on the ridge, just at the foot of the plateau where we were standing. From this point they could watch and take advantage of any movement on the part of the enemy. Lord Raglan's object was to place the cavalry in a position of safety, and at the same time prevent a general action coming on until the arrival of the 1st and 4th Divisions. I should mention that Barker's Battery of artillery, placed near Sir Colin Campbell and his infantry, had done good service against the flying enemy when they retired before the volleys of the Highlanders. The troop of horse artillery attached to the division of cavalry was stationed near the Heavy Brigade, under cover of a vineyard, ready to come into action at a moment's notice. The body of Russian cavalry that remained on the ridge between the two redoubts last captured had witnessed the defeat of their comrades. They now turned their attention to the English cavalry, and, seeing a portion of the Heavy Brigade without support, at once descended, and advanced at a rapid pace against them. Directly the Turkish garrison of No. 4 redoubt saw the enemy's cavalry in movement, fancying that it was to cut them off, they rushed out of the work towards our troops. The enemy, seeing this, sent a body of infantry to occupy it. Fortunately there were no guns in this work. Brigadier-General Scarlett, by Lord Lucan's order, immediately placed the Greys and Enniskillens in line, sent to the 5th Dragoon Guards to support them on the right, and to the Royals and 4th Dragoon Guards to attack on the left.

The Russian cavalry, consisting of Hussars and Dragoons in front, backed up by a host of Cossacks, mustering in all some 3000 sabres, came on, gradually slackening their pace as they saw the English cavalry advance towards them in such perfect order and confidence. The pace of the Russians got slower and slower the nearer we

Left above: A review for Omer Pasha.
Left below: The Zouaves come to the rescue of the English Guards at Inkermann.

approached, and, at the moment the two bodies met, the Russians were almost at a halt. The front line of the English cavalry was not able to meet the enemy at the pace that they wished, as they had to cross through what had been the camp of the Light Cavalry, and the ground was strewed with articles that had not as yet been removed, and consequently impeded the rapid movement of these two regiments. Nevertheless, our fellows went in with a will that told with striking effect on the enemy, and, after a moment's pause, we saw them disappear in the midst of the mass of Russians. For a second we were all anxious for the result: but a minute later and the 4th Dragoon Guards and Royals charged the enemy on the one flank, whilst the 5th Dragoon Guards attacked them on the other. The Russians made a momentary stand, and then you saw the entire body of men and horses move back a little; and after a minute or two the whole made a rush to the rear, our Dragoons cutting and slashing about them with an energy and force that must have been deeply felt on the heads and shoulders of the fugitive Russians. In this encounter our loss was scarce 20 casualties, whereas that of the enemy was put at over 200. When Lord Raglan saw the successful manner in which the charge had been made, he sent down an officer of his Staff to say "Well done!" to General Scarlett. It is much to be regretted that the Brigade of Light Cavalry, under command of Lord Cardigan, did not attack the enemy in flank and rear when they first met the Heavy Brigade, as the defeat would have been more complete, and numbers of prisoners might have been taken. Captain Morris, who commanded the 17th Lancers, pointed out to Lord Cardigan the opportunity that offered of charging the enemy; but the Earl said he was placed in that particular spot, and should not move without orders. In vain Captain Morris begged to be allowed to charge with his regiment alone. Lord Cardigan would not give his permission. *The Heavy Brigade were unable to pursue the Russian cavalry for any distance, as they came under the fire from the redoubts captured by the enemy.

Shortly after this successful charge a portion of the Turks who had bolted were led back by their Pasha into redoubt No. 5, which they had abandoned just before, and which had never been occupied by the enemy. The Russians were evidently very much cowed by the reverse their cavalry had met with, and all their forces were somewhat drawn back, and placed closer together.

At 11 a.m. General Canrobert and his Staff came up to Lord Raglan, and about the same time two squadrons of the Chasseurs d'Afrique moved under us to the left of the Turkish redoubts, and formed up across the Woronzoff road. The 1st Division of the French army had been ordered to join the English in the valley, together with two batteries of artillery; these arrived after a time, and were placed in reserve, under the heights on which Lord Raglan and General Canrobert had stationed themselves. The enemy still continued to place his troops on the

* The Earl of Cardigan has denied the whole of the above statement since the publication of the first edition of this work, and declared it to be "totally without foundation;" adding "that Captain Morris never gave any advice, or made any proposal of the sort;" that "it was not his duty to do so;" and that he "did not commit such an irregularity." The conversation, however, has been frequently related by Captain (now Lieutenant-Colonel and C.B.) Morris, in the presence of officers of high rank, at various times and places. Besides which, the author has been assured by other officers of the 17th Lancers, who were present at the time, of the truth of his statement, one of them adding that even the men in the ranks clamoured to be allowed to attack the enemy.

defensive. They brought a battery of eight guns, and posted it at right angles to the chain of redoubts, between No.2 and the Tchernaya river, so as to sweep the valley. On each flank they had also artillery; on that nearest the river eight guns, and on the opposite side, close under No. 2 redoubt, a battery of six. Behind all this artillery they had withdrawn their cavalry, in support of which were masses of infantry.

It now becomes my task to record the sad catastrophe of the day. If gallantry, courage, and daring can compensate in any way for the noble lives that were then sacrificed, we have every reason to be proud of the chivalry displayed. Indeed, I question whether we can look upon it as a disaster, when we think of the impression that noble little band must have made upon our foes. Although the result was not that of victory, still it will be remembered in future days as one of the brightest actions of British daring, and as a brilliant proof of how little our troops consider the odds opposed to them when 'duty points the way'. But to return to the action. It was now shortly after 11 a.m.: Lord Raglan, from the place that he occupied, commanding as it did so extensive a view of the whole of the valley of Balaklava and the position of the Russian forces, thought that he perceived a retrograde movement on the part of the enemy. Upon a closer examination with our glasses it appeared pretty evident that the Russians were removing our guns which they had captured in the forts. Lord Raglan, wishing, therefore, to prevent their object being attained, sent an order to Lord Lucan, to the effect that the cavalry were to advance and take any opportunity that might offer to recapture the heights. He also ordered the 4th Division, under the command of Sir G. Cathcart, to support them. This opportunity did not occur, according to the view that Lord Lucan took of the matter.

A pause of over half an hour ensued, after the lapse of which time Lord Raglan, still under the impression — whether erroneous or not it is impossible to say — that the Russians intended immediately to retire and take with them our guns, sent another order to Lord Lucan. The order was written by General Airey, the Quartermaster-General, who had been constantly at Lord Raglan's side during the day. It was in the following terms: *'Lord Raglan wishes the cavalry to advance rapidly to the front, follow the enemy, and try to prevent the enemy carrying away the guns. Troop of horse artillery may accompany. French cavalry is on your left. Immediate.'* This order was intrusted to Captain Nolan, aide-de-camp to General Airey, a cavalry officer of great experience. Previous to his departure he received careful instructions both from Lord Raglan and the Quartermaster-General. But before going any further, I must say that what follows is not meant in any way to disparage Captain Nolan. He was a man for whom I had a personal regard, and whose opinion, in matters of his profession, was generally respected. Poor fellow! he is now no more; and perhaps the best tribute we can pay to his memory would be to say that he died from an act of over-daring and courage. When the order was delivered to Lord Lucan he demurred for a moment to put it into execution, and asked Nolan what it was that he was to attack, who replied, I am told, "There, my Lord, is our enemy, and there are our guns;" at the same time pointing down the valley to where the enemy had the battery of eight guns, placed as I before mentioned, with artillery also on each flank.

Captain Nolan appears to have totally misunderstood the instructions he had just before received: 'the guns' in the written order, of course, alluded to those the

Sketch of Lord Raglan drawn by an artist visiting Headquarters.

enemy had captured in the redoubts, and which it was thought they were carrying away; and the direction which he (Nolan) pointed out to Lord Lucan was quite contrary to that intended by Lord Raglan. His manner also was scarcely that in which an aide-de-camp ought to address a general officer, and for which there was no reason or excuse. Lord Lucan appears to have considered that he was bound to charge the enemy, therefore made arrangements to carry out the object which he supposed Lord Raglan had in view. He consequently communicated with Lord Cardigan, and desired him to form the Light Brigade into two lines. Lord Cardigan remonstrated, and urged the uselessness of making such an attack; but Lord Lucan replied that his orders were imperative from the Commander-in-Chief, or words to that effect. The fatal order to advance was then given, and, to the horror of all of us on the heights above, we saw our handful of light cavalry advance down towards the Russian batteries. We all saw at once that a lamentable mistake had been made—by whose fault it was then impossible to say. Lord Raglan sent down two of his Staff to ascertain the cause of all this, so little was it his intention that an attack of this nature should take place.

But to follow the fortunes of the Light Brigade. It consisted of scarce 700 horses, although composed of no less than five different regiments. In the first line were four squadrons of the 13th Light Dragoons and 17th Lancers; in the second were four squadrons of the 4th Light Dragoons and 11th Hussars. Again, in their rear was one squadron of the 8th Hussars, as a sort of reserve. As they started into a trot, poor Nolan galloped some way in front of the brigade, waving his sword and encouraging his men by voice and gesture. Before they had gone any distance the enemy's guns opened on them at long range. Nolan was the first man killed: some grape-shot hit him in the chest: his horse turned and carried him to the rear through our advancing squadrons. His screams were heard far above the din of battle, and he fell dead from his saddle near the spot where the order had been given for the charge. The pace of our cavalry increased every moment, until they went thundering along the valley, making the ground tremble beneath them. The awful slaughter that was going on, from the fire the enemy poured into them, apparently did not check their career. On they went, headlong to the death, disregarding aught but the object of their attack. At length they arrived at the guns, their numbers sadly thinned, but the few that remained made fearful havoc amongst the enemy's artillerymen. Scarce a man escaped, except those who crept under their gun-carriages, and thus put themselves out of the reach of our men's swords. This was the moment when a General was most required, but unfortunately Lord Cardigan was not then present. On coming up to the battery (as he afterwards himself described it) a gun was fired close to him, and for a moment he thought his leg was gone. Such was not the case, as he remained unhurt; however, his horse took fright—swerved round—and galloped off with him to the rear, passing on the way by the 4th Light Dragoons and 8th Hussars before those regiments got up to the battery. I have said that the enemy's cavalry were posted in rear of their guns. On our advance some of their squadrons had been withdrawn to the higher ground on each flank, the infantry remaining in its old position, and these our cavalry had next to attack. The Russians did not wait to be assailed, but, on the approach of our men, a very large majority ran back to some brushwood behind them, and where our men could not follow. At this time the whole of our squadrons that composed the first and the greater portion of the second line were in considerable disorder. No blame was to be attached to anyone for this, as so many officers had been either killed, wounded, or had had their horses shot under them. The amazing number of riderless horses that were galloping about, many of them wounded and wild with fright, added also to the general confusion. Some of our cavalry chased the Russians almost down to the Tchernaya river, but then had to return on their exhausted horses to rejoin the brigade.

As soon as the Russians saw that all our squadrons had arrived at the guns, they sent a large body of Lancers, near No. 3 redoubt, to cut off our retreat. This was first observed by one of the officers of the 8th Hussars (which regiment, as may be remembered, was in rear of the brigade), who immediately rode up and informed Colonel Shewell, the commanding officer, of this movement by the enemy's cavalry. Colonel Shewell at once ordered his regiment to wheel about, which being done, he gave the word to charge, and was himself the first to enter the Russian Lancers. These unfortunates, completely surprised by the manoeuvre, offered but feeble resistance, and this single squadron of the 8th Hussars passed through the Russians,

Plan of the battle of Balaklava
Fought Oct. 25th 1854

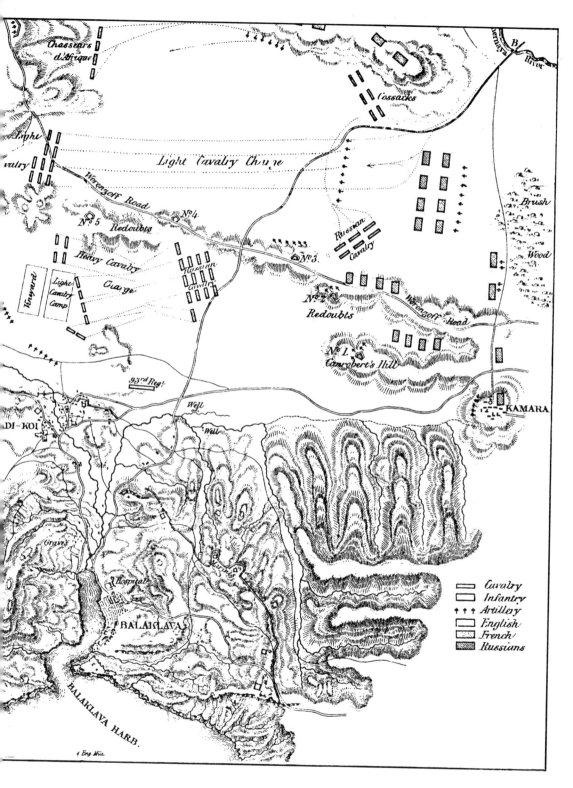

Chasseurs d'Afrique

Cossacks

Light Cavalry

Light Cavalry Charge

Worongoff Road

Nº 5 Nº 4

Redoubts

Heavy Cavalry

Charge

Vineyard

Light Cavalry Camp

Russian Cavalry

Russian Infantry

Nº 3

Nº 2

Redoubts

Brush

Wood

Worongoff Road

Nº 1.

Canrobert's Hill

KAMARA

93rd Regt.

Well

Well

DI-KOI

Graves

Hospital

Ruins

BALAKLAVA

BALAKLAVA HARB.

1 Eng Mile.

Cavalry

Infantry

Artillery

English

French

Russians

of four times their strength, cutting down all in their way, while the rest dispersed to the right and left. A way was thus cleared for the remainder of our cavalry to retire unopposed — but not unmolested, as the enemy opened upon them with grape from their guns, on both flanks, besides throwing out swarms of skirmishers, which combined fire made fearful havoc of the gallant remnant of the Light Brigade. Lord Lucan brought up the heavy cavalry to cover the retreat of their comrades, which they did with perfect order and regularity, although they suffered some loss of men and horses. I should have mentioned that, during the retreat of the Light Cavalry, the two squadrons of the Chasseurs d'Afrique, which up to that period had not been engaged, made a brilliant attack on the Russian battery on their left front, which was pouring its deadly volleys on the retreating groups of British heroes. They succeeded in silencing for a time several guns, and only retired when they found that they were opposed to an overwhelming fire from some Russian infantry, which was brought up to repel their attack. In this charge they lost two officers and over 50 men and horses killed and wounded. It was a daring act, and one well worthy of their reputed 'élan'. The losses our light cavalry sustained in this brilliant but unfortunate charge were very great.

	Wounded	Killed and missing	Total Casualties
Officers	12	9	21
Serjeants	9	14	23
Trumpeters	3	4	7
Rank and file	98	129	227
	122	156	278

Besides 335 horses killed in action, or obliged afterwards to be destroyed from wounds. It has since been ascertained that the Russians took many prisoners.

Directly it was perceived from the heights that the light cavalry were retiring, Lord Raglan, General Canrobert, and their respective Staffs, descended into the valley. Shortly after Lord Lucan came up to the Commander-in-Chief, and the first thing Lord Raglan said to him was, "Why, you have lost the Light Brigade!" or words to that effect. Lord Lucan denied this, and said he had only carried out the orders which he had received from Captain Nolan. Some more conversation ensued, in which Lord Raglan blamed Lord Lucan for not using his discretionary power, and for not taking advantage of the auxiliaries suggested to him in the last order, viz. 'Troop of horse artillery may accompany. French cavalry is on your left'. It would appear also that Lord Lucan did not see any connexion between that and the previous order, in which he was informed that the infantry (meaning the 1st and 4th Divisions) were also ordered to advance and support him in regaining the heights. In fact, the whole thing seems to have been misinterpreted by Captain Nolan to Lord Lucan, or at any rate misunderstood by him.

Lord Raglan now sent to Sir George Cathcart to desire him to occupy No. 3 redoubt, which had been abandoned by the enemy. This he immediately did, and placed riflemen in such a position that they caused the Russians in No. 2 great annoyance. The enemy seemed desirous of not renewing the action if possible, and contented themselves with the occupation of Nos. 1 and 2 redoubts. From this time they gradually withdrew their troops to the high ground beyond the village of Kamara, and towards dusk only a portion of cavalry and artillery remained in the valley, apparently to prevent their flank from being turned by any attack of the Allies. The allied Commanders-in-Chief now had a consultation together, when they decided that it would only be a useless sacrifice of life to attempt to retake the redoubts, as it was not their intention to occupy them again. They considered that they had not an adequate force at their disposal to defend in sufficient numbers so extensive a line of work. At the same time they arranged to augment the number of troops in the vicinity of Balaklava. Lord Raglan determined upon leaving the brigade of Highlanders at the disposal of Sir Colin Campbell; and General Canrobert ordered the 2nd Brigade of the 1st Division, together with a battery of artillery, to camp on some high ground on the left of our work situated near the village of Kadikoi. This brigade was under the command of General Vinoy, who was instructed to use his discretion in adopting any suggestion from Sir Colin Campbell in the event of an attack from the enemy. As to our unfortunate allies the Turks, they were to be placed in such a position that they should never have an opportunity of running away again. The only thing to be said in defence of their disgraceful conduct is, that they are so badly commanded, their officers being for the most part men entirely devoid of all education or experience in their profession. I understand that a large number owe their present appointments to having been *chibouqueji* (*i.e.* pipe-bearers) or attendants on Pashas, and have only lately left these servile employments. They can hardly be supposed, therefore, to understand military order and discipline. Their loss on the 25th was very considerable. I believe nine officers and upwards of 250 men were killed or wounded; of these at least two-thirds were struck down when running away after they had abandoned their works.

After dusk the brigade of Guards and the 4th Division returned to their respective camps, as also did the remainder of the French troops. It was dark when Lord Raglan and the Staff returned to Headquarters, all rather melancholy at the results of the day, and each mourning the loss of several dear friends and brother officers, whose lives had been uselessly sacrificed to a misconception of orders. *

The following morning (October 26th) Lord Raglan and the Staff rode down to Balaklava, in order to see in what manner it could be best protected against any attack of the enemy. We found Sir C. Campbell in the redoubt on the crest of the heights to the east of the harbour, where he had been all night, ready, in case the Russians should renew the attack on our position.

After some consultation with Sir Colin Campbell and the officers who are chiefs of the military departments, it was decided that a line-of-battle ship should be anchored across the upper part of the harbour, and thus bring an overwhelming battery of the heaviest artillery to sweep the usual approaches to Balaklava. Then all the works on the heights and in front of the town are to be materially strengthened. As our Turks do not appear to be able to fight, it was determined

* The loss of the Allies in killed, wounded, and missing, at the battle of Balaklava, was as follows: —

	Officers.	Serjeants, Trumpeters, and Rank and File.	Total Casualties.
English..	40 ..	.. .. 386	426
French	2 ..	.. .. 50 (about) ..	52
Turks	9 ..	.. .. 250 (about) ..	259
			737

that they should be employed chiefly in working parties, both at Balaklava and also in the trenches. For this purpose 1500 of them were sent up during the afternoon to go into our two attacks, and work there for the following night. The 42nd High-landers were placed in rear of the redoubt at Kadikoi, and the 79th, between them and the 93rd, on the eastern heights. These regiments are to strengthen the redoubt and construct a parapet and ditch across the valley to connect the works on the opposite side. The brigade of French under General Vinoy, camped to the east of Kadikoi, were ordered to fortify the ground they occupy, and complete the defence of the position before Balaklava.

On returning, half-way between Balaklava and Headquarters, Lord Raglan was met by a staff-officer sent by Sir De Lacy Evans, who begged to inform him that the Russians had made a sortie in force from Sevastopol on our extreme right, opposite Inkermann. Lord Raglan immediately galloped off to the 2nd Division, and, on his arrival, found that the enemy had been repulsed and driven back to the town. It would appear that soon after 1 p.m. a strong body of infantry, with two batteries of artillery and two squadrons of Cossacks, left the place, and advanced towards the heights on which our 2nd Division is encamped. This movement they made with such rapidity, that our outposts and pickets had to engage the enemy's skirmishers for some little time before any supports could be brought to them. Directly Sir De Lacy was informed of the Russian attack, he ordered out the 2nd Division, and the two batteries of artillery attached to it: in a very short time it was under arms, and instantly marched to the scene of action. In the meantime our pickets had been so hard pressed by the enemy's that they had to retire, and, on the division coming up, our guns opened with great effect. Shortly after, the brigade of Guards was brought up by H.R.H. the Duke of Cambridge in support of the 2nd Division; it was not however engaged, but the battery attached to it joined those already in action.

Our 18 guns now opened so destructive a fire upon the enemy's artillery, that it was driven out of the field immediately. They then turned their attention to the Russian infantry, which precipitately retired in great disorder and confusion, followed by our men, who kept up a sharp fire upon the retreating columns. It was with considerable difficulty that our soldiers could be recalled from the pursuit. As the broken forces of the enemy entered the Karabelnaia suburb, near the water's edge, they came within range of one of our Lancasters in the 5-gun battery, which opened up and caused them enormous loss. All this had taken up but little more than half an hour. We captured over 80 prisoners, of whom two officers and 17 men were untouched. I ought to state that General Bosquet, on hearing the cannonade, turned out five battalions of his division, and marched them in the direction of the firing, and sent an officer of his Staff to inform Sir De Lacy Evans of the fact; but before the French arrived the enemy had been driven back, consequently their proffered assistance was not required. On the following morning (October 27th) the prisoners who were not wounded were brought up to Head-quarters and examined by Mr. Calvert. From their account it appears that the guns captured before Balaklava on the 25th were brought round the same evening and paraded through the streets of Sevastopol, and it was generally circulated in the garrison that a victory had been gained over the English. Consequently the rejoicings were great, the church-bells were rung, and the Admiral gave a ball. The next day they decided upon making an attack, and, as the troops were told that the

English were quite disheartened, there was no difficulty in obtaining volunteers for that service. They consisted of 4500 infantry, with 12 guns and two squadrons of Cossacks. They must have been not a little surprised at the readiness with which they were met and repulsed by the British troops, whose number did not exceed 2000 men.

We buried yesterday (27th) 96 Russian corpses; many more were lying nearer the town, which the garrison would not allow us to approach. All the afternoon after the sortie and the following morning large fatigue parties were employed by the enemy in bringing in their dead and wounded. Altogether their loss is estimated at upwards of 600 casualties; our loss was two officers and 10 men killed, and five officers and 51 men wounded. One of the officers who was taken prisoner informed us that the Russian troops that attacked Balaklava on the 25th were under the command of General Liprandi, and consisted of 17,000 infantry, 5000 cavalry (of whom 2000 were Cossacks, the remainder being regulars), and 62 guns, of which 20 were guns of position. He said that he understood their loss was one General wounded, and 25 other officers, besides about 550 men, killed and wounded.

This morning (28th) Lord Raglan decided that a flag of truce should be sent to ascertain what prisoners the Russians had taken on the 25th. Accordingly he despatched an aide-de-camp to Lord Lucan, requesting him to send a letter by an officer of his Staff to the Russian General commanding the troops on the Tchernaya. Lord Lucan intrusted this mission to Captain Fellowes, Deputy-Assistant Quartermaster General of the cavalry division. He went, accompanied only by the trumpet-major of the 17th Lancers, bearing a white flag at the end of a lance. They rode up to our most advanced videttes, and then proceeded at a walk towards the Russian outposts, sounding every two or three minutes. As they approached they observed a party of some dozen Cossacks ride out towards them, who, when within 50 yards, halted, and two officers left them and rode up to Captain Fellowes. He addressed them in French, and informed them that he had a letter from the General commanding the English cavalry to the Russian General commanding the troops on the Tchernaya. He also stated the import of the letter, and added that he had observed many dead bodies lying on the ground on the scene of the Light Cavalry charge on the 25th, and begged they would have them interred, or allow us to send parties for that purpose. One of the officers, in reply, said that he would go and ask the General. He then rode off to the rear with a Cossack orderly. The other officer remained with Captain Fellowes, and, as he could speak no civilized language but his own, their conversation was necessarily limited. Nevertheless, they managed to fraternize by exchanging cigars and admiring one another's swords, etc. In a short time the first officer returned, accompanied by an old officer, who was evidently a man of rank from the respect shown him. He was at first not very civil, and appeared much annoyed at the remarks Captain Fellowes had made on the dead being left unburied. *"Dites à votre Général que nous sommes ennemis, mais que nous sommes Chrétiens,"* said he. However, he softened down when he found that Captain Fellowes had brought letters from Russian officers whom we had taken prisoners, and told him that, if he would return tomorrow at midday, he should have the names of the survivors of the 25th.

On October 29th Captain Fellowes went again with a flag of truce to the outposts of the Russians in the valley of Balaklava. He was immediately met by an officer who gave him a letter from General Liprandi in reply to Lord Lucan's of the day before; from which it appeared that they have only two English officers prisoners, namely, Lieutenant Chadwick, adjutant 17th Lancers, and Cornet Clowes of the 8th Hussars, both severely wounded; the former speared in the neck, and the latter in the back. Both had their horses shot under them, and it was in attempting to return to our lines that they were pursued by Cossacks, and wounded in the manner I have described. Several other wounded officers had been brought in to the Russian camp after the action of the 25th, but none had survived through the night. They had also from 30 to 40 men prisoners, the majority of whom were wounded. There was also a Piedmontese officer of the Sardinian army taken prisoner. He was one of several officers sent by his government, and attached to the Headquarters of the French army, and, having come with the French Staff on the 25th, foolishly joined in the charge of our Light Cavalry, had his horse killed under him, and was himself badly wounded. The Russian officer brought also a letter from Clowes to a brother officer of his regiment, in which he stated that they were very kindly treated, and received every attention and comfort that circumstances would admit, and that they were to leave for Simferopol that evening, to which place most of the other prisoners had already been taken.

We hear from deserters, and indeed we can see, that large reinforcements are daily arriving to the Russian army. It is said that the Corps d'Armée under General Liprandi counts upwards of 40,000 bayonets, and that he is expecting another division. General Osten-Sacken has arrived in the Crimea with a large force: accounts vary as to its strength, but probably it is not less than from 20,000 to 25,000 men. In the meantime the Allies are fortifying their position: the French are constructing considerable works along the edge of the plateau overlooking the valley of Balaklava; and the English have been unremitting in their exertions to strengthen the ground before that town. The *Sanspareil* screw line-of-battle ship has been brought round to Balaklava, and is now at the head of the harbour, anchored broadside on, so that her guns sweep the main entrances. For some time past General Canrobert has promised Lord Raglan to send a division of infantry to reinforce our troops on the extreme right, opposite Inkermann; but for some reason or other it has been put off from day to day, so that the much-wished-for assistance has never arrived. Sir De Lacy Evans has several times urged on Lord Raglan the necessity of strengthening our position at this point, and Lord Raglan, willing to give him every assistance and support in his power, induced General Canrobert to promise the troops before mentioned. Indeed, more than that — Sir John Burgoyne (Royal Engineers), the other day, took General Bizot (*Chef du Corps du Génie*) over the ground, and pointed out to him the desirability of increasing the number of troops at that place, which General Bizot admitted. With our present numbers it is impossible for us to construct any intrenchments. The men of the 2nd Division are much overworked, as the ground they have to defend is so extensive that there are necessarily many outposts and pickets to furnish. Although, with the exception of this weak point, our position begins to assume a formidable appearance, the line of defence is of such extent, that our force, as long as the siege lasts, is not numerous enough to defend it properly against a vigorous attack of the enemy, should they make it simultaneously at different points and in sufficient numbers. Though the Russians have a large disposable force, I doubt much

commencement of Sir Wm Wington
(on the other side are accurate
portrait of Percy Herberts cap)

D Rokeby

HW Barnard
May 16 1856

General Jones

Hugh Rose
May 16 1856

Sir H. Rose

C W Ridley
Brig Gel
May 16/56

General Ridley

Percy Herbert

R George Foley
May 16 th

Quick pencil sketches made during 1856. These are taken from a notebook and show fellow officers and some of the English Generals.

85

whether they will have determination and courage enough to overcome British firmness and French gallantry. All this makes it of great importance that the town should be taken with the least possible delay, especially as the troops begin to suffer from the coldness of the nights.

The 29th was the first really cold day that we have had since we landed in the Crimea, and the contrast to the previous warmth was very great. Far more men go into hospital from the night-work in the trenches than from any other cause; and even those not at work begin to feel the cold very much, being only under the cover of the tents, which are but poor protection against inclement weather. It is strange that there are many, even in high places, who think that we shall not winter in the Crimea; but I do not see how it would be possible to embark the allied armies with a large Russian force close by, unless we made up our minds to sacrifice all the artillery and cavalry, and even then there would be great difficulty in doing so.

I heard from a French officer that some of his men of the Zouaves had been feasting for the last few days upon some Russian horses which had been killed a few nights after the battle. This had been done by mistake: a picket of Zouaves, hearing the sound of galloping horses approaching, and fancying that it was a surprise by the enemy, fired with such effect that several horses were killed, while many others were caught. Upon examination, they discovered they were all without riders, although saddled; and it was evident, from the state of their bridles, that they had broken away from the enemy's camp, probably frightened by some rockets which the French had been throwing at the Russians. I expressed my surprise to the officer that the Zouaves should care about eating horse-flesh, when doubtless they were well provided with meat by their commissariat; but he replied, that, although they had plenty of *salt* meat given them, *fresh* meat was too great a luxury not to be taken advantage of when thrown in their way, as it was very rarely issued to the troops as rations.*

At daylight on November 1st the French at last opened their breaching fire, but with only 32 guns. They appeared to have considerable effect; and although the Russians answered them very briskly for about an hour, the predominance of the French fire was from that time very apparent, and, after some hours cannonade, the enemy ceased to reply altogether. The front line of the Russian works is in a very damaged state; but I suspect they care little for that, as they depend chiefly on the strength of their inner line of defence. They have been, for some time past, making very large earthworks in rear of the Redan and Bastion du Mât Batteries, and in spite of our incessant pounding they continue to increase the batteries in the neighbourhood of the Malakoff Tower. All these great inner works are but little affected by our fire, as their outer or front line of defence acts in a great measure as a screen to the inner one. I believe therefore the only thing that would silence the guns in there would be to bring an overwhelming vertical fire from mortars to bear upon them; but, unfortunately, we have but a limited supply of this ordnance.

* I remember Colonel Lagondie telling me that, when serving in Algeria during the winter of 1833–34, he lived for *six weeks* (!) on horse-flesh, as well as the greater portion of the French troops, because there was no other meat to be had. I think this was in the province of Constantine. I recollect, when I was travelling in that country, hearing from several French officers that they had often been obliged to eat horse-flesh from the scarcity of provisions.

CHAPTER 6

Battle of Inkermann

ON Sunday last, November 5th, 1854, we had another awful battle, far more desperate and bloody than that of the Alma. But before entering into any details, I must record that on the day before there was a grand Council of War of the allied Generals at the Headquarters of the French army. I am given to understand that it was then decided that a general assault on Sevastopol should take place on the morning of the 7th instant, as our batteries had so far got the upper hand of the enemy that it was at length thought practicable to do so. General Canrobert again assured Lord Raglan that he would send up the long-wished-for support and reinforcement to our extreme right, opposite Inkermann; and had that support arrived, as had been so *often promised*, before the 5th of November, it is impossible to say how many noble lives and gallant hearts might have been spared to their country. I have before mentioned that we had learnt from our spies that large reinforcements had already arrived to the Russian army in the Crimea, and that even greater were to be expected. Nevertheless, everyone under-valued this information, and all doubted their being able to bring up large bodies of troops in the time which the report specified; and it is only a new proof of how much we have all along underrated the strength and resources of the enemy.

The night before the battle of Inkermann passed undisturbed, save by the occasional shots which were fired from the different batteries on both sides. Some of the men, on the outlying pickets in front of the 2nd and Light Divisions, more than once fancied they heard the sound of wheels passing under the heights between them and the harbour. These sounds were reported to the officers commanding the outposts; but no heed was taken of them, as they supposed that it was merely provisions or supplies for the garrison, which would have required a regular attack in force to check. Little did the watchers think that the wheels which they heard rumbling in the distance were carrying the means for their destruction, and were forerunners of one of the bloodiest struggles in the history of modern warfare.

The morning was foggy; indeed a sort of drizzling rain had fallen throughout the night. It was 5.30 a.m when one of the pickets of the Light Division first saw the Russian infantry; their impression was that it was merely some parties of men who had mistaken their road from the thickness of the fog, especially as these appeared to be unarmed. Our picket of some 30 men stepped forward to meet them, but ere they had gone 20 yards they found themselves in front of a large body of men: it was the advanced guard of the Russian army. The pickets appear to have been almost paralysed with astonishment, as they were all, with the exception of two or three, made prisoners without firing a shot. These two or three men ran back and gave the alarm to their supports and to the neighbouring pickets. They all behaved admirably—immediately formed themselves up, and prepared to receive the enemy and contest every inch of ground, whatever might be the odds opposed to them. Fortunately, General Codrington had been visiting the outposts (a morning amusement of his, by the by), and had not as yet arrived in camp, but, hearing some musketry, turned to see what was the matter. A minute later he was met by some men from the outposts, who had been despatched by the officer in command to give notice to the Generals of the Light and 2nd Divisions that our position was being attacked by the enemy. General Codrington, without more ado, galloped off and informed Sir George Brown of the fact, who immediately turned out the whole of the available men of the Light Division; at the same time the 2nd Division was being got under arms by General Pennefather.

Scarce had the first shots been exchanged between the advancing parties of Russians and English, when the French sentries on the heights overlooking the valley of Balaklava became aware of the movement of Liprandi's troops towards the English lines before that town. Shortly after the enemy opened their guns on our works, but probably from the thickness of the fog they miscalculated the distance, as their shots fell many hundred yards short. The firing of these guns naturally aroused the whole of the camps along the line of our entrenchments; the troops were, therefore, everywhere turned out. Lord Raglan received information of the attack in force by the enemy on our extreme right about 6.20 a.m., and a few moments later intelligence reached him of the Russian advance on Balaklava. The horses were ordered out, and scarcely a quarter of an hour had elapsed before Lord Raglan and his Staff were mounted and ready to start for the scene of action. Lord Raglan was doubtful for a moment to which point he should go, as, having been informed of the advance of the enemy on the two extremes of our position, he was sure that one was intended as a feint. Knowing that the ground before Inkermann was our weak point, he felt that there his presence would be most required; besides, as he himself remarked, if the garrison of Balaklava, under such command as that of Sir Colin Campbell, was unable to defend itself, he could not assist it. Lord Raglan therefore decided to go to the 2nd Division, having first of all sent to General Canrobert to inform him of the state of affairs. He then despatched an aide-de-camp with orders to Sir George Cathcart (commanding the 4th Division) and Sir George Brown as to the relative support they were to give to one another. Colonel Steele (military secretary) was despatched to General Bosquet, commanding the French troops on the rear of our position, to beg him to send whatever reinforcements he felt able to spare to the support of the English troops on the extreme right. I was sent to Sir Richard England with instructions for him to occupy the ground in rear of our siege-works, and especially to render support on the left of the Light Division, so as to protect that part from any sudden attempt of the enemy to gain the plateau by coming up the ravines in force. To effect this purpose, Sir Richard moved up a portion of his division, under the command of Sir John Campbell, which was most judiciously placed on the ground specified, and there remained until the close of the day.

Lord Raglan and his Staff arrived at the field of battle, *i.e.* at the camp of the 2nd Division, at 6.50 a.m. I joined the Headquarters Staff a few minutes later, and found Lord Raglan, with several of his Generals, endeavouring to make out the enemy's force. Their object appeared to be to push up heavy columns of infantry, under cover of an overwhelming fire of artillery. Already the cannon-balls came tearing through the camp of the 2nd Division by dozens at a time. Tents were every moment being knocked over by shot, or blown to pieces by exploding shell. I saw several baggage-horses, tethered in a line, killed by one shot, which passed through them. The scene of confusion which the camp exhibited was frightful. Many bodies were lying about of men who had never even seen the enemy—possibly were hardly aware of their vicinity. The first one I observed was that of an officer lying flat on his back, with a cloak covering his face. I asked a servant who was near, and he told me it was Captain Allix (aide-de-camp to Sir De Lacy Evans), who had been killed by one of the earliest round shots from the enemy. I had been talking to him the night before; he was a dear good fellow, and one whose memory I shall always think of with affection.

Lord Raglan at once saw that the attack was serious, and said that it would give us much trouble and hard fighting to drive the enemy from off the ground they had already gained. The great difficulty was to see the numbers and placement of the enemy's troops, as, from the drizzling rain that was falling and the fog, the smoke from the firing hung close to the ground, and totally obscured everything around. But I should premise that previous to Lord Raglan's arrival some desperate fighting had been going on. Directly the outposts were driven in by the Russians, they placed their guns on the commanding ground at the distance of some 800 to 1000 yards in front of the camp of the 2nd Division. This high ground was known as Cossack Hill, from the fact that on our first arrival a picket of Cossacks was posted on it. By the time that General Pennefather had formed up his troops in line on the crest of the hill before their tents, the Russian infantry were advancing in heavy columns up the road from Inkermann and up the two deep ravines to the right of it. General Buller's brigade of the Light Division also, upon being marched towards the scene of contest, came upon a large body of the enemy in a ravine some little way to the left of the Inkermann road. The driving rain and fog were so blinding that it was not until they had come within 30 yards that they discovered one another; the men of the Light Division, true to their former valour, charged with the bayonet, and drove the astonished enemy down the ravine before them; having completely put them to flight, they moved on and gained the crest of the hill on the left of the line of regiments of the 2nd Division, already under heavy fire. General Pennefather ordered Brigadier-General Adams to take the 41st and 49th Regiments and three guns of Captain Wodehouse's battery, to advance to his right front, and hold the Sandbag Battery—a point of great importance to us from the fact that it was placed at the end of a spur of the heights before Inkermann, and completely overlooked two deep ravines on either side, both of which merged into the valley of the Tchernaya. This battery, as mentioned, had been made for two guns; they had been withdrawn after they had completed the service for which they were placed. Scarce had the 41st and 49th Regiments arrived at the battery when they found themselves assailed by a perfect shower of missiles from the enemy's artillery on Cossack Hill to their left front. Brigadier-General Adams ordered his men to lie down to escape as much as possible the effects of the shot; the three guns of Wodehouse's battery were under the command of Captain Hamley, and were placed so very advantageously by him that they continued to fire with deadly effect on the enemy's columns ascending the ravine and Inkerman road on their left.

The Russians now began swarming up the sides of the ravines towards the Sandbag Battery, and the cannonade from their artillery partially ceased; then commenced the first of the many bloody contests during the day for the possession of this small but important little work. The 41st and 49th held their ground for upwards of a quarter of an hour against ten times their force, but, although hundreds fell before their accurate fire, they were always replaced from the masses of infantry behind; and it was not until they found that the enemy were penetrating round their rear that the commanding officers found it necessary to order them to retire towards their own division, but in such regularity that they carried their wounded with them. The Russians instantly poured an amazing number of men in and about the battery, and evidently determined to hold it if possible. Brigadier-General Codrington's brigade was just marching up to join their comrades of the Light Division, when they were ordered by Sir George Brown to repel the advance of a Russian regiment which was coming up the ravine on the left. They were soon engaged in a sharp conflict, but this portion of the ground was so covered with thick brushwood that it was impossible to charge in line, and consequently the fighting was confined to musketry. A battery of artillery belonging to the 4th Division was sent to assist this brigade by order of Colonel Wood, R.A., who, from over-zeal and anxiety to post the guns where their fire would most cut up the enemy, had them placed too far away from their supports; and although the first few rounds must have told with murderous effect upon them, the Russian skirmishers from amongst the brushwood picked off our artillerymen and caused us severe loss. Major Townshend, who commanded the battery, was killed, as also were numbers of his men and horses; and a large party of the enemy making a rush upon the battery before the guns could be limbered up, four were captured, two of which, however, were spiked. Seeing this, some companies of the 77th and 88th Regiments, assisted by a portion of the artillerymen, advanced with a cheer and retook the guns, making several prisoners, and returned in triumph. Almost at the same moment that this incident took place on the left, H.R.H. the Duke of Cambridge arrived with a portion of the Brigade of Guards, under the immediate command of General Bentinck, on the right. The principal part of these men had only shortly returned from 24 hours duty in the trenches; they could hardly, therefore, be considered as *fresh* troops; nevertheless they marched into action with their usual proud step and bearing, regardless alike of Russian shot and shell, which was showered with deadly effect on them as they advanced to the brow of the hill. The 41st and 49th Regiments, as I have just mentioned, had been repulsed by the Russian columns from the Sandbag Battery, and were now formed on the right of the 2nd Division, keeping up a heavy fire on the enemy, who were collecting in force by the aforesaid work. It was of importance that they should not establish themselves at that point, and therefore without more ado the Guards were ordered to retake the battery. A cheer arose at this command, and the Grenadier and Fusileer Guards rushed down the incline, and dashed with irresistible force against the enemy. They, however, were in such numbers that nothing but the indomitable courage of the English could have overcome such overwhelming superiority. The Russians in a few minutes were driven out of the work, and none of them remained but the dead and

Col. Blanc

Sketch of Col. C. G. Blanc, possibly the Deputy Assistant Commissary General.

wounded. Up to this time the Guards had scarcely fired a shot; their whole attack had been made with the bayonet, but now their Miniés came into play, and the retiring troops suffered seriously from this destructive arm.

The Coldstreams now joined their comrades of the Guards, and the brigade was immediately formed up in the following order: the Grenadiers at right angles to the battery on the right, overlooking the ravine on that side; the Coldstreams in the centre, occupying the Sandbag Battery; and the Fusileers on the left, towards the regiment on the right of the 2nd Division, but, from the distance and nature of the ground, leaving a considerable interval between them.

Lord Raglan and his Staff had arrived just in time to see the attack of the Guards, and rode down towards the retaken work, to endeavour, if possible, to ascertain the force of the enemy. The fog, to a certain extent, had cleared off, but the quantity of smoke rendered it impossible to judge with accuracy of either the strength or disposition of our foes. Lord Raglan saw sufficient to convince himself of the enormous majority of the Russians over ourselves. He therefore determined to act for the most part on the defensive, and to maintain, at all hazards, the ridge which formed the natural cover across the front of the 2nd Division camp, and also

There were many bloody contests on one day for this battery. The 41st and 49th Regiments held their ground against ten times their force, but, although hundreds of Russians fell, they were always replaced and eventually the British had to retire.

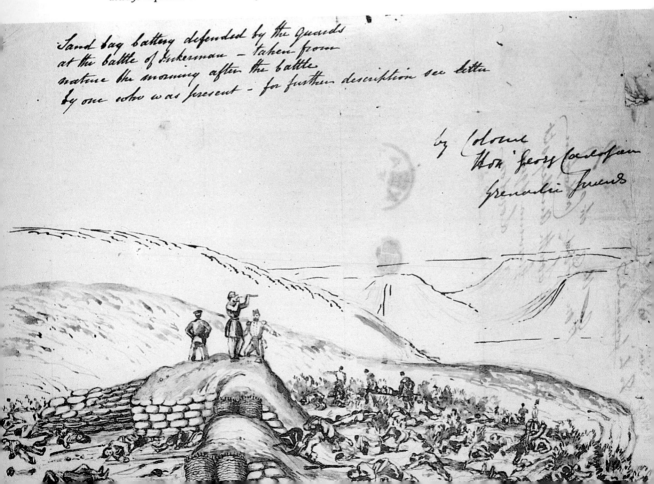

the Sandbag Battery. It was most desirable to hold this last, as it flanked all the more direct approaches to the ridge. The amazing superiority of the Russian artillery, both in number and calibre, made it more necessary to confine our efforts to repulsing only the *attacks* of the infantry than to move our troops about on the offensive, when they would be exposed to the terrible discharges from the enemy's guns. Our whole force at this moment opposed to the Russians did not exceed from 5000 to 6000 men; but Lord Raglan had ordered the 4th Division, under the command of Sir George Cathcart, to come in support of the brigade of Guards and the 2nd Division; he also momentarily expected to receive reinforcements from General Bosquet. On the first intelligence of the attack being made known to this General, he had immediately sent to know whether he could render any assistance; but I understand that both Sir George Brown and the Duke of Cambridge, to whom this offer was made, refused the proffered aid as at that time they imagined that the attack was not of the serious nature that it afterwards proved. General Bosquet, therefore contented himself with getting his regiments under arms, and distributing them in order along the edge of the plateau, overlooking the valley of Balaklava, to watch the movements of the enemy in that quarter. After 8 a.m. it became quite evident that the advance on Balaklava was intended as a feint: the enemy only firing occasionally from their field-guns, without any apparent object, as we did not lose a man here during the whole day.

It was not until General Bosquet had received Lord Raglan's message by Colonel Steele, begging him to support the British troops, that he moved a portion of his division towards the direction in which we were fighting. He had, however, to bring his troops a distance of two miles before he could reach us, and much of the ground that they crossed was covered with thick brushwood, consequently their progress was but slow. The enemy at this time appeared either to be at a loss what to do, or in preparation for another general attack upon our position, for, although their artillery kept up an unabated fire, their infantry were held back. Thus the battle was at a standstill for some little time. This was exactly what we could have most desired, as the grand object was to gain time to get up the reinforcements which were expected. The first to arrive was Sir George Cathcart's division, the first brigade of which, under Brigadier-General Goldie, was sent over the ridge to occupy the ground between the left of the Guards and the right of the 2nd Division; and the 2nd brigade was taken by Sir George Cathcart, under the command of Brigadier General Torrens, to the right rear of the Guards, where they were ordered by Lord Raglan to remain in support.

Now occurred one of the fatal errors of the day. Sir George Cathcart, seeing the inactive state of the Russian infantry, fancied that by descending the slope of the ravine, and turning round by the right of the Guards and the Sandbag Battery, he might attack the enemy's left flank and strike a severe blow, if not entirely throw them into disorder and confusion. I believe he sent one of his Staff to Lord Raglan, to inform him of his projected movement, but, without waiting for his Lordship's sanction, moved on the greater portion of General Torrens's brigade in the direction I have indicated. He soon discovered what a desperate error he had committed, for, on turning round the end of the spur on which was the aforesaid battery, he found himself under a heavy fusillade from the enemy's riflemen stationed on the opposite side of the ravine, next to the Inkermann road, and also, much to his surprise, he came upon a heavy column of infantry, which was advancing in order to retake the Sandbag Battery. These troops he had not before been able to discover in consequence of the formation of the ground at that point. Immediately the Russians saw our men they opened a heavy fire upon them, and poured volley after volley with most destructive effect, which decimated the brigade. In vain our men endeavoured to return the fire; most unfortunately the greater portion had but little ammunition with them, as they had come that morning out of the trenches without even going into camp. Sir George Cathcart showed his usual bravery, and called upon his men to charge the Russians with the point of the bayonet; but, although they did advance a few yards, the difficulties of the ground and the awful fire poured upon them prevented the movement from being attended with any success. Sir George found it would be necessary to retire, and the order was about to be given, when Brigadier-General Torrens, determined to make another effort, rallied the 68th Regiment, and prepared to try once more a charge up the hill. Sir George called out to him on the first advance, "Nobly done, Torrens; nobly done!" General Torrens was shot, a moment after, through the side, and fell, severely wounded, at the head of his men. They, seeing this, got disheartened, and wavered, and commenced firing again on the enemy, who replied to it with far greater severity, the advantage of ground being much on their side. Sir George was at this time shot through the head, and fell dead on the spot; his Assistant Adjutant-General, Colonel Seymour (of the Guards), a dear friend, who had served with him through the campaign in Kaffirland as his Military Secretary, on seeing Sir George fall, rushed forward to give him assistance, and in doing so was shot through the leg. Major Maitland (Deputy-Assistant-Adjutant-General) was also severely wounded. Our troops, completely over-matched, and their ammunition all spent, fell into confusion, and retired back along the side of the hill towards their former station, the enemy pursuing them in great force, keeping up a heavy fire all the time, and bayoneting our wounded as they passed by them. General Torrens had with great difficulty been carried back with his men. Sir George Cathcart's body had been left, and nothing that could be said would induce Colonel Seymour to leave his side; there he remained, and met a hero's death in endeavouring to protect his friend and General's person from insult.

The Russians, having completely overcome this attempt to turn their flank, advanced to recapture the Sandbag Battery, swarming up the hill on all sides. The Coldstream Guards, who, as I before mentioned, had been placed to defend the work, held it for a long time with the utmost determination and vigour: with five times their force opposed to them, they continued to fire on the Russian masses with such coolness and accuracy that the ground was covered with dead and wounded. But no amount of slaughter seemed to check the enemy's onward course; they showed a reckless bravery and stubborn determination for which we had never before given them credit. Numbers at length overcame in this unequal struggle; and the Guards, after having lost a third of their officers and men, and exhausted their ammunition, slowly retired out of the work, without, however, turning their backs upon the enemy, but leaving behind them many wounded, amongst others Captains Sir Robert Newman and Neville, Grenadier Guards, and Lieutenant Greville, Coldstream. The Russians once again poured into the battery, and, it is generally believed, committed the most barbarous atrocity by murdering our

94

wounded as they lay defenceless on the ground; for when the work was afterwards retaken, the above-mentioned officers, although left but slightly wounded, were found quite dead, and their bodies bayoneted in several places, besides being horribly mutilated. The Duke of Cambridge, on seeing his men retire, galloped across their front, and urged them to stand firm and fire upon the enemy, but he was met with the unanswerable reply, that they had no more ammunition. His Royal Highness had his horse shortly after shot under him, but was fortunately not hurt, though a bullet passed through the sleeve of his coat; of his Staff, Major Macdonald (who particularly distinguished himself) and Captain Clifton had their horses killed under them; the latter was also wounded. A few minutes later and Captain Butler (Deputy-Assistant-Adjutant-General) was shot through the head, and fell dead. General Bentinck was also wounded in the arm, and had to leave the ground. In such a state of things there was nothing for it but to rally the men, place them in the most advantageous position to prevent the enemy from making a sudden rush to carry the ridge, and immediate orders were given to bring up the reserve ammunition with the least possible delay. The Russians did not attempt to advance upon our men, but continued to concentrate masses of infantry in and about the neighbourhood of the often-contested Sandbag Battery. Had they followed up their success with their previous determination, and pursued our men, the mere weight must have penetrated through the thin line of British troops. Our right flank once turned, the issue of the day would indeed have been doubtful. Probably their already enormous loss had to a great extent disheartened them from attempting to renew the attack.

It was now 10.30 a.m., and at this important moment of the battle General Bosquet arrived with a battalion of Zouaves and another of Tirailleurs Indigènes, and almost at the same time General Canrobert and his Staff joined Lord Raglan. He brought with him four strong squadrons of the Chasseurs d'Afrique, and immediately informed Lord Raglan that he had ordered up another brigade of infantry, with two batteries of field artillery. He placed these troops entirely at Lord Raglan's disposal, and begged he would give whatever orders concerning them he thought proper (a very high compliment, by the by, to his Lordship, as showing what entire confidence General Canrobert had in his judgment and discretion). Lord Raglan, therefore, requested that the battalions with General Bosquet might be placed so as to support our right, where the Brigade of Guards and the remnant of General Torrens's brigade of the 4th Division still remained. As these fine troops advanced to their appointed station, the Zouaves leading the way, they were greeted with loud and prolonged cheers from our wearied soldiers. In the meantime a considerable quantity of ammunition had arrived, and had been served out to those of our men who required it. A general advance on the right was again ordered, and the brigade of Guards, the French troops, and those of the 4th Division who were available, marched down towards the Sandbag Battery. The enemy, seeing a column of French infantry with our troops, doubtless supposed that we had received large reinforcements; their former determination left them, and they abandoned the redoubt with scarcely any resistance.

The Allies having advanced at a rapid pace, the work once more was occupied, and remained in possession of the British, who poured upon the retreating masses a heavy fire, which mowed them down by dozens. Nevertheless our troops at this time, the French especially (from the fact of their being in column), suffered severely from the terrible cannonade which the enemy continually hurled upon them from their artillery placed on Cossack Hill. This cannonade had indeed been playing upon the whole extent of our front ever since the commencement of the action; the heavy ordnance of the enemy had from the first told against us. Their artillery consisted of 24 heavy and 16 light guns, all arranged in two lines upon Cossack Hill; besides this they had three field batteries, placed on some commanding ground which overlooks Careening ravine: in all they mustered about 60 pieces of artillery in action. Independently of the above the enemy kept throwing up every minute numbers of large shot and shell (chiefly 32-pounders) from two Russian steam frigates, the *Vladimir* and the *Chersonese*, which were placed high up the harbour of Sevastopol. Occasional shots also were fired at a great elevation from the Russian batteries near the Malakoff Tower; but these last, for the most part, fell short into Careening ravine, and consequently did us no harm. To reply to at all this enormous weight of metal we could bring into the field only six 9-pounder batteries; in all, 36 pieces of ordnance. But in spite of this preponderance the British artillerymen continued to serve their guns with a steadiness beyond all praise. Their losses were heavy, especially in horses, which caused great confusion, and prevented the reserve ammunition being brought up with the quickness and regularity desirable.

Lord Raglan, wishing, if possible, in however small a degree, to equalize the contending artillery, bethought himself of bringing into action any guns of position that we might have unemployed in the siege-train. He inquired of an officer on the artillery staff what guns there were in the right siege-train, and was told that there were two iron 18-pounder guns of position. Lord Raglan immediately despatched an order for them to be brought up. The order was, by some mistake, delivered to Colonel Fitzmayer, who commanded the artillery attached to the 2nd Division, but who had been erroneously thought to have under his care the two 18-pounders in question. Colonel Fitzmayer replied that it was 'impossible' for him to bring up the guns. This answer was brought back to Lord Raglan by the officer of the artillery staff who had taken the order, without his first ascertaining Colonel Fitzmayer's reasons for making such a reply.* Lord Raglan was much annoyed, and, turning to the Assistant-Adjutant-General Royal Artillery, one of Headquarters Staff, said, "Adye, I don't like the word *impossible*; don't you think the guns can be brought up?" Major Adye said he was certain it could be done. Lord Raglan then sent to Colonel Gambier, commanding the siege-train, to bring the two 18-pounders into action with the least possible delay.

As it was some little time before these guns could be moved up, I will describe what had been going on in other parts of the field. But first I must say that, on General Canrobert bringing forward the Chasseurs d'Afrique, Lord Raglan sent for

* In justice to Colonel Fitzmayer, it should be stated that the two 18-pounder guns had only been under his charge for 48 hours, a fortnight previous to the battle of Inkermann, when they were returned to the park of the left siege-train, and were subsequently placed in a redoubt constructed midway between the camp of the 2nd Division and the rear heights overlooking the valley of Balaklava, and were actually in position there at the time of the battle. The 18-pounders brought into action on that eventful day were two remaining guns in the right siege-train, and consequently were not, and never had been, under Colonel Fitzmayer's command.

the Light Cavalry Brigade, or rather the remnant of it, as it did not muster more than 350 horses. They were placed near the French cavalry, but neither were engaged, although several men and horses were knocked over by the shot that came bounding over the ridge from the enemy's guns on Cossack Hill, and also from the shells thrown up from the steamers at the head of the harbour. At the time that the enemy advanced and retook the Sandbag Battery, causing the Coldstream Guards and Torrens's brigade to retire, they pushed on two columns of infantry, one by the Inkermann road, and the other up the ravine next to it. They advanced steadily towards the ridge, under cover of their numerous artillery on Cossack Hill; when within 150 yards they were received with well-directed volleys from our men of the 2nd and Light Divisions, and General Goldie's brigade of the 4th Division: these last, were placed obliquely between the Guards and the 2nd Division. They suffered dreadfully from the Russian column nearest to them; numbers of officers and men were shot down, and, among others, Brigadier-General Goldie was mortally wounded. The 2nd Division again came in for a large share of desperate fighting, most gallantly directed by General Pennefather, who continued throughout the day to cheer and encourage his men by his brilliant example. Brigadier-General Adams, who commanded a brigade, was badly shot through the leg, and rode towards the rear; he passed close by Lord Raglan, who was anxiously watching the battle. General Adams appeared to be suffering agonies from his wound, and was lifted off his horse and carried to the nearest field hospital. Colonel Carpenter also, who commanded the 41st Regiment, was most horribly wounded, and would have been killed on the spot, had not a soldier of the 55th Regiment most gallantly come to his rescue, attacking several Russians who were plundering and maltreating him while lying helpless on the ground, killing two of them, and protecting the Lieutenant-Colonel until the arrival of some of the men of the 41st Regiment, who carried him to the rear.* The Light Division acted on the left flank of the 2nd, and on this advance of the Russian infantry materially assisted in checking the enemy's progress; but as they were exposed, perhaps more than any other division, to the hostile cannonade, their loss was fearfully great. Sir George Brown was shot by a musket-ball through the arm, and had to retire, severely wounded, out of action.

This unequal contest could not last long; our ranks were sadly thinned, and the inexhaustible reinforcements of the Russians prevented our men from doing more than just holding the ground on which they stood. Indeed Goldie's brigade of the 4th Division had suffered so severely that they had given way on their right, and thus left the Guards with their flank uncovered. Some guns of the artillery were now brought most judiciously to bear on the columns of the enemy, and then only did they cease to advance. This, however, was done without any hurry, as they only retired step by step down the slope of the hill for about 100 yards, and still kept sending showers of bullets at our diminished line of troops. In return for this repulse of their infantry the enemy brought up fresh guns on Cossack Hill, and the whole opened, if possible, with renewed vigour upon the entire length of the ridge. The ground was ploughed up in all directions, as the shot came smashing through the brushwood, throwing about the dust and dirt. As there was no object to be

* The name of this gallant soldier well deserves to be recorded — Private Thomas Beach. He has since received the Victoria Cross for his distinguished conduct on this occasion.

gained by our troops remaining as mere targets to the Russian artillerymen, Lord Raglan ordered the whole of our troops to lie down, as far as practicable.

At this time the Headquarters Staff suffered severely from the fire of the enemy, and had especially to mourn the loss of one of its principal members. General Strangway (R.A.), when in the act of receiving orders from Lord Raglan, was struck by a round shot, which carried off one of his legs just below the knee. He turned round and asked in a calm voice for someone to help him off his horse. General Estcourt, who was riding next to him, instantly dismounted and went to his side, as did also Major Adye. With their help, the gallant old man was assisted off his horse, and, reclining in General Estcourt's arms, was laid on the ground. Major Adye then hurried off to procure a stretcher to carry him to the rear. Almost at the same moment that General Strangway was mortally wounded, a shell entered Colonel Somerset's horse just behind the saddle, and burst inside, covering him (Colonel Somerset) with blood, and splashing several of the Staff around. Wonderful to say, Colonel Somerset escaped unhurt, except a slight bruise. Colonel Gordon also had his horse killed under him by a round shot at this place. Major Adye had some trouble in procuring a stretcher, as all the men who were going backwards and forwards from the ambulance to the battlefield carrying wounded belonged to regiments in action, and, when asked by him, said their orders were to confine themselves to removing the wounded of their own corps. At last, with the promise of a couple of sovereigns, he got two men to come with a stretcher, and on it General Strangway was carried to the hospital of the right siege-train. The surgeons considered it useless to torture him with an amputation, as at his age he could not survive the operation. Towards the close of the battle, when the Russians were retiring, Lord Raglan received intelligence that the poor old General was fast approaching his end. Lord Raglan immediately rode to the hospital-tent where he lay, and, going in, found him rapidly sinking. He pressed the old man's hand, and told him we had gained the day. A faint smile passed over the dying veteran's countenance, but he was too weak, from loss of blood, to speak. A few minutes after, and his spirit fled to rest.

But to return to the battle. General Canrobert, when engaged in watching the advance of his infantry on the right, had his horse killed under him by a shot, and was himself wounded, though but slightly, in the arm, by a piece of shell. He went to the rear to have it dressed, but later in the day rejoined Lord Raglan. The moment had at last arrived when the battle was to turn decidedly in favour of the Allies; for at this instant the two 18-pounders were being brought into action. They were dragged up, not without considerable difficulty, by horses and men under the command of Colonel Gambier. This gallant officer was proceeding with these pieces of ordnance towards Lord Raglan, when a spent shot (comparatively speaking) ricocheted off the ground and struck him on the chest. He was knocked down senseless and carried to the rear (as it was thought at the time) a mortally wounded man. His place was taken by Colonel Dickson (next senior officer), who brought the guns into action, and continued till the end of the battle in command of them. They were placed in a particular spot, which Lord Raglan himself indicated, in front of the 2nd Division camp, and which gave them the advantage of ground over the enemy's artillery on Cossack Hill.

Immediately after the guns opened, the Russians discovered the fact of their presence, for they concentrated their fire upon this point, and sent a perfect shower of balls, in the hope of silencing them. Lord Raglan remained for some little time watching the effect of our practice, and by his coolness and *sang froid* encouraged the men in serving the guns. I think, while he was there, five or six men were killed and wounded close to him, besides several horses; but, although a man of the kindest heart and warmest sympathies, Lord Raglan, in action, never allows his attention to be taken off by the casualties around him, and therefore, though in the midst of this great slaughter, neither his voice nor manner was apparently changed. Indeed, to such an extent is this indifference carried, that it is a common saying among his Staff, that "My Lord rather likes being under fire than otherwise."

It was now about midday; we received another reinforcement in the shape of two batteries of French artillery and three battalions of infantry; the former were placed, by Lord Raglan's direction, to the right of our heavy guns, with orders to fire upon the Russian infantry, and good service they did, for there they continued until the close of the action, firing with accuracy and rapidity. The infantry Lord Raglan ordered to be posted so as to support the centre of our troops, that is in rear of the 2nd and part of the Light Divisions, which were, for the most part, still lying down to escape the enemy's cannonade. The French advanced up towards the ridge in good order, presenting a broad front and formed in a line of four deep. The moment they reached the crest of the hill they came under the direct fire of the Russian guns, and lost in the first minute a number of men. This threw them partially into confusion; they were seized with a panic, and the large majority retired down the hill, in spite of the bugles sounding and the drums beating the *pas de charge*. The French officers, under these trying circumstances, behaved remarkably well; begged, entreated, and swore at their men, to induce them to return; but for the moment it was of no avail: they did not run far, as a short distance back they were formed again by their officers, and led up into action. This time (if I recollect right) they were in columns of companies instead of a line four deep as before. On regaining once more the crest of the hill they were received by a most murderous discharge from the enemy's artillery, and, for a second, there appeared to be some wavering in the ranks. At this critical moment two English staff-officers, Captain Glazbrook (Deputy-Assistant-Quartermaster-General, 2nd Division) and Captain Gubbins (aide-de-camp to Sir De Lacy Evans) went in front of the panic-stricken troops, and cheered them on into action, the former crying out, "*En avant, mes braves! en avant, mes amis!*" Captain Gubbins I also remarked for his gallant bearing and zealous exertions, and I regret to say he was afterwards severely wounded. Our allies, when once face to face with the enemy, seemed to recover their steadiness, and remained, giving their support to our troops, and fighting with them, until the Russians retreated.

I cannot describe the sinking sensation one felt on observing our allies give way; our first impression was that they had retired, beaten back by the overpowering masses of Russian infantry, and consequently that our thin line of troops had been broken through, if not annihilated. It was the only time that I ever observed Lord Raglan's countenance change. I confess, myself, that for the moment I thought the day was lost. Lord Raglan, with an exclamation of astonishment and annoyance at the retreat of the French, immediately despatched an aide-de-camp to General Pennefather, who was on the left of the line of the 2nd Division, to ascertain the cause of this, and also to find out how we were getting on in that quarter. General Pennefather sent word in reply that he could hold his own perfectly well, and that he saw symptoms of retiring on the part of the enemy's infantry. If this movement proved to be a general retreat, and if he could be reinforced with fresh troops, he said, he would follow the enemy up, *"and lick them to the devil."* Lord Raglan was delighted at this spirited answer, and, riding over to General Canrobert, translated General Pennefather's words literally to him. General Canrobert, who had just remounted his horse, after having his arm bound up, exclaimed, *"Ah! quel brave garçon! quel brave homme! quel bon général."* Lord Raglan, wishing as much as lay in his power to further General Pennefather's views, shortly afterwards sent him up some companies of the 20th Regiment and about 200 of the Guards. These, for the most part, were men who had some little time before come to the rear to replenish their pouches, their ammunition being exhausted, and the rest had been brought off pickets, which, in the emergency of the moment, were thought

Unfinished drawing of the French review given to General Lüders.

unnecessary. Another brigade of French infantry (mustering 3000 men) and two more batteries of 12-pounders had before this arrived, but, by General Canrobert's wish, they were kept in reserve and did not go into action at all.

Sir De Lacy Evans about this time rode up to Lord Raglan; he had come from Balaklava, where he had gone from illness, and, on receiving intimation of the battle, had insisted on returning to the front, although not in a fit state of health to do so. He appeared to take a very gloomy view of matters, and even at this time seemed to think that the issue of the day was doubtful. His division being under such able command as that of General Pennefather, who had held it during the heat and burden of the day, Sir De Lacy Evans had the good taste and kind consideration not to deprive him of it; so that the honour of commanding the division during the entire action might remain with him who had already so brilliantly distinguished himself.

Our 18-pounders had not been in action half an hour before their superiority was shown by the enfeebled reply of the enemy's artillery. Indeed, at one time, a great number of their guns ceased firing, and we were in hopes that they were finally silenced. Our expectations on this point were disappointed, as shortly after they all opened again; probably they had merely ceased from a temporary want of ammunition. Their fire, nevertheless, continued to decrease and was far less accurate. It was evident that they had lost many of their best artillerymen. On the other hand, although our loss in gunners had been very great, especially among those serving the iron 18-pounders (17 of whom were killed or wounded), we received fresh men from the right siege-train, and if anything our fire became more and more accurate. I never saw such beautiful practice; the greatest praise is due to Colonel Dickson for the admirable manner in which he directed his men. Shortly before 1 p.m. it became perfectly evident that the Russians only continued their cannonade in order to cover their infantry, who began to retire in heavy columns. The day cleared with our prospects, and as we gazed on the battlefield, and compared our small force with the still huge masses of our retreating foes, we felt indeed greatly relieved that we had no longer their legions opposed to us. The might duel of artillery continued for some time, the enemy drawing off their guns by fours every ten minutes or so, until but two batteries remained on Cossack Hill. These were severely knocked about by our 18-pounders, but Lord Raglan sent an aide-de-camp to Colonel Dickson to desire him to cease firing, as he wished to advance some infantry, and thought that the enemy would be glad of an excuse to withdraw their guns. Colonel Dickson begged to be allowed to have a few shots more, as he said he had the range so perfectly; and, to verify his assertion, the guns, which were then loaded, were fired, and the shot went crashing through two Russian carriages. A minute or two later he ceased firing, an example which the Russians immediately followed, and then we had the satisfaction of seeing the last of their artillery limber up and gallop off the field.

Thus terminated the battle of Inkermann, for, although they fired at us from the Russian steamers occasionally, and we also sent a few shots after the now distant columns of infantry, yet no more actual fighting took place. Lord Raglan was very anxious that, as soon as their artillery was withdrawn, the Russians should be pursued down the Inkermann road; thinking that their panic would be thus increased, and many prisoners made, besides causing them heavy loss. In all retreats troops are invariably more or less in a state of disorganization; and there could be no doubt that, had this been done according to Lord Raglan's wish, a greater blow might have been struck upon the enemy. Moreover, as almost the entire Russian force retreated over the Tchernaya river by a single bridge, there was good reason to suppose that they must have been in great confusion, from the masses of men who had to pass over in so narrow a space. Unfortunately there was no British infantry that could be sent on this service; all our available troops had been engaged—all had suffered a heavy loss, and but very few had partaken of any nourishment since the previous day; consequently they were exhausted by the protracted struggle that had taken place, and it would have been unfair to expect troops to do more than they had already accomplished. This was not the case with all the French: the Zouaves and others had suffered severely, and had shared with us the honours of the day, but there was still a brigade of 3000 men and two batteries of artillery which had never been under fire. Lord Raglan pointed out to General Canrobert the great results which might accrue from the pursuit of the enemy, and most strongly urged that the French troops, then on the ground, who had not been engaged, should be employed for this purpose. For some reason unknown to me, General Canrobert did not agree with Lord Raglan, and, when again pressed by the English Commander-in-Chief, proposed that, if they went, the Guards should go with them, as he said his infantry had such confidence and admiration for 'les Black Caps'.

This, however, was quite out of the question. The Guards now consisted of but a handful of exhausted men, and these had still to perform the onerous duty of removing their many wounded, who had fallen too far in advance to be carried to the rear during the action. After more conversation and repeated urging on Lord Raglan's part, General Canrobert consented to send a battalion of infantry, with a battery of guns, to the high ground which the enemy had just abandoned; this commanded the bridge over the Tchernaya river and the causeway across the valley of Inkermann. The two Commanders-in-Chief, and a portion of their respective Staffs, accompanied the French battalion and guns; but so much time had been lost by General Canrobert's indecision, that, when they arrived at the place indicated, they found that the enemy had, in the most masterly manner, almost completed the retreat of his infantry across the bridge, and had from this point deployed to the right and left, so that the fire from the battery of French artillery on the heights just mentioned did him, comparatively speaking, but little harm, and his forces were completely out of range of small arms. It is much to be regretted that General Canrobert, in the first instance, did not accede to Lord Raglan's proposal to follow the Russians down the Inkermann road. Had he done so, even with the battery of six light guns, great chastisement might have been inflicted on them. Indeed General Canrobert admitted his error, and expressed to Lord Raglan the regret he felt at not having at once followed his advice. Lord Raglan had been desirous to bring forward the two 18-pounders, which had already done such good service, to the brow of the hill, where the French battalion was afterwards placed; but on inquiry, it appeared that it would be almost impracticable to move them, as our losses in artillerymen and horses had been especially great, and those of the latter, that were then available were knocked up by the continual work they had to perform in bringing ammunition, etc., backwards and forwards. So anxious, however, was Colonel Dickson to carry out Lord Raglan's proposal, that soon after, seeing some artillery horses a short distance off, he ordered them to be attached to one of the 18-pounders, which being done, they moved forward. But as the ground was very rocky and full of inequalities, besides being covered with thick brushwood, their progress was slow, and before they could reach the spot indicated by Lord Raglan, they met the French troops returning from their tardy pursuit.

The allied Commanders now rode over the field of battle, and horrible, indeed, was the sight that everywhere met their gaze. Mangled corpses of friend and foe lay in every direction; such heaps of slain! In some places down the Inkermann road, where our shot and shell had fallen into the retreating columns of the enemy, the way was literally blocked up with dead and dying. The spots where artillery had been placed could be easily traced by the circle of dead which lay around the position of each gun. Behind every bush one discovered a body; some so terribly smashed that one could scarcely credit that they had ever been human forms. On visiting the Sandbag Battery the most awful scene presented itself. Within the circumference of a few yards round the work upwards of 700 dead were lying, the majority of them torn with the most ghastly wounds; for here had raged the most desperate hand-to-hand conflicts. Upwards of 200 British soldiers were stretched upon the ground which they had so nobly held until death.

Outside the parapet of the battery the Russians appeared to have piled some of their dead, probably with the idea of using their bodies as a sort of *banquette* for them to stand upon to fire into the battery. In each embrasure were the bodies of two Russian soldiers, who had evidently been endeavouring to enter the work; in front of them were the bodies of guardsmen. In the empty magazine of the battery were found several corpses, probably of some poor creatures who had been wounded, and who had crawled in there to be under shelter. While we were there the French cacolets arrived, and were speedily loaded with our poor wounded. This was a kind thought on the part of General Bosquet, who ordered them to be sent down to the battery, from whence but few of our wounded had been yet removed, in consequence of its advanced position. The English ambulance-waggons consist of great lumbering vehicles, which are far more difficult to move over broken ground than even a heavy piece of ordnance; but the French cacolets, carried on mules, are both easier for the wounded, and are able to go into places impracticable for carriages. Lord Raglan, anxious to alleviate the sufferings of our wounded enemies as soon as possible, ordered a fatigue party of 500 of the Turks to bring them at once into camp, so that before dusk upwards of 700 wounded Russians were more or less provided with surgical aid. On leaving the field of battle, Lord Raglan went to General Pennefather to make the necessary arrangements for the better protection of our position on the right, in case the Russians should attempt a renewal of the attack. It was determined that a parapet should immediately be constructed along the ridge which our troops had held throughout the day; and to effect this purpose large working parties of Turks, under the direction of some officers of the Royal Engineers, assisted by a party of sappers and miners, were ordered to set to work so as to complete it by the following morning. The iron guns of position were retained on the spot where they had already done such good service; and two other guns of the same metal and calibre were to be brought up and placed on the left of this parapet.

Lord Raglan was shortly after joined by Sir De Lacy Evans, who took upon himself to give his Lordship the most wonderful counsel and advice which, perhaps, ever fell from the lips of a British General. He urged upon Lord Raglan the utter uselessness, and indeed impracticability, of attempting to hold our present position, supposing the enemy's attack to be renewed, of which there was every probability. He therefore gave it as his opinion that there was nothing to be done but for us to raise the siege, embark the troops in the best way we could, and evacuate the Crimea. Such was the meaning, if not the actual words, used by one of the oldest and most experienced Generals we have in the army out here! Lord Raglan never for one second entertained such a project; but with his usual courtesy he took the trouble of pointing out to Sir De Lacy the absurdity of his proposition. In the first place, even admitting we had gained no victory, that could not justify the abandonment of our siege-train and material to the enemy, which we should necessarily be obliged to do, from the impossibility of embarking it. In the second place, supposing that we had transport enough to carry all the English troops, what was to become of the French, as we had brought certainly half their present force to the Crimea? Besides this, there were the Turkish troops unprovided for. Would Sir De Lacy Evans counsel that our allies should be left in the lurch? not quite an English mode of dealing with our friends! Altogether there is no way of explaining this most extraordinary plan of Sir De Lacy Evans. One can only account for it by the fact that he was in a feeble state of health, and that possibly his illness may have affected his mind as well as his body.

After this discussion Lord Raglan proceeded to several different camp-hospitals to inquire after the wounded, and had the satisfaction of hearing that almost all the English sufferers were already under the care of the surgeons of the army. The numbers, however, were so great that necessarily many had to lie with wounds undressed for a considerable interval of time. No blame could be attached to the doctors for this, as they worked with a zeal and earnestness for which, indeed, they are always remarkable.

Lord Raglan arrived at Headquarters shortly before 7 p.m. in the evening, having been on horseback more than 12 hours. Soon after this about 200 Russian prisoners were marched under escort into the Headquarters camp. Mr. Calvert (chief of the Intelligence Department) set to work to collect from them any information they could afford, especially as regards their force, the object of their attack, the Generals who commanded them, etc. He ascertained that the Russian force consisted of three regiments of the 10th, 11th, 16th, and 17th Divisions respectively, that is 12 regiments of four battalions each, or 48 battalions. These properly should consist of 1000 men each, but, from the great losses which the 16th and 17th Divisions sustained at the Alma, that number had been considerably reduced; but, putting their casualties in battle and sickness at 8000, the Russian infantry at the battle on the 5th instant must have probably consisted of 40,000 men. To these must be added their enormous force of artillery, which mustered, according to the accounts of the prisoners, 24 heavy pieces of ordnance, guns of position (probably equal to our 32-pounder howitzers), and 10 batteries of field artillery; and as each battery consists of eight guns in the Russian service, that will give 80 field-pieces. But of these, probably three or even four batteries may not have been engaged. Perhaps in all we may safely put the Russian army at the battle

Plan of the battle of Inkermann. Fought on the 5th November 1854.

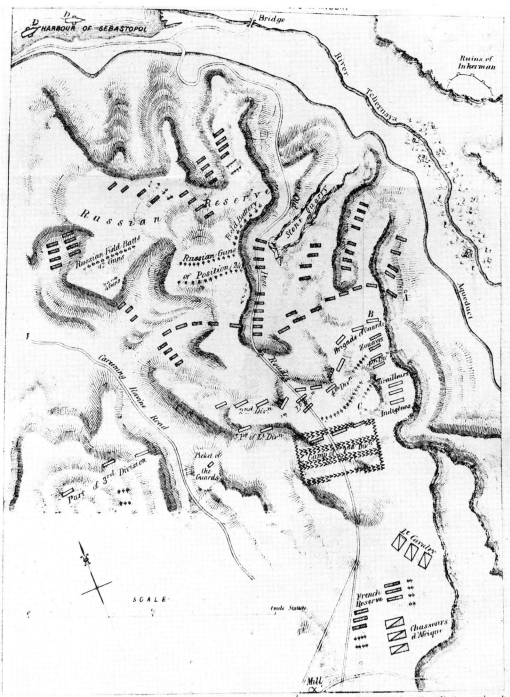

A Near here Sir G Cathcart & Col! Seymour were killed & B! Gen! Torrens wounded — B Sandbag Battery taken by the enemy several times but finally held by the Guards here the greatest slaughter took place upwards of 1100 dead were found after the battle within the space of a few yards — C Two 18 pounders, guns of position placed by order of Lord Raglan on this spot — These guns turned the battle in favour of the Allies, causing the enemy to retreat with enormous loss — D Russian Steamers "Vladimir and Chersonese — E Cossack Hill.

of Inkermann at 50,000 men. It appears that the whole force was divided into three great columns.

Prince Menchikoff appears to have had the command-in-chief of the whole: but as the columns were at a considerable distance apart, a system of semaphores was established on the heights above Inkermann and on those above the village of Tchorgoun. It seems that the object of their attack was to take possession of, and establish themselves on, the high ground in front of our 2nd Division camp, and, in the event of not succeeding in the first instance in driving off the English, that at any rate they would be able to construct batteries on the position which they took for granted would be captured from us; and from thence with their guns to enfilade the English camps, compel us to withdraw our troops and consequently raise the siege. To effect this purpose, they brought up a large quantity of intrenching tools, as well as gabions and fascines to erect batteries. The plan of attack seems to have been as follows: — General Soimonoff's column was to leave the town an hour before daylight, and to proceed up the Careening Bay ravine, which he was to follow, and enter the English position at that point, thus cutting off our extreme right from the rest of the ground we occupied.

General Pauloff's column was to march from the northern side of the harbour of Sevastopol, across the valley of Inkermann and the Tchernaya river, by the causeway and bridge, and there divide into two bodies; the left — to follow the course of the Inkermann road and ravines adjoining it, and thus gain the right of our 2nd Division camp; the right — to ascend the high ground after leaving the Tchernaya, and, crossing near Cossack Hill, penetrate to the camp of the 2nd Division on its left. The main portion of the artillery was to be posted on Cossack Hill, as it was known that the camp of the 2nd Division was within easy range of it. To render their success more certain, it was determined to make two false attacks on the extremes of our position; one by a formidable sortie from the garrison of Sevastopol on the left of the French siege-works; the other by General Gortschakoff's column, which was to threaten Balaklava and the rear of our position, in the hope of preventing the withdrawal of troops from that quarter to our assistance during the grand attack at Inkermann. The whole of these arrangements appear to have been carried out, except that, according to the prisoners statement, General Soimonoff's column did not take the proper turn after entering the gorge of the Inkermann ravine, and that consequently, instead of cutting off our 2nd Division from any reinforcements, they arrived near Cossack Hill on the right of General Pauloff's column, thus crowding the ground with troops. General Soimonoff was unfortunately killed, so that probably this will ever remain a mystery. The whole scheme was certainly most cleverly planned, and, had it not been for the indomitable courage and determination of the British troops and the well-timed assistance of the French, the Russians no doubt would have succeeded in attaining their object. *

* Many statements have been made as to the probable reasons for failure on the enemy's part at the battle of Inkermann. It has often been alleged, and indeed by Prince Menchikoff himself in his despatch of the battle, that the defeat was caused by General Soimonoff not taking the proper side of the ravine from the head of the Careening Bay. It appears never to have occurred to anyone that a considerable portion of this ravine was enfiladed by the English 5-gun battery; and I doubt very much whether any column of troops, necessarily confined and crowded together in so narrow a space, could ever have faced the fire which would have been poured upon them from this battery.

The prisoners state that their loss has been something frightful; but I do not see how they can be good judges of this, though no doubt they are right, as in the heat of battle you never can know the loss you have sustained at the time, except immediately around you. They also report that two sons of the Emperor, the Grand Dukes Nicholas and Michael, arrived on the 4th instant at Sevastopol, for the avowed purpose, they declare, of seeing the Allies driven into the sea!

Late in the evening Lord Raglan sent an aide-de-camp to General Canrobert to propose to him that a heavy cannonade should be opened from all the allied batteries on the following morning against the enemy's works. Lord Raglan calculated that the intelligence of the defeat and rout of the Russian army would not be generally known to the garrison of Sevastopol until the following morning, and that the fact of their being assailed with a heavier cannonade than usual, on receiving the first news of this disaster, would probably add to their panic and consternation, and materially tend to the effectual carrying out of an ulterior scheme which I shall presently mention to you. General Canrobert at first hesitated whether to comply with Lord Raglan's proposal or not, as it appeared from his explanation that they (the French) are very short of ammunition—indeed have not enough for a single day's heavy firing in their artillery parks. However, he finally consented to open upon the Russians at daylight what he called 'un feu de joie' for the victory at Inkermann. The same evening Lord Raglan received reports from all the different divisions engaged in the battle, that to the best of their belief all the wounded British troops had been brought into each of the camp hospitals, although probably (as indeed was afterwards shown in a few instances) some might yet remain in obscure parts of the field.

I was up early the following morning (6th), and rode off to the right, first of all, to inquire after the wounded, among whom were many friends, and then to ride over the field of battle. I was shocked to find several officers, who the day before had been reported severely wounded, had died during the night. Among others, Brigadier-General Goldie, Colonel Blair of the Guards, and Colonel Carpenter of the 41st Regiment, besides many others whose loss will be greatly felt. On riding over the scene of sanguinary contest, it was sad to see what frightful numbers of bodies were everywhere lying about. Now that the excitement of the battle passed off and one could look calmly around, the fearful aspect of the field was far more striking than before. The same peculiarities were to be observed as those I have mentioned at the battle of the Alma—I mean those shot through the head and heart all appeared to have died so easily, and really almost in every instance with a smile upon the lips; and on the other hand, those wounded in the body, especially when from the bayonet, invariably showed on their countenances the agonizing death they must have suffered. It was wonderful, too, the numbers who had their arms stretched upwards, as if imploring aid. Altogether the ground presented a most horrible and sickening spectacle, and one which I shall never forget. A good number of Russians who had been wounded on the previous day, and who had crawled as far from our camp as their strength would allow, were brought in during the morning. Fatigue parties were also removing the few wounded of the French and English who had been accidentally left on the field.

The cannonade I have spoken of was opened on the morning of the 6th from all the English batteries, and was kept up with unremitting energy by our artillerymen for several hours. The French confined themselves to firing sharply for the space of half an hour, and after that time only continued at the usual rate.

A general return of killed and wounded was sent in to the Adjutant-General's office, amounting to, in the English army, close upon 2600 casualties. The French state their loss in killed and wounded at 1760 men; but I understand that this number includes the repulse of the Russian sortie from the right of the town, and this is stated to have cost them upwards of 1100! The Russian loss it is difficult at present to calculate—it is stated at from 10,000 to 15,000 men; indeed many aver that 20,000 would be nearer the mark. This, however, is a matter of conjecture, as it will be days before we can collect the numbers of Russian dead lying about on the field of battle.

There was a Council of War during the morning at the English Headquarters; present—Lord Raglan, General Canrobert, Sir John Burgoyne, and General Bosquet. This was partly to arrange the reinforcement that General Bosquet should give to the English troops on the right. It was resolved to occupy all the ground on which the battle of Inkermann had been fought, and to construct a system of redoubts for the better protection of this part of our position. These works will take considerable time and labour to make. In the meanwhile a strong brigade of 4000 French troops are to camp in the immediate vicinity of our 2nd Division, and indeed they have before this established themselves thereon. It was also decided at this Council of War, that a letter should be addressed to Prince Menchikoff by the allied Generals, complaining of the Russian soldiers stabbing our wounded men when lying on the ground unable to defend themselves, as it was alleged that this had been done in numerous instances during the action on the 5th, whenever the Russian troops gained any advantage over us. The Commanders-in-Chief demanded an explanation, and inquired whether the war was to be carried on in such an inhuman and barbarous manner as would disgrace any civilized nation.

Lord Raglan had expressed his wish to attend the funerals of Sir George Cathcart and General Strangway. Arrangements were therefore made that they should be interred at 4.30 p.m. on the top of the hill in front of the 4th Division camp, and inside what appears to have been an old redoubt. Lord Raglan and his Staff arrived at the time appointed, and witnessed the last honours paid to the remains of these gallant veterans. Sir George's body had been removed from the battlefield to his own tent, so that it had only to be carried from thence a few yards to its last resting-place. General Strangway had died in the field hospital of the right siege-train, and his body was conveyed from there to the place of interment on a gun-carriage, escorted by a troop of horse artillery. Strange to say, it was this very troop which he had commanded at the battle of Leipzig in 1813, the commencement of his military career, and where he had the first opportunity of distinguishing himself. Sir George Cathcart is a loss to the army and country at large; he had great military talents, and was one on whom many looked as the beau-ideal of a military commander. General Goldie had been buried earlier in the morning near the same spot. Most of the general officers whom duty did not prevent were present on this melancholy occasion. Lord Raglan was much moved, as he had a great personal friendship for both the deceased Generals. After it was all over he went and sat for some little time by the bedside of General Torrens, who was lying most severely wounded in his tent, and later in the day he visited several of the field-hospitals and made the best arrangements in his power for the speedy removal of the wounded to Balaklava and from thence to the Bosphorus. Lord Raglan traversed the whole battlefield, and was as much astonished as anyone at the enormous heaps of the Russians slain.

Yesterday morning (7th), another Grand Council of War was held at the English Headquarters, at which a number of Generals of both armies were present. It had been the intention to have assaulted the town on the morning of this day, and indeed Lord Raglan was still anxious for it to be carried out. General Canrobert was strongly opposed to it, and maintained that it would be utterly impracticable to attempt to storm the place with our present small force, while the enemy had so large an army in the field, and which at any moment might again attack us on any point of our rear. He therefore counselled that we should wait for reinforcements, which are shortly expected; and that in the meantime we should not make any offensive movement against the enemy, but confine ourselves to acting on the defensive, holding our present works without making any absolute advance. For the better protection of the right of our position, he (General Canrobert) engaged that the French troops should construct the greater portion of the new works to be erected there, and also that they should occupy the same. Lord Raglan, although utterly opposed in every way to the first part of this scheme, had no alternative but to accept it, as the English army was now reduced to little more than 16,000 bayonets. It was also finally settled that, as now there could be no doubt of the army wintering in the Crimea, and probably on their present ground, measures should be immediately taken for hutting the troops; and for this purpose it was resolved to despatch vessels to Constantinople, Sinope, and other parts, where it was likely that they would be able to procure wood and the necessary materials for housing the army. There were certain Generals present who thought so badly of our actual position that they proposed that the siege should be raised, and the troops withdrawn to different ground, if the idea of the army being embarked was impracticable; and I understand that the Duke of Cambridge advocated this measure, and advised that, as far as the English army was concerned, it should occupy the heights round Balaklava.

This morning (8th) 1000 Turks were ordered to be employed in collecting the Russian dead on the field of Inkermann, as up to this time only the dead of the allied armies have been interred. This, although it may appear rather a menial office, was not without considerable danger, as the enemy had never ceased since the close of the action to throw up occasional heavy shot and shell, from steamers which they had stationed for this purpose near the head of the harbour, upon any groups they could discover. The enemy must have been perfectly aware of what we were about, as the distance was not too great to discover with the naked eye the burying-parties occupied with their melancholy duties. This also is made a subject of complaint by the allied Generals in their letter to Prince Menchikoff.

Yesterday and the day before the Turks were employed in bringing in the Russian wounded; and of these we have in camp nearly 1100. We are now able to judge to a certain extent of the losses of the Russians at the battle of the 5th. There are said to be nearly 4000 corpses lying on the field; so that, if one allows three wounded men to every one killed (which is very much inside the usual calculation), their loss at that proportion would be 16,000 men. With us the proportion has been about four and a half wounded to one killed, both at the battles of the Alma and Inkermann. But independently of the dead left on the field, the Russians appear to have lost numbers who have since died; for during the last two days large working-parties have been employed on the further side of the valley of Inkermann in making great pits for the reception of their dead; and by the aid of a telescope we could see numbers of corpses perpetually brought down from the camp on the heights above. They had placed close to where they were working a large black flag, and put up a high white cross, I suppose to show us what they were about, so that they should be unmolested. I need hardly say that nothing was done by the Allies to prevent their performing the last rites to those who had fallen for their country's sake. It is strange that they should not have the same regard for us.

Captain Fellowes (Deputy-Assistant-Quartermaster-General) went in today with a flag of truce from our lines in front of Balaklava to take the letter of which I have spoken. He was received by two Russian officers at their outposts, who informed him that an answer should be sent as soon as possible.

I will end by giving the general total of our dreadful losses on the 5th instant: —

English.	Killed.	Wounded.	Missing.
Officers	43	103	1
Sergeants	32	122	6
Drummers, and rank and file	387	1727	191
	462	1952	198

Grand total, 2612 casualties.*

* This includes the losses in the trenches on the 5th, as well as those in the battle.

CHAPTER 7

Russian deserters

IT has rained in torrents for the last two nights and almost the whole of today, November 10th 1854. We begin to fear that the weather is breaking up. The trenches in places are knee-deep in slush, and to avoid this the men have continually been walking out of the trench, and have thus exposed themselves to the fire of the place, and several, I am sorry to say, have been killed or wounded from this cause. Stringent orders have been issued to prevent the men exposing themselves unnecessarily, and the engineers are endeavouring, as far as possible, to drain the trenches. This can only be partially done, in consequence of the formation of the ground. A reply came from Prince Menchikoff, late last night, to the letter of the allied Generals of the 8th instant, in which he states that he thinks that our Generals are misinformed about the Russian soldiers stabbing and maltreating the English wounded when on the ground. He says that it is contrary to the character of a Russian soldier, and that, although unfortunately there are in all armies men who will commit any atrocity, still it is quite the exception to the rule, and that he should doubt many instances being found of it amongst his troops.

After speaking much more upon the horrors of war, and the probability of there being men who, in the excitement of battle, allow themselves to commit acts of which, in their cooler moments, they repent, he concludes by complaining that the French have committed a great sacrilege in burning a church, at the head of Chersonese Bay, on the 5th instant, which has made the Russian troops very indignant, as it was a spot that was held especially sacred by them. Thus it would appear from the general purport of Prince Menchikoff's letter, that, although he does not admit the acts of barbarity complained of, yet he makes the burning of a church a sort of set-off against it. As regards this deed of the French, I need only state that it was purely accidental, and, indeed, it is hardly likely that they would burn a building which might serve them for many useful purposes. The Court of Inquiry, which had been ordered to ascertain the truth of the accusations made against the enemy's troops, concluded its labours today. The charge was clearly established by the testimony of 52 witnesses, officers and soldiers; some of whom died from the wounds they had received when lying helpless on the ground, and whose evidence was taken on their death-beds. No less than six officers, and twice as many sergeants and privates, it was proved, had been murdered by these inhuman cruelties on the part of the Russian troops.

I rode into Balaklava in the afternoon of November 11th. A great many shops had been established there, chiefly provision stores. They are mostly held by Maltese, who ask the most exorbitant prices for everything. The 62nd Regiment arrived there today from Malta, quite unexpectedly; it musters over 700 men. A wing of the 97th Regiment also arrived, and the rest are shortly expected. In all, today we have received upwards of 1100 men. The roads between the plateau and Balaklava are shockingly bad; at places knee-deep in mud, and almost impassable for wheeled conveyances; consequently, all the provisions and stores for the army have to be brought up to the front on baggage-animals, and of these we have not too many. Difficult, indeed, will be the task for the Commissary-General to provide the army with its requirements during the forthcoming winter, when he has entirely to depend on animal transport. Last night a trench for musketry was commenced; it runs about 300 yards in front of both our attacks, and is nearly 900 yards in length: in this trench are to be placed numbers of our best marksmen, and it is to be hoped that by this means we shall keep under the fire with which the enemy now annoy us from their rifle-pits. These they have established in considerable numbers along the front of the whole line of their works. Several deserters came in today; they were brought up to Headquarters, and were examined, as usual, separately. On being asked about their losses on the 5th, they all agreed that General Soimonoff and two other general officers had been killed, and from 225 to 240 other officers killed and wounded. As to their losses in men, they varied much in their statements. One said they had buried nearly 3000 men, and had 6000 wounded, but 7000 more were missing. Another told us that they had 5000 killed and 8000 wounded, but more missing. A third quietly informed us that they had lost 20,000 men. Altogether, it was difficult to come to any accurate conclusion from their statements; but, considering the numbers that we have buried and the small proportion of wounded that fell into our hands, I think their loss may be safely estimated at 15,000 men.

Some deserters who came in from the camp on the north side, by Inkermann, said that since the battle they had been daily employed, with other soldiers, in parties of 50, in digging pits for 500 bodies, and that several of these had been excavated in various places in the valley of Inkermann; and it was when on this duty that they had managed to run away. Some informed us that on the evening of the 5th it was generally believed by the garrison they had gained a great victory over the Allies; but, on the following morning, handfuls of men, representing the remains of regiments, returned to the town; and that, when they became aware of the great losses they had sustained, a perfect panic ensued. It was with difficulty that the men could be kept to serve the different batteries, as they momentarily expected to be assaulted by the Allies; and, in consequence of this feeling, large numbers of men had been sent into the town from the north side to reinforce the garrison, so that now they are numerically stronger than they have been before. This is only another proof of how accurate Lord Raglan is in his calculations, and how much it is to be regretted that he has not a larger force under his command, which would give him the power of overruling the objections raised by the French Generals.

At Inkermann, one feature peculiar to that battle was that the English troops were all in their great-coats, and not in red as usual, in consequence of their having turned out before daybreak in that dress on account of the rain; the majority of the Guards and 4th Division had come out of the trenches, where they had been on duty for 24 hours, and were also in great-coats. I know but of one exception to this, in the person of an officer who greatly distinguished himself both at the battles of the Alma and Inkermann, Captain Lindsay, of the Scotch Fusileer Guards.* It certainly was a great disadvantage to those in command, as, what with the fog and smoke, it was difficult to distinguish, beyond a few yards, friend from foe. The whole of our force engaged with the enemy during that eventful day did not amount to more than 8000 men. The brigade of Guards, who suffered more than any other, consisted only of 1230 rank and file, viz: the Grenadiers had in action 380 men; the Fusileers and Coldstreams together, 750; besides these, there was one strong picket of the Grenadiers, under the command of Prince Edward of Saxe Weimar, guarding the Careening Bay ravine; there were also two or three pickets of the Fusileers and Coldstreams overlooking the valley of the Tchernaya. But none of these pickets could be said to be actually engaged. The 2nd Division scarcely amounted to 2000 bayonets; the 4th Division only brought into battle 1400 men; while the Light Division consisted of about 1900 men. The Royal Artillery may perhaps have had, at the very outside, 1200 men engaged; we may add to these the brigade of Light Cavalry of 350 horses, but they can hardly be considered as sharing in the battle, as, although they were much under fire, they never met the enemy. The whole of this number together, which I am sure is quite the outside, amounts to 8080. According to the French return, they had actually engaged, including artillery, 5700 men; later in the day, as you may remember, a brigade of 3000 bayonets and two batteries of guns were brought up to the field, but were kept in reserve, and indeed were never under fire.

One may perhaps wonder how it was that we could bring so few men into action, but it must be remembered that the brigade of Highlanders, mustering over 2000 men, was down at Balaklava; the 3rd Division, of 3400 men, occupied the heights in rear of our trenches, to give support in the event of the enemy making a sortie from the town, which it was thought was not unlikely to be done. Besides these, men to the amount of 3600, who belonged to the divisions engaged at the battle of Inkermann, were in the trenches on various duties; to these must be added 2000 more, employed as regimental camp guards, officers' servants, etc., in all 11,000 men, who were not engaged, which, added to the 8000 in action, will give the amount of the British army before Sevastopol *effective* at that time.

I must relate an instance of Lord Raglan's great coolness on that eventful day. He was sitting on horseback, in the midst of a battery of artillery, watching our men working the guns. A very heavy fire was being directed against this part of the field, both from the enemy's cannon and also from small-arms. One of his Staff suggested the propriety of his not putting himself in quite so dangerous and conspicuous a place, especially as it appeared from the number of bullets which came singing by us that he was a mark for the enemy's riflemen. Lord Raglan merely said, "Yes, they seem firing at us a little, but I think I get a better view here than in most places." So there he continued for some time, and then, turning his horse, rode along the whole length of the ridge at a foot's pace, and consequently exposed him-self as much as ever. It was stated by several officers of the artillery (with what truth I can't say) that the Russians had a battery of guns which always kept firing at the Staff. This might easily be the case in spite of the fog, as they were the only body of

* Captain Lindsay has received the Victoria Cross for his gallant conduct on these two occasions.

horsemen, with the exception of the artillery, that could have been seen by the enemy; and certainly the number of casualties that occurred round Lord Raglan would seem to confirm this statement.

I should also tell of great *sang-froid* on the part of a hospital sergeant, I think of the 7th Fusileers. It was towards the close of the battle, and Lord Raglan was returning from taking leave of poor General Strangway, and was going up towards the ridge. A sergeant approached us carrying canteens of water to take up for the

General Bouat, Commander of the 1st Division which was employed as covering force during the siege of Sevastopol in 1855.

wounded, and, as Lord Raglan passed, he drew himself up to make the usual salute, when a round shot came bounding over the hill and knocked his forage cap off his head. The man calmly picked up his cap, dusted it on his knee, placed it carefully on his head, and then made the military salute, and all without moving a muscle of his countenance. Lord Raglan was delighted with the man's coolness, and said to him, "A near thing that, my man." "Yes, my Lord," replied the sergeant, with another salute, "but a miss is as good as a mile."

One of the most painful things during the action was the number of wounded horses. Some of the poor creatures went grazing about the field, limping on three legs, one having been broken or carried away by shot; others, galloping about, screaming with fright and terror. At times, some would attach themselves to the Staff, as if desirous of company; and one poor beast, who had its nose and mouth shot away, used to come in amongst us, and rub its gory head against our horses' flanks; he was ordered to be killed by one of the escort, which was of course done.

I must now record a great disaster which has happened to us by sea and land. We have had one of the most destructive hurricanes that can well be imagined; indeed, I think it is a wonder that we have any ships left, and, considering how entirely the army depend upon the transports and fleet generally for their resources, it is a mercy that it was no worse. Shocking accounts came into Headquarters of the sufferings of the troops in the trenches and outposts of the army during the hurricane. Many men were carried into camp on stretchers from being paralysed by cold, and several died in consequence. A man of the 8th Hussars was found dead in the morning from cold, and several others died on the heights above Balaklava from the same cause. 24 horses of the Royal Artillery, and 35 of the cavalry division, died during the day and night of the 14th. Numbers of men had to go into hospital with paralysed limbs.

The first desertion from our army, that we know of, took place yesterday afternoon: a private of the 79th Highlanders went over to the enemy before Balaklava. He was not seen by our sentries until he had got some little way off, and, although fired upon several times, managed to get away apparently unhurt.

The Commissary-General, Mr. Filder, came up to Headquarters, and had a long conversation with Lord Raglan and General Airey, Quartermaster-General, as to the losses the commissariat had sustained by the gale, and to see what steps could be taken in order to replace that which had gone down. Lord Raglan at once decided that an officer of the Quartermaster-General's department should immediately go to Constantinople, and purchase everything in the shape of great-coats and covering that could be found, and Mr. Filder was to use every effort to replace the provisions, by sending officers to different places to procure them at any price.

On November 16th, Lord Raglan received a communication from Sir Edmund Lyons detailing further losses incurred by the transport service off the Katcha river, where also the greater portion of the English fleet was lying. Five transports had gone ashore between the Katcha and Cape Constantine, but the crews were saved from all. The greater portion of the cargoes were all saved by the boats from the English fleet. Two, that did not go to pieces, were set on fire by orders of the Admiral, and burnt to the water's edge, so that they should not fall into the enemy's hands. Of the English fleet Her Majesty's ships *Trafalgar*, *Queen*, *London*, *Spiteful*, *Vesuvius* and *Sampson*, were all considerably damaged; the three first lost their rudders, and were otherwise a good deal knocked about. The French loss at sea, during the gale, it is difficult at present to estimate. At Kamiesch Bay upwards of 20 of their transports were driven on shore, but, as they were all very small, probably most of them will be got off again without very much damage. Two of their large transports, outside the bay, foundered with their crews and cargoes. The French fleet, off the Katcha, suffered in about the same proportion as ours: four ships of the line were more or less badly injured; at Eupatoria they suffered more severely, for there they lost the *Henri IV*, three-decker, of 100 guns, and also the *Pluton*, steam sloop of war, both of which went ashore between four and five miles south of that town. However, they lost but few men, as the gale abated shortly after they were stranded. A line-of-battle ship of the Turkish navy foundered off Eupatoria, with almost her entire crew. Our Mahometan allies also lost another line-of-battle ship and a large frigate off the entrance of the Bosphorus.

Yesterday we had several deserters who came in from the town and north side of Sevastopol; they all gave us accounts of misfortunes that had happened to them, similar to those which had befallen us, and they said that the *Gabriel*, 84-gun ship, had been sunk at the entrance of the harbour, to fill up the place of the *Silistria* (80 guns), which had been driven out of its position during the gale of the 14th. Except this they gave us no information worth speaking of, but one, a Pole, asked if it was true that 'the English always cut off the ears of the prisoners they took', as he had been informed in Sevastopol. When we laughed at this, and asked who had told him, he replied that their officers had asserted it on parade! Several others of the deserters concurred in this.

It is some time since I referred to the siege: one may almost say that it is at a standstill. We never fire into the town except in reply to the enemy, and it is now apparently an acknowledged thing that each side just answers the fire of the other, and directly one ceases the other does so also. This only refers to our guns, for a smart fusillade is continually going on between the sharpshooters in our musketry trenches and the Russian rifle-pits. It is difficult to say who has the best of it: our men are very sanguine, and declare they are perpetually '*bowling over*' the Russians. We have daily a few casualties from their riflemen. The enemy continue to repair and improve the defences of the town, so that they appear just as perfect, and probably more formidable than ever. They have placed *abattis* in front of the Round Tower, Redan, and Flag-Staff Batteries, but this is not looked upon as any great impediment, as a few rounds of gun-shell would make openings at any part.

I think it is very problematical, when we shall take the town; certainly not for a long time. The good people of England are much too sanguine, and have no idea of the difficulties to be overcome before we can hope for a successful result. They seem quite to forget how small our force is for so great an undertaking; besides, we have an army of the enemy in our rear, much more numerous than the Allies, with certainly as much artillery, and *ten* times as much cavalry; the town we are besieging is of great extent, and with unparalleled resources in men and the munitions of war.

Several Polish deserters came in to us again on November 23rd from the town; the following is a summary of what they said:—The garrison of Sevastopol are getting very tired of the siege; their losses have been immense: out of the crews of the ships, which mustered on our arrival nearly 15,000 men, the larger portion of whom have been since that time employed in working the guns in the batteries opposed to the Allies, not more than 7000 men now remain. The rest have been killed, died of disease, or are in hospital sick or wounded. They also said that in some of the batteries their losses had been so great that the men employed there declared that, if the siege lasted much longer, they would spike their own guns sooner than remain to serve them. They added, they had been told by their officers that the Emperor hinself was coming with a whole Corps d'Armée of 47,000 men, and then he would drive the Allies into the sea. It appears, too, that General Lüders arrived with a portion of his division from Odessa, two days ago, at the Russian ¹camp on the north side of the harbour of Sevastopol, and the remainder is expected in a day or two. They state that this division musters 18,000 bayonets, and that in a few days it is to come into the town and relieve the same number of men now forming a part of the garrison; and that an order has been issued that every month's duty in Sevastopol shall count as a year's service; but, as the men very naively remarked, "what is the good of that, if we were to remain to be killed?" One man told us that our three-gun battery on the left of our left attack, which fires up the ravine between the French and English trenches, does them more harm than any other, as it continually throws shot and shell into the arsenal and dockyard, where large bodies of men are constantly employed in making gun platforms, carriages, etc. He said that we ought to have eight or 10 guns there instead of three, and that he would point out the places where the guns would do most damage. He informed us also that the Russians have constructed what are called *fougasses pierriers** in the front of all their principal works, which of course would be exploded in the event of our assaulting the town. This same man stated, like a former deserter, that, had we attacked the town after Inkermann, we might have taken it with ease, as the garrison found out on November 6th the frightful losses they had sustained. He said that one battalion returned with only 90 men, that had gone out before the battle 650 strong. All intelligence given by deserters must not be taken *au pied de la lettre*, as they often invent things which they think will please us, and it is also possible that occasionally the enemy may send in men on purpose to give us false information, in the hope that we may be misled by their statements. Still, one can generally ascertain the truth by comparing the evidence of different deserters.

Two Russian soldiers were found on November 20th in one of the ravines near Inkermann half hid in a sort of hole. They had been wounded in the battle on the 5th instant; one had a shattered knee, and the other a bad contusion in the leg; both were therefore unable to crawl any distance. They had lived during these 15 days on the bread and arrack with which Russian troops are always provided.

On the night of November 21st a very spirited attack was made upon a large Russian rifle-pit, called by us 'The Ovens'. It is a sort of half-cavern in the side of a ravine, with stone huts about it, and in these for the last few days have been placed a considerable number of Russian sharpshooters, who have not a little annoyed the men in a portion of our trenches in the left attack, and caused numbers of

---

* *Fougasse pierrier* is a small mine in which the chambers are placed a few feet under the ground, and the axis of whose crater is inclined to the horizon at an angle of 45°. It is filled with heavy stones, which, when the mine is fired, blow outwards against any advancing body of men.

casualties among the French in their advanced parallel. There might have been room for some 200 men in the 'Ovens'. The attack was made by a strong company of the Rifle Brigade, under the command of Lieutenant Tryon; they advanced in the most determined manner, and drove out the enemy, who were probably taken by surprise. A good deal of fighting ensued, in which the Russians suffered severely, leaving behind them many killed and wounded. Poor Tryon, when in the act of firing at the retreating troops, was himself shot through the forehead and fell dead on the spot. The command then devolved upon Lieutenant Bouchier,* a very young officer, who showed considerable ability and judgment in the way he directed his men in repelling the repeated endeavours of the Russians to retake the post. They came back several times during the night in considerable force, but were met with such steady fire from these men of the Rifle Brigade, that they never regained for a moment any portion of the contested ground. Lieutenant Tryon is a great loss to his regiment, where he was much beloved; he was one of the best shots in the army, and it is stated by many men of his own company that he had himself killed over 100 Russians. At the battle of Inkermann he had the command of a party of men on some ground to the left front of the 2nd Division camp, and employed himself during the whole day in firing at the Russian artillerymen; he had two of his men to load for him, and they say that he knocked over 30 Russians, besides wounding several others. We lost in this affair last night seven men killed and 10 wounded. All this day the Russians have been shelling our left attack and the newly captured ground, thus showing their disgust at our success. Fortunately, their heavy fire did us but little harm.

Still horrid weather; rain day after day, with occasional slight falls of snow. Some of the troops are beginning to make huts for themselves in their spare time. The general mode of constructing them is as follows: they dig a trench some 20 feet long, 10 broad, and three deep; then build a wall of loose stones inside the trench, and raise it two feet above the ground, and then the earth is thrown outside the wall, and banked up against it, so that the sides of the hut are quite air-tight. A roof is put on in the usual way; it is made with planks, when procurable but more frequently, from the want of the former, brushwood is used, supported on small rafters, and afterwards covered with earth, plastered down. The hut is then completed, as no fireplace is put up, it being usually made in the centre of the hut, the smoke escaping, after the Irish fashion, by the doorway.

Sickness is greatly on the increase, and the cholera has, I am sorry to say, broken out very badly in the 3rd and 4th Divisions; the 44th Regiment has lost 19 men dead since yesterday morning, and from 12 to 15 have died in other regiments from the same cause. Every morning men are brought in, who have been either on picket or in the trenches during the night, with paralysed limbs; consequently our hospitals are crowded with inmates, and it is with the utmost difficulty that they can be removed from the front down to Balaklava for shipment to Scutari, on account of the dreadful state of the roads.

* Lieutenant (now Major) Bouchier has received the Victoria Cross for his gallant conduct on this occasion.

CHAPTER 8

Onset of winter

ON December 2nd, 1854, Lord Cardigan sent in his resignation to Lord Raglan on the score of illness, and consequently a medical board was ordered to assemble and report upon his case; and it has decided that, as he is much reduced in strength, and considering the serious character of his complaints, he should proceed home for the recovery of his health. He therefore returns to England immediately. I may as well mention that, on the 1st, Lord Lucan reported officially to Lord Raglan that the division of cavalry was not capable of further active service. Lord Raglan therefore informed General Canrobert of this unfortunate fact, and ordered the Brigade of Light Cavalry to move down to the valley of Kadikoi, to which place they marched yesterday. They have the advantage of being sheltered from the cold winds of the Chersonese, and have a better chance of being provided with forage, which, since the hurricane of the 14th, has been issued in but scanty quantity.

Lord Raglan rode down to Balaklava yesterday and visited the hospitals: they were not in the most comfortable state, but great excuses are to be made: the constant change of the weather, which precludes the possibility of keeping the floors clean—the difficulty of getting the bedding cleansed;—all these, together with the dreadful disorder from which most of the patients are suffering, namely, cholera (in all its stages), prevent that order and comfort which are so necessary to the recovery of the sick. Lord Raglan gave several directions, and made various suggestions to the medical officers for the better regulation of the hospitals, and went round to the majority of the sick, and had for each a word of kindness and sympathy. The cholera broke out with increased violence a few days ago in the army; yesterday between 70 and 80 men died of it, and near double that number went into hospital for treatment. General Pennefather, to the great grief of everyone, was taken ill with it this morning, and is in a dangerous state. However, the medical men say that the cholera is not of the same virulent order that it was at Varna, and when we first arrived in the Crimea; so we must hope for the best. Our losses from this dreadful scourge dishearten the men far more than the hardships they have to bear, and the constant dangers to which they are exposed.

The statement made by some of the newspapers that 'we have set a great hospital in Sevastopol on fire, burning 2000 men in it', is all nonsense. It is extraordinary how these lies are originated, and how easily you good people in England are led to believe in them. Special inquiry has been made of all the deserters from the town, and they have invariably stated that the wounded are removed daily across the harbour to their hospitals on the north side. There are several buildings in the town appropriated as temporary hospitals; but the two principal of these, we understand, are in Fort Paul, in the Karabelnaia suburb, and Fort Constantine, in Sevastopol. I believe both these great forts are almost, if not quite, out of range of our guns, and certainly too far off for us to do them any serious injury.

The 90th Regiment, 750 strong, have arrived at Balaklava from Dublin direct in the *Europa* steam transport, having been only $17\frac{1}{2}$ days coming out, including a delay at Malta and Constantinople of nearly 48 hours. For the present they are to be encamped close to the town. General Pennefather is so far better today that he has been taken down to Balaklava in Lord Raglan's carriage for change of air.

For a wonder it did not rain today, but last night it poured in torrents, with very heavy hail. The brigade of Heavy Cavalry on the high ground in rear of our Headquarters moved down today to the valley of Kadikoi, where the whole of the division will be together. Temporary stables are to be erected; but there are such difficulties in the way, that I doubt much whether they will be finished before the worst part of the winter is over. If they could be supplied with plenty of good forage, I think the horses would do perfectly well, without being under regular shelter. As it is, they get little or no hay and but a small ration of barley, consequently not a day passes without many falling down from sheer weakness that never rise again.

Four Polish deserters came in on December 8th from the Russian division opposite Balaklava. They say that they are getting very short of provisions and have been for some days on half-rations, as their supplies have not been brought up for the last fortnight from the interior, in consequence of the badness of the roads. They told us that the artillerymen of the 3rd Corps have arrived in Sevastopol from Perekop, to relieve the sailors who work the batteries, and who are quite worn out with their constant duties. They also stated that numbers of Turkish soldiers come over to the Russians from Balaklava, and that they say that we (the English) do not feed them well enough. On inquiry, I find that we give the Turks attached to our army a ration of biscuit and rice daily, and fresh meat once or twice a week according to the supply. They might have salt meat every day, like our own troops; but they refuse to eat it, as they fancy all salt meat is pork! It would be impossible for our commissariat to give them fresh meat every day, without taking it from the English troops, who only have it twice or three times a week.

The Russians made two sorties during last night, both of which were complete failures: one—on the French trenches in the earlier part of the night, when they were driven back by our allies immediately, and so closely followed up that the French got possession for a short time of one of the enemy's advanced batteries, but, as it was of course impracticable to remain there, they soon had to return to their own works; the casualties on either side were trifling: the other—at midnight, on the English left attack, when they endeavoured to retake the 'Ovens' and rifle pits, but were forced directly to retire by our men. They left three men killed on the ground, but carried off their wounded. We had one man killed and two slightly wounded.

The Russian troops in the valley of Balaklava retreated this morning to the other side of the Tchernaya river, having previously set fire to their huts, and overturned the two old Turkish redoubts which up to this time they have occupied. This confirms to a certain extent the statements made by the deserters yesterday of the difficulties of bringing up provisions etc.

On the night of December 6th, about 8 p.m., one corporal and five men of the 55th Regiment, on picket at the bottom of the Inkerman road, a few yards from the head of the harbour, were taken prisoners by a party of the enemy. One of our soldiers contrived to escape a few minutes afterwards, and from his statement it would appear that the Russians came over the water in a boat, and our men, fancying that they were going to desert, allowed themselves to be surprised by an armed party of greater strength than their own. Lord Raglan and the Staff went today all round the works of Balaklava, which now present a very formidable appearance. From the extreme point of the heights to the south of the town, a magnificent view was obtained of the whole of the valley and the plateau of

Infantry and cavalry on reconnaissance in difficult terrain.

Mackenzie beyond. The Russian troops, now all encamped and hutted between the Tchernaya and the last-mentioned plateau, were relieved this morning by a fresh body of men; as near as we could judge, they consisted of about 7000 infantry, 28 guns, and some squadrons of Cossacks. The large force of cavalry which was in the plain of Balaklava until only a few days ago has entirely disappeared. The enemy have thrown up a strong redoubt on the farther side of the Tchernaya, to cover the Tractir bridge; and from this it may be inferred that they have no intention of again occupying any part of the valley with their troops. A picket of Cossacks remain alone at the village of Kamara, and have two videttes on the old works on Canrobert's Hill and that west to it. The 34th Regiment, 800 strong, arrived today at Balaklava from Corfu.

On December 8th I saw the parade state of the English army in the East. The grand total of all ranks is 39,360. This appears a very formidable force, but the following deductions reduce its effective strength nearly one-third, viz. —

		Men.
Sick and wounded	.. ..	10,400
Cavalry (not effective)	.. ..	1,200
On command at Scutari, Varna, and other places	.. ..	3,600
	Total	15,200

—which only leaves 24,160 of all ranks effective: of these 2900 belong to the Royal Artillery. So you see, in spite of the almost daily reinforcements we have received since the battle of Inkermann, amounting to upwards of 8000 British troops, we are now scarcely 5000 men stronger. The number of deaths since the same period has been very large. Last week they averaged from 80 to 100 per day: but I am glad to say this week they are but half, being from 45 to 50 per day: this includes those killed in action and dying of wounds, but the greater portion are from cholera or diseases of that nature, Colonel Simmons goes this afternoon, and returns to Bucharest, carrying despatches to Omer Pasha from the allied Generals.

The mail from England arrived this morning, December 9th, and by it we are informed that Lord Raglan is made a Field-Marshal: this, I need hardly say, gives general satisfaction. It also brought us the receipt of the telegraphic despatch sent from Constantinople about the battle of Inkermann. General de Montebello, aide-de-camp to the Emperor Napoleon, arrived at Kamiesch yesterday, and today came up to the English Headquarters to congratulate Lord Raglan from the Emperor upon the successes that have attended the allied armies. He has also come out to give certain decorations in the French army; but the chief object of his mission is to report on the progress of the siege. A strong reconnaissance was made by a portion of the garrison of Sevastopol this morning in the direction of the Light and 2nd Division camps, but was immediately driven off by our pickets. It was probably to ascertain the strength of our works on the field of Inkermann. During the whole day numbers of waggons and baggage-animals were brought down with different things to the water's edge on the north side of the harbour, and three steamers were seen taking troops backwards and forwards from one side to the other. In consequence of all this there is a general impression that the enemy intend to try another attack on us tomorrow; but Lord Raglan says, *No*; he thinks it is merely a relief of a portion of the garrison. A flag of truce was taken by one of Lord Raglan's aides-de-camp today to the Russian outpost in front of Balaklava, with a letter from his Lordship to Prince Menchikoff in reply to his acknowledgment of the arrival of Captain Kousowleff, of the Russian artillery, captured by us at Mackenzie's Farm on September 25th. He has been given up in exchange for Lord Dunkellin, who was taken prisoner.

Soon after 5 a.m. on December 10th, we were all turned out and got on our horses, in consequence of a report that the Russians were advancing in large force opposite the Light Division, and to the right front of our right attack. However, it turned out to be only a false alarm. About midday, General Canrobert and General Bosquet each came, with their respective Staffs and escorts *en grande tenue*, to the English Headquarters, to pay Lord Raglan a visit of ceremony and to congratulate him on being made a Field-Marshal; also to thank him for the handsome manner in which he had spoken to them in his despatch of the battle of Inkermann, of which it appears they were informed by a telegraphic communication from the French Government. In the afternoon Lord Raglan rode through several of the English camps; and as before this time, the general order informing the army of his advancement had been made known to them, the men off duty crowded round and cheered him wherever he went.

A telegraphic message in cipher arrived from the Duke of Newcastle, via Vienna, Bucharest and Constantinople, informing Lord Raglan that intelligence from an authentic source has reached the English war minister, that Prince Menchikoff has reported to the Emperor of Russia that he has had 800 men at work for the last three months constructing mines in every part of Sevastopol, and that the whole town is now like a charged shell. Last night and today it has been clear and frosty, so that several heavy guns and mortars which have lately arrived were brought up from Balaklava to the artillery park of the left attack.

During the night of December 12th, the enemy made two sorties, one upon the French trenches, and the other upon us; the former was partially successful, as they penetrated into their advanced parallel, spiked several guns, and carried off a small mortar. The French covering-parties, on coming up, drove the enemy back to their works: the loss of men on either side was but trifling. The sortie upon us was made very early in the morning by a strong body of infantry coming up the Woronzoff road, doubtless with the intention of getting between our two attacks, and then taking them in reverse; fortunately our pickets stationed on the road saw them in good time, and, opening a brisk fire upon the advancing column, made them retire in a hurry. We had only one casualty, that of a private who was slightly wounded. What the Russian loss was it is impossible to state, as they carried off whatever men were killed or wounded. Lord Raglan rode this afternoon to one of the advanced posts of the French, in front of the Maison d'Eau, from whence he could obtain a good general view of both English and French trenches, and also of the enemy's works round the town.

On December 13th, all the ordnance for the left attack was reported as having been brought up to the left siege-train, consisting of 36 guns and 10 mortars. The last few days have been fine, which has reduced the sickness in the army considerably, and enabled us to bring up a large quantity of stores, etc., from Balaklava. I forgot to mention before that General Airey (Quartermaster-General) has been very ill with fever, and is reduced to a very weak state; but I am glad to say that his recovery seems now probable, which was more than doubted a few days ago. In spite of his sufferings, he has continued to direct the business of his office, instead of leaving it entirely to subordinate officers. His illness has been a great loss to the army, as his unceasing energy and indefatigable exertions have been wanting in many arrangements connected with his department, and which invariably go on more satisfactorily when superintended by the chief of the office.

Two privates of the Guards were taken prisoners on December 14th by some Cossacks in the plain of Balaklava. It appears that four guardsmen started from the town and thought to make a short cut to their camp by crossing the valley instead of keeping to the usual track inside our lines, and, when in the plain, they mistook their road in the fog, and were all at once attacked by four Cossacks, and, as none of our men were armed, they could make no defence. Two escaped, but the others were taken off by the Cossacks, who put cords round their necks and led them away in that undignified manner. An hour or so after this two deserters came in to Balaklava from their camp by the Tchernaya; they said they had met the two guardsmen being taken into the Russian camp. They had but little information to give us, except accounts of the privations the Russian troops were suffering from the want of supplies of every description, caused by the wretchedness of the weather and bad state of the roads. They said that enormous field-hospitals for several thousand men had been established in the woods over the Belbec river north of Sevastopol, in consequence of the impossibility of transporting the sick and wounded to Batchi-Serai and Simferopol, where the main general hospitals were situated.

The 89th Regiment, 670 strong, arrived on December 15th at Balaklava from Malta. A private of the 62nd deserted over to the Russians, by Inkermann; our sentries allowed him to pass them, as he said he was going to cut wood: he contrived to creep down to the bank of the Tchernaya, which he crossed, and then ran towards the Russian outposts. He was not observed by our sentries until he had passed the river, and was then quite out of musket-range. The blackguard was afterwards seen shaking hands with the Cossacks and walking off with them. Two soldiers of the French infantry tried to desert about the same time from the rear of our position across the valley of Balaklava. However, they were seen and pursued by a picket of cavalry, which speedily caught and brought them back to their lines: one was immediately shot, and the other is, I understand, to be also executed.

I must mention a story that was told of Sir Edmund Lyons and the Port-Admiral of Sevastopol, Admiral Istomine. It appears that Sir Edmund, when English Minister at Athens, had been very friendly with Admiral Istomine, who was there in a like capacity from the Russian Government. A few days ago a flag of truce was sent into Sevastopol from the fleet to return Captain Kousowleff, who had just come up from Constantinople, where he had been a prisoner. Sir Edmund Lyons thought he would send Admiral Istomine a present of a Cheshire cheese, and accompanied his gift with a little note, saying, he was sorry they were on their present terms, but, knowing his partiality for English cheese, took this opportunity of sending one, instead of a round shot! Three days ago a flag of truce came in from Sevastopol to our fleet, about some English sailors who had fallen into the hands of the enemy during the hurricane of November 14th. Admiral Istomine at the same time sent to

Right: Bersaglieri troops. Their proper dress was a blue cloth tunic, but the grey capote was adopted instead by all their troops for the Crimean War.

Sir Edmund Lyons a roebuck, in return for the cheese, and also a letter, thanking Sir Edmund for remembering him, and saying he often thought of the old and happier days they had passed at Athens together, and the numerous battles at whist which they had fought. He said he had *heard* the splendid *Agamemnon* on October 17th last, but there was too much smoke for him to see her on that day; he trusted Sir Edmund Lyons admired the bravery of the Russian sailors, as much as he (the Russian Admiral) did that of the English; and he only regretted they had not the opportunity of shaking hands once more, but he hoped that the day might yet come. These little civilities between two great chiefs of the contending powers form an amusing episode of the war.

Late on the night of the 20th the Russians made a strong sortie from the town in two columns, one on each of our different attacks; that against our left attack came on with considerable noise and shouting, and with bugles sounding and drums beating. They were speedily repulsed by portions of the 38th and 50th Regiments who drove them back with considerable loss: we too suffered severely. The attack on our right attack was made in perfect silence by the Russian troops, who, favoured by the intense darkness of the night, succeeded in arriving to within a few yards of our trenches before they were discovered. Our men (part of the 34th Regiment), completely taken by surprise, fell back before the enemy, who got into our advanced parallel: however, they did not remain there above a few minutes, as the covering party of a portion of the 97th Regiment came up, and together with that of the 34th advanced and retook the parallel. Our loss was heavy considering: Major Möller, killed; Captain Frampton and Lieutenant Clarke, 50th Regiment, and Lieutenant Byron, 34th Regiment, taken prisoners; four men killed and 13 wounded. This is the only thing of importance that has occurred lately.

We have been having thorough Christmas weather; a little snow at night, but, generally speaking, bright, frosty days. The men appear to hail this weather with delight, as, at any rate, they have no difficulty in making fires, and thus are able to cook their fare, which, Heaven knows, is not too luxurious, poor fellows! Another great advantage of frosty weather is, that we are enabled to bring up large supplies of warm clothing and provisions and huts from Balaklava, so that I am glad to say that our men are better off now than they have been for the last month.

On December 30th the 18th Regiment, 1100 strong, arrived at Balaklava direct from Dublin. They are all dressed in the new winter clothing, with fur caps and high boots; so I hope they will not suffer from going into camp at this time of the year, which must be very trying to men who have been accustomed to warm, comfortable habitations. The sickness in the army continues very great. As an instance I may quote that this month the 3rd Division has lost over 400 men: the other divisions have suffered in proportion almost as much, but it can scarcely be wondered at when one considers the hardships the men have to encounter. A man is said to have died of the cold in the trenches on Christmas night: this was the first really severe frost that we have had.

The mail which arrived on the 26th brought us out the promotions and rewards for the campaign. The fortunate ones are of course delighted, but there are numbers who grumble at not being remembered. I have read with great interest the speeches in both Houses of Parliament upon the 'carrying on the war'. The Government proposal to engage foreigners, as soldiers to serve in the British army, will be,

I should think, a most unpopular movement. We see daily how little faith can be placed in the services of men who have no other interest than their pay to make them fight. The French have here two battalions of their *Légion Etrangère*, which is a corps they raised some years ago for service in Algeria. I remember when travelling there, this time two years, hearing some of their officers say that the authorities had so little confidence in their foreign corps, that they were only used to garrison the unhealthy stations; and certainly I recollect myself finding them in two of the most out-of-the-way and least agreeable localities in the whole country. I also hear from French officers that numbers have deserted over to the enemy; two were caught in the act, and have been shot: and I was told the other day by one of their staff-officers, a man of considerable rank and standing, that it had been a question whether it would not be wiser to send these two battalions back to Algeria, and that General Canrobert would have done so had not the want of troops been so great.

I recently had rather an interesting interview with a Russian officer. I received orders in the morning to go with a flag of truce to Inkermann to give over some letters and money from Russian prisoners, and also letters and money to some English officers who are in the hands of the enemy. As there is no trumpeter attached to the escort at Headquarters, and the cavalry are some way off near Balaklava, I was directed to take a trumpeter from one of the batteries of artillery nearest Inkermann, and to manufacture a flag as best I could. Accordingly, I started, mounted on my best horse, and in my best attire: I got a trumpet-boy from Major Morris's battery; he also lent me a towel, which we fastened to the end of the *side* of a stretcher: this the trumpet-boy carried, and we started together down the Inkermann road. Directly we got up to our advanced sentries, I told the boy to sound, upon which he favoured us with the 'stable-call', and, no notice being taken of us by the Russian sharpshooters at the ruins of Inkermann, we trotted on down the road, which takes a winding course to the bridge over the Tchernaya, sounding several times on our way. I had hardly arrived there before I observed two horsemen approaching me from the other side of the valley along the causeway; they proved to be two Russian officers, and, when a few yards off, one advanced alone. I did the same, and we each continued approaching one another, until we stood on the opposite sides of the river (for the Russians had broken down the bridge after they had retreated over it on November 5th). We both made profound bows, and I then stated in French the object of my coming, and, as it was not possible to throw either the letters or money across, the Russian officer said it would be necessary to send for a boat from one of their ships-of-war in the harbour, which would come up the river to where we stood. He accordingly despatched the other officer with orders to that effect: he told me that I should have to wait for nearly an hour before a boat could arrive; we therefore both dismounted, and sat on the edge of the broken bridge, holding our horses. We looked at one another for some minutes without speaking; but it struck me that this was an unsociable way of spending an hour, and I thought I might as well try and get into conversation; so I began by making the truly British remark that it was a fine day; to which he replied, "Thanks to God, it is." Then a long pause ensued, which I again tried to break by telling him that I had the pleasure of knowing several Russian officers, whom I named and asked after. This rather thawed him; he appeared a good deal astonished that I had any

Russian acquaintances, and we were soon in animated conversation. He told me he was a Colonel of cavalry on the Staff, and had command of the outposts, and had been present at all the battles. He said he admired the English troops very much, that he thought the Guards were the finest infantry in the world, but that the Russian artillery was superior to the English. This, of course, I could hardly admit, although in the scientific part of that arm I think they are quite equal, if not superior to us. I should tell you that during this time a pretty brisk fire was going on from the Russian battery close to the lighthouse above the end of the harbour, against a work which the French are constructing to counteract the effects of this very battery. It so happened that, just after my Russian friend had been extolling his artillery, two shells were fired and both exploded far short of the mark. We were both watching the flight of these missiles during our conversation, so when I saw this bad firing I laughed, and asked my friend if that was a specimen of their practice. He took it very good-naturedly, and said we often made quite as bad shots from our batteries. He spoke in anything but praise of our allies; laughed at the Turks, and said the French infantry were inferior to the Russian. Possibly this may have been said to please me. Shortly after we saw a boat in the distance pulling towards us, so he said, "Here comes the boat from the *Vladimir* steamer." "Ah!" I replied, "I know the *Vladimir*, I have been on board her before now at Nicholaieff." This astonished him not a little, and he said that it seemed I had been everywhere. I then told him I had travelled through Russia, and had always received the greatest civility and kindness from his countrymen, and should entertain the most pleasant remembrances of my sojourn amongst them. This seemed to please him greatly, and he said, "The Russians like the English much; we ought never to have gone to war with you, but it was the will of God." The boat soon arrived; from its size it was evidently a barge, and the crew of 14 men were very smartly dressed in blue jerseys with red edgings. The Russian Colonel came across to me, and I gave him the letters, etc., and, after shaking hands, we parted with mutual expressions of hope that we should meet again before long. I then returned to the camp.

CHAPTER 9

No progress either side

IT may be of interest to record the strength of the British army on the first day of 1855. The following is a general summary which I made from the parade state this morning.

				Sick						
	Sick Field Officers.	Captains.	Subalterns.	Regimental Staff.	Serjeants, Drummers, Trumpeters.	Men fit for Duty.	Present.	Absent.	On Command.
Cavalry	6	14	23	20	149	762	111	237	41
Artillery	6	54	59	18	477	2,421	450	510	62
Sappers and Miners ..	2	3	23	4	45	503	60	31	0
Infantry	76	190	407	197	2372	19,948	3330	8128	1684
Total	90	261	512	239	3043	23,634	3951	8906	1787

Besides these, there are the soldier-servants of the officers and the clerks in the different military offices, amounting to 1331 men, which gives a grand total of 43,754 men of the English army in the East.

It is bitterly cold, the thermometer down at 21° Fahrenheit; the snow upwards of a foot deep, and drifting with a high wind in a manner that nearly blinds one. The troops suffer dreadfully from it; every endeavour is being made to get them under better shelter than canvas tents. The wooden huts have arrived in great numbers at Balaklava, but, unfortunately, their great weight renders it a service of considerable difficulty bringing them up to the plateau.

I see from the newspapers that the reaction against the English army has already begun. I thought the outcry in our favour was too great to last. *The Times* seems to abuse everything and everybody out here, and to pooh-pooh the difficulties with which the commissariat have to contend, and to find fault with the endeavours made by the authorities, who, I am sure, do all in their power, as far as circumstances will admit, to alleviate the overwork and sufferings of the soldiers.

Omer Pasha arrived here two days ago, and yesterday had a long interview with Lord Raglan, chiefly about the transport of his army from Varna to Eupatoria. At the present moment there are upwards of 16,000 Turkish troops in garrison at Eupatoria, the greater portion of whom have arrived during the last fortnight; and, if we can give more transport, Omer Pasha promised Lord Raglan that in the course of a month he would have 45,000 men there. I do not think the allied Generals expect much from these Turkish troops, except as making a diversion in our favour; indeed, already the enemy have sent a very large cavalry force to the neighbourhood of Eupatoria, the Headquarters of which are at Sak.

I am sorry to hear that the government have an idea of forming a corps of Bashi-bazouks. I am perfectly convinced that they will never be an efficient body of troops, and, from their propensity to plunder friend or foe, whenever they get the opportunity, they will only bring discredit on the British arms. I believe a Bashi-bazouk by nature is a coward; at least, I have never seen an instance to the contrary yet, nor heard of one either. I know Omer Pasha, who has had greater opportunities, perhaps, than anyone else of judging of these ruffians, entertains the profoundest contempt for them as troops in the field; and, as a proof of this, I may mention that when he crossed the Danube, and entered with his army into the Principalities, he would not allow any of the Bashi-bazouks to accompany him, as he said they would only murder and rob the inhabitants.

Omer Pasha and Staff leave Balaklava this afternoon, January 6th, in H.M.S. *Inflexible* (steam-frigate) for Eupatoria, where he takes command of the garrison. A deserter, who came in a few days ago from the town, said that there were frequent rows between the troops and convicts in Sevastopol. It appears that the latter have been allowed to go at large, as they volunteered to work at the batteries, etc. Three days ago Sir John Campbell (commanding the 4th Division) told me that the night before he had heard, when in our trenches, a great deal of musketry-firing and shouting going on in the town, and part of the time they could see the flashes in the streets. It was quite evident that there was a great riot among the garrison; doubtless it was some disturbance created by the convicts. Calvert told me the following story of one of these Russian forçats, who appear to be desperate fellows. About two years ago, a gang being at work in the dockyard of Sevastopol, one of them attacked a passer-by without any provocation, knocked him down, smashed in his face with the manacles on his hands, then jumped upon and trampled him to death. The act had been so sudden that the occurrence could not be prevented. It was thought by the authorities that so brutal a murder should be visited with some peculiar punishment, as an example to the others, for, if the man was hung or shot immediately, the circumstance would soon be forgotten. The case was made known to the Emperor Nicholas, who, on hearing of it, ordered an iron wheelbarrow made, and chains from its legs to be attached to those of the man. This was accordingly done, and, of course, the man could not even move a yard without wheeling the barrow in front of him. It is said that a week after he had been thus punished, he begged to be put to death, as it made his life a burden to him. This, of course, was not listened to, and three months after the wretched man died, raving mad! It was a novel but horrible punishment.

The cold is not so severe today, although the thermometer is lower; but there is not a breath of air, and consequently one does not feel it. The regiment I mentioned before as having suffered so much (63rd) is now reduced to only seven men! It came out from England, 1080 strong, with the rest of the 4th Division, which, as may be remembered, never landed at Varna, but arrived off that town a day or two before the expedition to the Crimea started. At the battle of the Alma they were not engaged; at Inkermann they had 113 casualties; and, allowing for as many more in the trenches, they will have lost 850 men from sickness. I fear much of this is from want of proper attention and care on the part of the officers. There are some strange stories about of the slovenly manner in which they have conducted themselves; and inquiries have been ordered to be instituted to ascertain the reasons for this conduct.

It is strange that the severity of the weather should have led to the English and Russian sentries fraternizing. It was in this way: a few nights ago, when very cold, our men on sentry in front of Inkermann observed several Russian soldiers coming towards them without arms, and they naturally supposed them to be deserters; but, on their approaching nearer, they made signs that they wanted a light for their pipes, which one of our men gave them, and then they stayed a few minutes talking to our sentries, or rather trying to do so, the conversation being something like this:

1st Russian soldier. — "Englise bono!"

1st English soldier. — "Ruskie bono!"

2nd Russian soldier. — "Francis bono!"

2nd English soldier. — "Bono!"

3rd Russian soldier. — "Oslem no bono!"

3rd English soldier. — "Ah, ah! Turk no bono!"

1st Russian soldier. — "Oslem!" making a face, and spitting on the ground, to show his contempt.

1st English soldier. — "Turk;" pretending to run away, as if frightened, upon which all the party go into roars of laughter, and then, after shaking hands, they retire to their respective beats.

I hear, a night or two ago, after one of these little conversations, some of the Russian sentries brought our men some firewood, of which they stood much in need. One may now see the English and Russian sentries, at a distance of some 60 or 80 yards apart, trotting up and down their beats to keep themselves warm, without thinking for a moment of molesting one another; whereas, only a few days ago, the sentries on both sides were always crouching down behind the bushes, and, if either saw his enemy, bang went his rifle, and probably he either killed or wounded him. This sort of fighting is perfectly useless, and is only an unnecessary sacrifice of life.

The article of *The Times* of December 23rd, against Lord Raglan and his Staff, has caused considerable commotion at Headquarters now that it has reached us. Lord Raglan, knowing as he does how totally false the whole tenor of the article is, treats it with the contempt it merits, and says it is nothing more than what any and every public man always gets when he does his best to serve his country, but he was very indignant at the attack made on his personal Staff. It is very easy for a man to sit down in England, and write an article against everybody in authority in the Crimea, without knowing one half the difficulties with which they have to contend.

Last night (January 11th) the Russians made a sortie upon the lines of the Allies before the town. I am sorry to say that this was perhaps the most successful of the many sorties which the enemy have made against us. Soon after 1 a.m. the Russians opened a furious cannonade from all their batteries; perhaps one of the quickest fires that we have had since the opening of the siege: it was probably to cover the

on the evening of the 7th and when the bombardment was at its height whilst looking on at the Pickett house I saw a lady walking with an officer who was evidently pointing out to her his point of attack, for next day – the orders were already out – she was very pretty and looked so sad that I could not help asking who she was – it was Mrs H——.

Below: The next day the artist heard that she met her husband's body near the same spot.

advance of their troops, for a heavy column of men came out of the town, between the Redan and Malakoff Batteries, and did this with such rapidity that a picket, of one sergeant and 12 men, were taken prisoners without firing a shot. They continued their advance, and got into a portion of our trenches, and, taking our men by surprise, drove them out without meeting with much resistance. In about six or eight minutes the covering parties came up, advanced with the guard of the trenches, and re-occupied the portion of our parallel which we had lost, the Russians retiring without attempting to hold it any longer. In this affair we had four men killed, and one officer and seven men wounded. What damage we did, if any, to the enemy it is impossible to say, as they had time to carry off any killed or wounded they may have had. Our allies fared no better than we did, for the enemy got into one of their batteries and spiked several mortars, but were speedily driven out again, leaving five dead and two wounded in the hands of the French. Their own loss is somewhat severe, being variously stated at from 20 to 30 casualties. The truth is, that, as far as the English army is concerned, the men are overworked, and consequently it is almost impossible to keep them as alert and active as the advanced posts and parallels before a besieged town require. I think, too, the intense cold makes one's sense of hearing and seeing, especially at night, difficult: one gets so benumbed that all one's faculties are more or less paralysed. I understand that the four men killed last night were bayoneted by the enemy when wrapped in their blankets fast asleep, their comrades not being able to wake them in time before the Russians got into the trench. The enemy have the advantage of coming out of warm habitations, and not unfrequently full of warm spirits; so that it can hardly be wondered at if they are successful in their sorties.

A deserter came in today from the town; he told us that the Emperor of Russia has ordered that every man who brings in the following things from the Allies shall be paid accordingly; viz. for a blanket, four paper roubles; for a musket, eight silver roubles;* and for a prisoner, 50 paper roubles. And he also said that the men who had spiked some French guns and mortars in their different sorties got 100 paper roubles each; and those that carried off some small mortars (cohorns) got 150 paper roubles each. A man of the 19th Regiment deserted today: he went down the Woronzoff-road ravine towards Sevastopol. When a little past our advanced sentries he was discovered: the picket was turned out and fired a volley at him, and he was shot through the back, and fell badly wounded. As he was too near the Russian outposts for our men to go to him, he lay there for several hours unassisted, and our sentries would not allow any of the Russians to approach him. When it got dusk a party of six men were sent to try and recover him, but were met by a strong picket of the enemy, consisting of some 30 men; he was abandoned to his fate.

About midday on January 15th, I was sent with a flag of truce to take in the letter which they would not receive two days previously. I accordingly went down the Inkermann road as usual, accompanied by a trumpeter belonging to a battery of artillery. When I reached our advanced picket on the road, I made him sound: but before he had finished his flourish a great 32-pound shell came crashing down some fifty yards to my right, and exploded with a noise that made the valley ring again,

---

* A silver rouble was worth 3s. 4d. in English money and was used as the basis of all financial transactions in Russia, no higher denomination being employed in accounts. The value of a paper rouble varied, but it may be generally put at about 10½d.

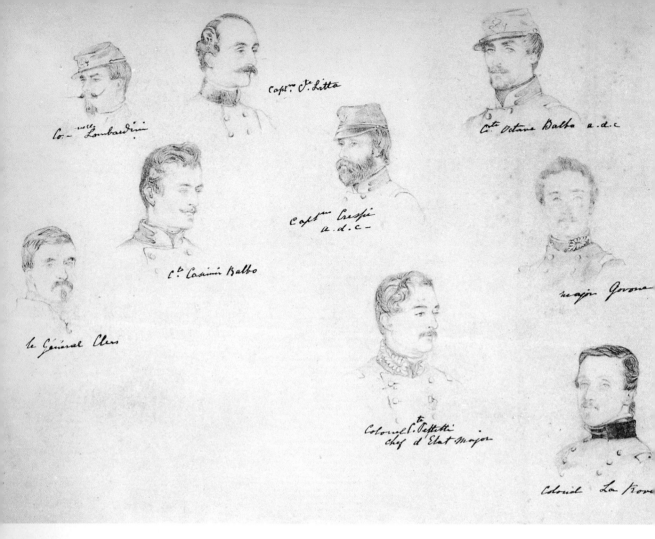

Quick sketches of fellow officers drawn during off-duty hours.

throwing up a little volcano of earth and stones. This was not a very pleasant way of being received; however, I ordered him to sound again, which he did. An instant after a 32-pound shot came whizzing towards us and struck the road about five yards in front of us, giving us a shower of dirt and snow. Our horses were very much alarmed; indeed I must confess that we were also. There was nothing for it but to sound again, and, as after that we were not fired at, we continued our way to the bridge, sounding at every turning. Both shell and shot were fired from two guns at the Lighthouse Battery, above the head of the harbour, on the north side. I waited for an hour and a half, and was just thinking of returning to camp when I saw two officers, and a soldier carrying a white flag at the end of his musket, walking towards me along the causeway from the other side of the valley. For some reason or other the Russians had cut the causeway across, about a quarter mile from the bridge, since they received the last flag of truce: it looked as if they fancied that some night we might attempt to move troops across the valley by the causeway, and this would put another obstacle in our way. The two officers came up shortly after and apologised for keeping me waiting, but said that there was no officer of sufficient rank to receive a flag of truce, and that they had to send across to Sevastopol for instructions; but that a boat would soon be sent with a superior officer authorised to take my letter. These two officers belonged to the guard of the Lighthouse Battery. I complained to them that I had been fired at twice: they expressed their regret, and said that the gunner who fired at me was '*un homme bête*', who did not remark that I came with a flag of truce — a poor consolation to us, if we or our horses had been either killed or wounded. They congratulated me on my fur coat, and wanted to know if we had all got the same sort of thing; to which I replied, that all those who had not got them would receive them. The Russians said they wished they had the same chance. They were both very indifferently clothed, and appeared to feel the cold much. In course of time a naval officer of some rank arrived in a boat. I gave him my letter, and then he told me that "The General" — "What General?" I said. "The General commanding in the town," he replied (he was too sharp to let out his name, in reply to my query*), "wished in future for flags of truce to come in from the English to the town, as it is inconvenient to receive them at Inkermann, and difficult to discover their approach from the battery at the lighthouse." After a few commonplace observations and compliments we bowed and separated: I returned to Headquarters.

This morning a woman, the wife of a corporal belonging to the 23rd Regiment, was confined of a daughter, in a hole excavated out of the ground, covered in with a small dog-kennel tent; both mother and child are doing well, as people say. Lord Raglan, with his usual kindness, sent his own doctor to see after her, and some little comforts from his kitchen that he thought might be acceptable.

The Times continues to abuse us, I see, and talks much of the discontent of the officers and men in the English army out here. It is a notorious fact that the officers who grumble the most are those who have lately arrived, and who have not gone through any of the hard fighting; the brigade of Guards have got some of the greatest grumblers of the army among them, but I believe the worst are those who have joined within the last month. It is surely to be especially regretted when officers comparatively high in command, and who may otherwise have greatly distinguished themselves, should so far forget the *first quality* and consequent duty of a soldier as to set an example of grumbling and discontent at the hardships which all have to endure alike, instead of showing a steady determination to make the best of everything.** I cannot fancy a greater fault on the part of one in command than to exhibit in his own conduct a disposition to criticise and censure those in authority, and, in point of fact, one may almost say to sanction a spirit of insubordination among his men. In making these remarks I have no wish to disparage the brigade of Guards generally: they have displayed on every occasion before the enemy a courage and devotion to their country which will ever be

* It was of importance to ascertain who commanded in Sevastopol, as it had been reported some time before that General Osten-Sacken was expected from Odessa with reinforcements, and was then to take command of the garrison.

**La première qualité du soldat est la constance à supporter la fatigue et les privations; la valeur n'est que la seconde. La pauvreté, les privations, et las misère sont l'école du bon soldat. — Maximes de Guerre de Napoléon.

remembered with admiration by all who witnessed it. It is, therefore, the more to be lamented that men who showed such bravery and indifference to danger in the battlefield should not exhibit more firmness and resolution in facing the hardships of a winter encampment; for since the battle of Inkermann, the Guards, in consequence of their severe losses, have been excused from all trench-duty.

I see also it is stated in *The Times* that 'the Commander-in-Chief does not go amongst the troops, and that many officers and men who landed in the Crimea in September have never seen Lord Raglan'. To this I can only say that it is false from beginning to end.

There is a report here that the Emperor of Russia is dying: this intelligence was brought to us by some Tartars, who had come from the interior of the Crimea, and who said that prayers are ordered to be offered up for him both in the Greek churches and also in the mosques, and that in Simferopol and Batchi-Serai pictures are shown about and sold representing the Emperor in bed holding a cross in one hand and a sword in the other, and underneath an inscription to the effect that he will fight for the true faith till the 'last hair of his head'. They also told us that the Tartar population are *ordered* to contribute to a fund that has been opened for 'carrying on the war'; but at the same time they are assured that, when the invaders (the Allies) have been driven into the sea, the Emperor guarantees them advantages and improvements they never even dreamed of before. Poor devils, if these are the conditions, I fear their chance is poor indeed.

January 16th was the most disagreeable day we have yet had; a high north wind making the frozen snow drift in clouds, which almost blinded one; indeed at times it was next to impossible to face it. The thermometer was at 20° Fahrenheit. Lord Raglan, accompanied by only two of his aides-de-camp, rode out to the Light Division camp, principally that he might take some little comforts and warm things to the poor woman who was confined yesterday. On arriving at her miserable habitation, Lord Raglan got off his horse, and himself gave the things he had brought to the woman and her husband the corporal. The man was so overcome by his Lordship's kindness that he had no words to express his thanks, but Lord Raglan, with his usual good-nature, endeavoured to relieve his embarrassment by talking about his child, etc.

Next day it began to thaw rapidly. The Russians made two sorties last night, at different times, on the French trenches—the first, on their extreme left; the enemy were repulsed by a portion of the *Légion Etrangère*, not without considerable loss to them. The second sortie was made more on the centre of their works; here, too, considerable fighting took place; the enemy were soon forced to retire, leaving several of their dead behind them. The loss of our allies is stated by themselves to be 32 men killed and wounded. It appears that for the last few days the Russians have been adopting a new method of taking prisoners; they have employed the *lasso*, and I understand that the French have lost several men in this manner; and it is said that last night they took six or seven prisoners, who, after having driven in the Russians, were lassoed round the body, leg or arm, and forcibly dragged into the Russian batteries. I hear today that General Canrobert intends sending in a

Right: One of the Tartars is wearing the normal black sheepskin cap and a gaudy sash round his waist. Both wear the usual handsome jackets and wide breeches.

Tartars of the Crimea
(from nature)

letter to General Osten-Sacken, protesting against this mode of warfare, as being barbarous.

On the morning of January 21st the French at length gave us their long-promised assistance on the right. A brigade of infantry of the 1st Corps camped close to our 2nd Division; and in the course of the day all our pickets and guards right of the Careening Bay ravine were relieved by the French troops, thus freeing us of a duty which took no less than 1600 men daily; which will consequently give our men employed in the trenches at least one night a week more off duty.

We are all very indignant, and much disgusted at the repeated attacks made on Lord Raglan and those in authority by several of the English newspapers, especially *The Times*. The mail came in this morning, and brought us the public journals up to the 7th instant. In *The Times* of 2nd, 3rd, and 4th instant, there is each day a letter purporting to be written by officers out here, of a character so discreditable to them as holding Her Majesty's commissions, that one can hardly believe in their really being the productions of English gentlemen. I notice these three in particular, as being written by officers; those which are published as being letters from soldiers and amateurs are unworthy of notice, as men of that class rarely have the opportunity of judging with any fairness of the motives of those in authority. Every man can make out a grievance for himself; but I hope readers are not misled by these letters, especially those written by civilians, who, it would really appear, come out here for the sole purpose of finding fault with everything and everybody.

It may not be out of place here for me to give you some idea of the daily labour of the English Commander-in-Chief. Lord Raglan is generally up in the morning by 6 a.m., and at this time of the year writes by candle-light for an hour or more before his breakfast at 8 a.m. After that is over, he sees the general officers of the Head-quarters Staff, who bring to him the morning reports. First of all the Quarter-master-General, then the Adjutant General, then the General of Engineers, then the officer commanding the Royal Artillery, and twice or three times a week, according to circumstances, the Commissary-General and the Inspector-General of Hospitals, or head of the medical department; so every morning of his life Lord Raglan has to see four, and very frequently six officers, heads of the different departments of the army. The length of time that it takes to discuss business with these officers of course varies very much; sometimes they may be disposed of in an hour, at others each may take as long. He then writes till 1 or 2 p.m., at which time he receives any of the different Generals or other officers who may wish to see him on duty. He then usually rides out till dusk to the different camps, where again he invariably has some object in view, of perhaps visiting the field-hospitals or the officers and men of any particular brigade or regiment. On returning home, his Lordship generally writes till dinner-time, which is usually about 8 p.m. Most days he has several officers from the camps to dine with him, after which he does business with different members of the Staff, and almost always writes till past midnight. I will answer for it, that although his Lordship has not the same fatigue to go through, there is no officer in this army who is so constantly at work, or who gives himself so little relaxation. I may also mention here that from the Field-Marshal's dislike to anything approaching parade or ostentation, he usually rides out accompanied only by one of his aides-de-camp and one mounted orderly, so that his appearance to the uninitiated would be only that of any other General of division or brigade, and would consequently not be remarked except by those who pass close by him. When I have mentioned that 'Lord Raglan went out, accompanied by *the* Staff', I mean that he was accompanied by officers not only of his personal Staff, but also by others belonging to Headquarters, as, for instance, the Quartermaster-General and some of his department, the commanding officers of Engineers and Artillery, etc.; but on these occasions there are rarely more than three or four orderlies, so that even then the cortege is not numerous. The escort of cavalry attached to Headquarters, of which I have before spoken, are used as mounted orderlies for the different military departments at Headquarters, and a hard time they have of it, as some of them are perpetually carrying letters, etc., day and night. In the French army it is invariably the custom for a general officer to go about at all times and seasons accompanied by a cavalry escort, whether it be in a French garrison town or on service in the field. General Canrobert, whenever he goes out, is always accompanied by six or eight officers of his Staff and an escort of some 20 Hussars, preceded by a *porte-drapeau* bearing the French flag, independently of one or two Spahis,* his personal attendants. This cortege, of course, attracts attention, rendered remarkable, as it is, by the *porte-drapeau* and the peculier dress of the Spahis.

Early on January 29th arrived from Constantinople several nurses, under the superintendence of three ladies, the first of whom is styled the 'Mother Eldress', who has the general direction of the others. These kind-hearted women have petitioned Lord Raglan to allow them to go at once into the hospital at Balaklava, and have also asked to be allowed to attend the field-hospitals in camp. The former Lord Raglan has granted, and has given directions for immediate arrangements to be made for lodging them close to the hospital, with such conveniences as circumstances will permit. Their latter request Lord Raglan very properly refused, as he said he could not allow them to be exposed to the hardships and trials of camp life. I hear that this morning a ship-load of navvies has arrived at last in Balaklava harbour, so I suppose that the railroad will be now commenced. Considering that the Duke of Newcastle said that the navvies would be here by the 20th of December last, and in three weeks from that date construct a tramway that would carry all the requirements for the siege and army up to the plateau—and that up to this day nearly six weeks have elapsed before the first detachment of navvies have arrived—I think some of the abuse so liberally showered on the authorities here by the British public for their want of arrangement and forethought might fairly be transferred to those at home, who have none of the difficulties to contend with which so embarrass our chiefs.

On the 25th Lord Raglan, accompanied by two of his personal Staff and the commanding officers of the Royal Engineers and Royal Artillery and their aides-de-camp, went through the whole of our trenches, examining everything in detail connected with the batteries, and inspecting minutely our most advanced works, and even going into some of the rifle-pits. The enemy were very civil upon the

---

* The Spahis are a corps of cavalry, raised by the French in Algeria, in 1834; it consists entirely of Arabs. who find their own horses and accountrements, but receive arms and a certain amount of clothing from the French Government. They are dressed in the native Arab costume, but wear a crimson cloth burnous instead of the usual one of brown wool. The superior officers of the corps are Frenchmen, the remainder native Arabs.

Russian prisoners being marched into captivity.

whole, and scarcely fired a single round shot during the four hours Lord Raglan was in our two attacks: as usual, he had several narrow escapes from the rifle-balls of the Russian sharpshooters. He frequently would remain looking over the parapets for some minutes at a time in places where he fancied he gained a new or better view of any of the enemy's works, and consequently exposed himself much.

CHAPTER 10

Attack on Eupatoria

TWO deserters came in from Sevastopol late on January 29th, 1855, at different parts of our trenches; both were Poles in the Russian artillery. One was a cadet, acting as a subaltern officer (the first who has deserted over to the Allies), and the other a bombardier. They informed us that the Grand Dukes Nicholas and Michael both arrived in Sevastopol two days ago, and had been inspecting all the works of the town, and reviewing the troops, giving those who had distinguished themselves decorations and money. They stated that yesterday the Grand Dukes made a reconnaissance from the town of the ground in front of Inkermann, in the dress of private soldiers, so as not to attract the attention of the French sharpshooters. The bombardier said he thought that the Russians intended to make another attack on the English right, and try and force their way into our camp at the same point which they had hoped to have attained at the battle of Inkermann, viz. by the Careening Bay ravine; but the cadet said that it was not at all likely they would attempt anything of the sort, as there was only one battery of field-artillery in the town, all the rest having gone in relays to Simferopol, to be repaired and recruited for future service. The latter part of the cadet's statement was fully confirmed by a Tartar spy who had been sent out by Mr. Calvert, and who returned from Simferopol late last night. He states that the Russians are repairing quantities of field-artillery at that town, where a great establishment has been formed for the purpose, and that a large number of wheels and different parts of gun-carriages have been sent from Nicholaieff and other towns in the south of Russia, together with artificers and workmen.

In the afternoon of February 1st, Lord Raglan rode out to the 3rd Division, and visited the hospitals. In the official report this morning I see that no less than 6500 men have been sent down sick to the general hospital at Scutari during the month of January.

During the night of February 3rd it froze harder than it has yet done this winter, the thermometer going down to 10° Fahrenheit. A French artilleryman was found frozen to death this morning, just outside the English Headquarters. Lord Raglan and the Staff rode down to Balaklava, and went through the hospitals. He found the eight nurses in full employment; and the medical officers said they were of great assistance to them, as they made slops and messes for the sick. With the exception of the three ladies, they are none of them young, all rather fat and motherly-looking women, and quite come up to one's idea of orthodox nurses.

A man of the 9th Foot (batman to an officer) was found this morning dead on the road-side between the Col and Balaklava; he had evidently been murdered, as his body was stripped. His head had been much knocked about with some blunt instrument, and his face was covered with blood. There were also marks round his neck, which looked as if he had been strangled: suspicion, from this last fact, falls on its having been committed either by a Turk or by one of the Tirailleurs Indigènes, as with them it is a common way of putting a man to death. Inquiries have been instituted, and a large reward offered for the apprehension of the murderer.

When out riding today I met some sailors, one of whom was leading a pony, rather a good-looking beast, so the following short dialogue ensued between us: —

I. — "Who does that pony belong to?"

He. — "It's mine, yer honour."

I. — "Where did you get him?"

He. — "Why, I found him, yer honour."

I. — "And what are you going to do with him?"

He. — "Why, sell him, yer honour; may be you'd like to buy him; he's cheap at a pound."

However, not wishing to become a purchaser of *found*(?) goods, I rode on. Cool hands these blue-jackets; they bag no end of ponies and animals every day, and then sell them to anybody for a sovereign. Indeed, it has become such an established fact that the sailors are very handy at appropriating stray cattle, that if an officer loses a baggager he always goes or sends his servant to the Naval Brigade camp, where he not infrequently finds his missing property. But Jack invariably demands a fee for taking care of what he calls the 'dumb baste'.

All the men have now got plenty of warm things, indeed more than they want, for *several* commanding officers or regiments have applied to the Quartermaster-General to return some of their clothes into store. The other night, when it was very cold, I asked a sentry at Headquarters if he was comfortable, to which he replied, "I should be, Sir, only I have got on such a b— —y lot of clothes." This will give you some sort of idea of the feeling of the men about it.

I see in one of the last *Times* to arrive here it is stated that we had borrowed from the French 25,000 great-coats for the use of the troops; this is totally untrue: when the winter clothing for the French army arrived, General Canrobert sent Lord Raglan *two* sheepskin coats as specimens of that article provided for the French. I suppose this is the foundation of *The Times* correspondent's report. Then the same newspaper informs us that 'the French and Turks are nearly all hutted, but none of the English'; two or three days ago 270 huts, capable of holding between 5000 and 6000 men, were officially reported as having been put up in the English army. I have never yet seen a French hut, except a few at the French Headquarters for the use of the general Staff, but I understand that some have arrived a few days ago at Kamiesch. As to the Turks, they certainly have got a great number of their men in burrows, but this plan would appear hardly advisable for us to adopt, as the awful mortality among our Mahometan allies is attributed by the medical men in a great measure to their living underground.

The other day I saw the official return of the number of deaths in the general hospitals at Scutari during the month of January; I am sorry to say they amounted to no less than 1461 British soldiers. I may mention what was told me yesterday by a staff-officer attached to the French Headquarters, to show that the losses of our allies in sick have been in proportion as great as our own.

The French have commenced opening a fresh attack against the defences of the town, from the Malakoff Tower to the harbour of Sevastopol; it will be a work of considerable time and labour before completed sufficiently to open fire against the enemy's batteries. I understand that this resolution on the part of General Canrobert was finally adopted by the advice of General Niel, who differs altogether with General Bizot (Chef du Corps du Génie) as regards the proper point of attack for the reduction of the town; General Bizot's opinion being, as I some time ago mentioned to you, that the Bastion du Mât is its vulnerable point. On the other hand General Niel takes the view which Sir John Burgoyne has held from the very first, viz. that the Malakoff is the key of Sevastopol. The consequence of this is, that at last the French will adopt the first plan proposed to General Canrobert by Lord Raglan at the suggestion of Sir John Burgoyne. It is now much to be lamented that our allies did not in the first instance give way to Sir John's arguments, as there can be no doubt of the capture of the town, if his propositions had been carried out.

The new attack against the town between the Malakoff Tower and the harbour was commenced by the French on the night of February 7th, who broke ground on the right of the second parallel of our right attack. Two heavy batteries, one of eight, and the other of 15 guns, are to be constructed. At present it is proposed that they should be armed with English ordnance and manned from the Royal Artillery, but the trenches are to be guarded by French infantry. This arrangement will probably be changed. Lord Raglan received a telegraphic message from London this afternoon announcing that Her Majesty's Ministers had resigned in consequence of a motion having been brought forward in the House of Commons by Mr. Roebuck of 'want of confidence in the Government by the Houses of Parliament'. For the Government, 146; against, 305. Majority against, 159. The message went on fully to explain, that the Queen had sent to Lord Derby to form an administration.

On the morning of February 13th, Lord Raglan sent Colonel Steele, his military secretary, down to Lord Lucan with a despatch from the Duke of Newcastle, in which he was informed that he was recalled from the command of the cavalry in the Crimea. As far as I understand, the reason of this is, that Lord Lucan objected to an expression in Lord Raglan's despatch of the battle of Balaklava, and wrote a remonstrance to him on the subject. Lord Raglan recommended Lord Lucan to withdraw his letter, but on his refusal it was forwarded to the Duke of Newcastle (Minister of War), who with the concurrence of Lord Hardinge (General commanding-in-chief) decided that it was necessary for him to be recalled; for it would be incompatible for Lord Raglan, as Commander-in-Chief, to retain a Lieutenant-General in an important command, after he (the Lieutenant-General) had thought proper to censure his judgment. I hear Lord Lucan was very much annoyed at his recall, more especially as the date of the Duke of Newcastle's despatch is of January 27th, only two days before the Duke was out of office by the resignation of ministers. Lord Raglan went out this afternoon and visited the 3rd and 4th Division camps.

Last night the enemy only fired two round shots at our trenches, one of which took off the *left legs* of two men posted as double sentries; the one in front had his

Le Général Cler
formerly commanding the Zouaves
(... in the Zouave Costumes)

leg taken off above the knee, and the other below it; the latter screamed so dreadfully from pain, that he was heard by the sentries in camp: both men were immediately carried in, and had their shattered limbs amputated.

A Tartar spy sent out by Calvert on February 11th returned this morning from Simferopol and Batchi-Serai. He represents the Russian soldiers as suffering very much from want of meat, for they get nothing but black bread. He says that the road between Batchi-Serai and Sevastopol is strewed with loaded waggons full of powder and clothing for the besieged, as all the draft-horses have died from overwork and want of forage; but that large quantities of cattle dragging waggons full of forage were daily expected from the interior. He overtook on the road a body of 12,000 infantry on march from Simferopol to Eupatoria. He told us also that every now and then reinforcements arrive from Russia of 500 to 1000 men each, belonging to the 6th Corps. He represents the number of sick at Simferopol and Batchi-Serai as being something quite prodigious; the cholera has broken out amongst them, and the poor creatures suffer dreadfully both from want of doctors and medicines; they consequently die daily by hundreds.

On February 18th, Lord Raglan received despatches from Eupatoria, informing him that at daylight yesterday morning the enemy advanced in great force against the entrenchments round that town. The attack was made with great determination; and, under cover of the fire of 80 pieces of artillery, the Russians advanced to within a few yards of the works of the place. They continued their attack for upwards of four hours, but were finally driven back in great confusion by the garrison. Omer Pasha commanded the defence in person. It would appear that he was aware, ever since his arrival in the Crimea, of the probability of an attack from the enemy, and it was reported that positive orders had been received by the Russian Generals, from the Emperor Nicholas, to drive the Turks into the sea, and raze Eupatoria. A very indifferent line of earth fortification had been constructed round the town, and at the time of the attack, was in an incomplete state. The undulating nature of the steppe in the immediate neighbourhood of the town favoured the enemy in concentrating their troops within a short distance, without the garrison being in the least aware of their vicinity. The chain of Russian videttes prevented the possibility of making any reconnaissance except in force. On the night of the 16th, under cover of darkness, the enemy placed 80 pieces of artillery in a curved line round the front of the town, about 300 paces from the most advanced Turkish work. At the point of day, (shortly after 6 a.m.) on the morning of the 17th, the Russians opened a heavy cannonade from their artillery against the defences of Eupatoria, and continued firing without intermission for upwards of two hours, during which time they considerably damaged the earthworks, and succeeded in dismounting nearly a third of the guns of the place. The Turks behaved with the greatest courage and endurance, especially in the most advanced earthwork, which, armed with only three field pieces, was under the command of Selim Pasha, the chief of the Egyptian troops, who himself set an example of heroic bravery. He was unfortunately killed during the action.

The Russians had sharpshooters placed in rifle-pits, which had been constructed during the previous night on either side and between each of their guns. These

Left: General Clérs of the Zouaves who proved himself a worthy chief of those fine troops.

men, aiming at the Turkish embrasures, did great execution amongst the gunners. During their furious cannonade, the enemy's infantry had been formed up in heavy masses for the assault of the town on three different points. The column to attack the left, was preceded by a large body of cavalry, who were severely knocked about by the well-directed fire of two field-guns, judiciously brought to bear upon them as they advanced. These field-pieces were commanded by Lieutenant-Colonel Cadell, a young English officer of the Hon. East India Company's service, who is attached with some others to the Turkish army. The Russian cavalry also suffered considerably from some shells thrown at long range into their flanks, from H.M.S. *Valorous*. This cross-fire checked their further progress and compelled them to retire, the column of infantry following their example. Upon this Colonel Cadell turned his field-pieces against the Russian artillery, and placed them so advantageously as to enfilade a portion of their line of guns. The enemy finding themselves taken in flank, sent up a reserved field-battery to counteract their effect, but in spite of this, the Turkish gunners managed to hold their own until ordered by Omer Pasha to another position.

During this time, a far more important assault had been taking place on the extreme right. The enemy advanced heavy masses of infantry, under cover of the fire of two troops of horse artillery, and passing through a cemetery which afforded them partial cover, pushed on with determined resolution up to the edge of the ditch, surrounding this portion of Eupatoria. They had brought up scaling-ladders and materials for filling up the ditch to facilitate the crossing of their troops, but they were destined to succeed no further, for the volleys poured into them by the Turkish infantry, who lined the parapets at only a few yards distance, threw them into complete disorder. Their confusion was augmented by some shells fired into their left rear from H.M. gunboat *Viper*, and also some rockets from a boat of H.M.S. *Furious*.

Nevertheless, with great determination, the column of attack was to a certain extent reorganized, and they again advanced to the assault, but without any more success than before. This time, a portion of the Turkish troops sallied out and pursued them for a considerable distance, killing every unfortunate man they overtook, without attempting to make prisoners. The Russians, seeing the utter failure of their two attacks on the left and right of the town, declined attempting any further assault, although they had a heavy column in their centre, formed up apparently for that purpose. Accordingly, about 10 a.m., they began a general retreat, which was accomplished in perfect order, and carried with them their wounded, and even a large portion of their killed. To the last their line of artillery kept up a heavy cannonade, succeeding in almost entirely silencing the guns of the place. From the statements of the few prisoners taken, it would appear that it was the intention of the enemy, if they succeeded in penetrating into any portion of the town, to have set it on fire; and for this purpose, every infantry soldier was provided with a small faggot of wood, thousands of which were found strewed about the ground after the Russians had retreated.

On the afternoon of February 19th Lord Raglan rode down to Kadikoi, and had a long talk with Sir Colin Campbell about the proposed attack upon the Russian force near Tchorgoun tomorrow morning. It was settled that Sir Colin should take with him the Brigade of Highlanders, and the 14th and 71st Regiments, with

300 horses of the cavalry division, and one battery and a troop of horse artillery (both 9-pounders), in all about 3600 men; that they should march tomorrow at 1 a.m. from Kadikoi, and proceed to some high ground overlooking the village of Tchorgoun and the entrance to the valley of Baidar, and so contrive as to arrive there before daylight. They are there to wait until they hear the French commence the attack on the enemy's camp by the Tchernaya river, upon which Sir Colin is to attack the Russians in the rear; and by this means it is hoped that the whole of the enemy's force will be captured.

The French are to be commanded by General Bosquet, and will consist of three brigades of infantry, mustering upwards of 9000 men, the brigade of Light Cavalry (Chasseurs d'Afrique), and three batteries (12-pounders) of artillery; in all, their force will be little under 12,000 men. They are to descend about 1 a.m. from the heights on the rear of the plateau, then traversing the valley of Balaklava remain on the heights this side of Tractir Bridge till daylight, at which time they are to advance rapidly, and endeavour to surprise the Russian force at Tchorgoun.

Notwithstanding the inclemency of the weather, Sir Colin Campbell got his force in motion soon after 2 a.m. on February 20th: they marched with great difficulty, as it was excessively dark, the snow blowing right in their faces, and consequently their progress was but slow. The column was formed with the light infantry (71st Regiment) in advance; then a battery of artillery; then the three Highland and 14th Regiments; then the troop of horse artillery, with the cavalry on the left flank and the rear, together with the spare ammunition and ambulance waggons. The whole force arrived at the appointed spot soon after 5 a.m. some time before daylight; and, according to orders, Sir Colin remained waiting for the French until shortly before 9 a.m., when an aide-de-camp came up with orders from Lord Raglan for the troops to return immediately to their camps. The reason was, that General Bosquet found the weather so bad at 2 a.m., that, although he had reached the plain of Balaklava with his troops, he thought it impossible to go on, and decided on returning, sending one of his Staff to inform General Canrobert of the fact. The latter instantly despatched Major Foley (aide-de-camp to General Rose, English Commissioner) to Kadikoi to acquaint Sir Colin Campbell that the intended attack could not take place in consequence of the weather. Unfortunately Major Foley missed his road and wandered about in the dark until near 5 a.m., when he found himself at the English Headquarters. On Lord Raglan being informed of the state of things, he ordered one of his aides-de-camp to go with Major Foley to Kadikoi, and if he found Sir Colin had gone on to follow and give him orders to return. Sir Colin on receiving Lord Raglan's order retired without loss of time, and re-entered our lines at 9.45 a.m. Not a man fell out during the whole march, though several went into hospital with frostbites, but I understand none are of a severe nature. General Vinoy, on ascertaining that Sir Colin's force had gone unsupported by the French General Bosquet, turned out his brigade of infantry, and marched to meet him in case of his requiring assistance. However, he met the English returning just as they passed under Canrobert's Hill, so his friendly aid was not needed.

I was sent down upon duty to Balaklava this morning just after our troops returned, and I must say I never felt anything equal to the intensity of the cold. The day became worse instead of improving, and at 1 p.m. the wind was so high that the drifting snow at times literally blinded one. It was with the greatest difficulty that I could make my horse face the storm: wherever the snow fell upon me it froze hard, so that one was covered with cakes of ice; my beard and mustachios were frozen up into a sort of lump, and my eyes feel at the present moment as if they would be sore for days to come; altogether I never remember having suffered so much from the severity of climate.

We have received the London journals up to February 9th. I see that Lord Cardigan has been fêted at the Mansion-house, and made a speech on that occasion which has afforded considerable amusement and merriment amongst the officers of the Light Cavalry here, who naturally know better than anyone else the very *prominent* part which his Lordship took at the celebrated charge of Balaklava. I *never* read a more egotistical speech in my life, to say nothing of the wonderful way in which Lord Cardigan indulges his imagination.

I have not mentioned the railway for some little time. It is getting on, and at the present moment brings up all the heavy ordnance for the siege, and also a considerable amount of commissariat stores, from Balaklava to Kadikoi; thus saving over a mile of animal transport.

CHAPTER 11

Councils of war

ON the morning of February 24th, 1855, after the repulse of the French by the Russians, Lord Raglan strongly urged upon General Canrobert the importance of renewing the attack, and even offered the co-operation of some of the English troops. General Canrobert very properly said, that, as the work was in no way opposed to our trenches, it was a purely French affair; besides which, he felt that it would be a slur upon the French troops to call in the aid of the British merely to capture an unfinished work. Accordingly, I understand that it was the intention of General Canrobert that the redoubt should again be assaulted the following night, and for this purpose upwards of 10,000 men were sent into the French trenches of the Inkermann attack. But for some reason which I am unable to explain, this attack never took place.

On the morning of March 3rd, General Canrobert sent a written communication to Lord Raglan, to the effect that the Russian works opposite the French attack on Inkermann are of such strength that he thought them almost unassailable under existing circumstances, and he therefore proposed that the allied Generals should send to Omer Pasha, and request him to come with 20,000 of his Turks from Eupatoria; and, when thus reinforced, a general attack should be made by the English and French against the north side of the harbour, which, if successful, would complete the investment of Sevastopol. A proposal of this magnitude would require great deliberation; Lord Raglan therefore decided that a general Council of War should be held.

Two deserters came in from the Russian troops on the Tchernaya. One was an officer in the infantry, and the other a private of the same regiment, who had been degraded from the rank of officer, as he states, for some political offence. He speaks French very well. They escaped by persuading some Cossack soldier to lend them their horses, that they might go to the outposts to look at Balaklava, and when they had arrived at their farthest vidette, coolly galloped over to the English cavalry-picket on this side of the valley. When they got a short distance the Cossacks, perceiving their object, pursued them; but being fired upon by our Dragoons they retired, and allowed the deserters to come over to us without further ado. The officer states that he has been employed in one of the military offices in Sevastopol, drawing plans of the defences of the town, etc., and has also been engaged in a military survey of the surrounding country; and to confirm his words, he has brought with him some maps and drawings of the enemy's position along the Mackenzie Heights. Mr. Calvert anticipates gaining much useful information from him, especially as regards the by-roads in the hilly country between this and Batchi-Serai. If his information proves accurate, it is proposed that he shall be employed at Headquarters to revise and alter our maps of the surrounding country.

Lord Raglan, after visiting the Light and 2nd Division camps, rode on to our new three-gun battery, constructed, as I before mentioned, for the purpose of firing upon the Russian steamers at the head of the harbour. Finding this battery completed, his Lordship gave orders that the three guns should open upon them this morning at daylight; red-hot shot were to be prepared, in the hope of setting the vessels on fire. Wishing to see the effects of our fire, several officers of the Staff and Royal Artillery, myself included, left Headquarters soon after 4 a.m., and rode over to the 2nd Division camp, where we dismounted, and proceeded on foot to the advanced French sentries, overlooking the Inkermann bridge. We established ourselves in a comfortable little nook, from whence we should be able to see the whole of the harbour of Sevastopol, as well as our battery. It was still quite dark, and not a sound was to be heard, except the occasional booming of the guns from Sevastopol, on the extreme left of the allied position. Shortly after day broke we could perceive the two steamers lying perfectly motionless on the water, and with our glasses could distinctly make out two persons pacing the deck of each, one of whom was probably the officer of the watch. We waited with anxious expectation some little time, as it was useless firing from our battery until the objects were perfectly distinct.

At seven minutes after 6 a.m. (20 minutes after daylight) the first gun from our battery fired at a range of 1600 yards against the nearest steamer; the shot fell too short. The range was then changed to 1800 yards, and that shot fell beyond. The other steamer was so far off that after the first few minutes they gave up firing at her and turned all their attention to the nearest. Within three minutes after our first gun the whole crew on board the steamer were turned up on deck, and seven minutes after our opening fire replied to us from a heavy gun in the stern. By this time the batteries on the north side, whose guns could be brought to bear upon our three-gun battery, opened fire with shot and shell, some of them at enormous range. It was not until our 12th shot had been fired that any took effect; this carried away a portion of the counter of the steamer: the 17th shot hit her between wind and water, just in front of her paddle-wheel, port-side: the 18th hit one of the paddle-boxes, and the 30th and 31st shots also took effect on her. I believe that was all, though some of the officers of the Royal Artillery asserted that she was struck several times more. We continued firing until 7.15 a.m. (altogether throwing 60 shot, 20 of which were red-hot), by which time she got her steam up, and, although apparently, from the slow progress she made, her machinery was damaged, she managed to get round a point of the harbour out of sight of our three-gun battery. The steamer behaved very well, and in reply to us fired 14 immense shot from her two heavy guns. The Russian batteries on the north side kept up a brisk fire upon us, firing in all 163 shot and shell, but ceased directly we did; wonderful to say, although our battery was much knocked about by them, and two shells burst actually in the trench of the battery among our artillerymen, we had not a single man killed or wounded.

I thought our practice indifferent, but the officers of the artillery would not allow that such was the case, as from the fact of our battery being on such high ground, the fire from thence was necessarily plunging, and consequently the object was far more difficult to strike than if they had been able to make their shot ricochet on the water.

The most important news to reach us is that of the death of the Emperor Nicholas. Lord Raglan received a telegraphic despatch on the evening of March 6th (after the post went out), during the time the grand Council of War was sitting, and he not a little astonished the general officers present by reading out the message, which had been forwarded by steamer from Constantinople. It was as follows : —

'Berlin, March 2nd.—Lord John Russell to Lord Raglan.—The emperor of Russia died this day at 10 minutes past 12. No reason is given for this, but Lord Raglan can depend upon the information.'

I need hardly tell you what commotion this news excited: many declare that we shall immediately have peace; others say that when it is known in Sevastopol, there will be such a panic that we could take the town without any difficulty. Up to the present time the garrison of Sevastopol do not appear to be aware of it, although a day or two ago three Poles who deserted from the town, upon being asked the question, said that they had heard of the death of the Emperor eight days previous! that is two days before it took place!

During the morning of the 7th, one of Lord Raglan's aides-de-camp (Lord Burghersh) was sent with a flag of truce to take some letters and parcels for some of our prisoners. He went to the extreme left of the French trenches, opposite the Russian Quarantine Fort, and, after sounding and showing the white flag in the usual manner, the firing on both sides, at this part of the lines, ceased. He then went over the parapet and walked up towards the Russian rifle-pits, and was shortly met by two Russian officers. After delivering his letters, etc., he told them that we had received intelligence of the death of the Emperor of Russia: they neither of them seemed exactly surprised, but replied, "that it was not true—that it was a mistake—a false report." Yesterday a Polish officer in the Russian service deserted from the town over to the French, and upon his being asked, he said he had not heard anything of it. One would imagine that the first announcement of His Imperial Majesty's death would have been transmitted to the Grand Dukes Nicholas and Michael, who are now in the neighbourhood.

In the afternoon of the 7th, Lord Raglan went over to the Headquarters of the 1st French Corps d'Armée to visit General Pélissier, which command he had taken some days ago. Lord Raglan subsequently visited several other French Generals, who all appeared to appreciate the honour done to them. The following day the Field-Marshal, accompanied by the two British Admirals (Sir Edmund Lyons and Admiral Houston Stewart), and the Generals of Engineers and Artillery, and their Staffs, went through the whole of our left attack, and minutely inspected the works.

According to the statement made a short time back in the House of Lords by the War Minister, it seems that 56,000 men have been sent from England and our colonies to compose the army under Lord Raglan's command since the commencement of the war, consequently it has lost the services of 10,604 officers and men, who have been killed in action, died of disease and wounds, or have returned home invalided. It must also be remembered that, although many of our sick and wounded may not be fit for service again, still many more will, so that certainly the army is not in so bad a state as the good people of England fancy.

I saw in one of the newspapers the other day a statement that the English soldiers before Sevastopol moved about in wretched spirits, as if they were miserable and unhappy. This is certainly not the case: the men are always cheery, and, although when the weather is bad one may hear a few hearty curses and complaints, still this is quite the exception to the rule.

Now that our men have not such hard work, one cannot ride into any of the camps on a fine afternoon without seeing a number engaged at various games, such as football, leap-frog, running races, etc. In short, the men look anything but miserable and unhappy. It was only three days ago that I happened to be in one of the camps when Lord Raglan came up. He spoke to some of the men who were playing at football, and directly a crowd of soldiers gathered round him; when he moved on they hurrayed, upon which all the regiments in the vicinity turned out, and, seeing the Commander-in-Chief, cheered him most vociferously, numbers running along by the Staff, throwing their caps in the air, and shouting in a manner which proved the strength of their lungs. So much for Lord Raglan's alleged unpopularity in his army.

Much has been done on both sides in the last few days: by the Allies as regards extending and increasing their approached to Sevastopol; and by the enemy, in throwing up and improving their advanced works, in order to retard our progress. It was not until daylight on March 11th that it was discovered the enemy had commenced a very considerable earthwork on a mound or hillock in front of the Malakoff Batteries. This is known by the French as the Mamelon Vert; and that name has been pretty generally adopted by the Allies. Ever since the 11th the work has increased in size and importance, and is now a most formidable redoubt.

We hear from deserters that no less than 30 heavy guns are to be placed in it, which from its great size may easily be the case; but they add that it will be some days before they will be ready to open fire. Immediately the enemy's intention was discovered, two batteries were ordered to be constructed in the English right attack, and also a number of guns were placed in the French Inkermann attack, for the simple object of throwing the enemy's work back as much as possible. Besides this, it was decided that a communication should be established between the most advanced portion of the English right attack and the French Inkermann attack. This communication, or parallel, as it may be properly termed, was commenced by us on the night of the 11th, and by our allies on the night of the 12th; but in consequence of the difficulty of working in a rocky soil, it took several nights before the trench could be completed, as during the day it was impracticable to work at it, on account of the fire kept up by the enemy's sharpshooters in their rifle-pits. It is now finished, so as to afford tolerable cover between the two attacks; but it will be some time before the parapet will be of sufficient thickness and strength to render it, comparatively speaking, safe for the passage of troops to and fro during the daytime. Although the fire of the batteries and the French guns have caused the Russians considerable loss, they have been working steadily onwards until the present time.

I think the Russian engineers have displayed great cleverness and ability in the manner in which they have up to the present time conducted the defence of Sevastopol. For some time past the deserters who have come over to us have perpetually mentioned the name of Todtleben as the chief director of the works of the town. He appears to have been only a captain of engineers at the commencement of the siege. At the first sitting down of the allied armies before the place, when the Russian Generals were completely at a loss how best to defend the town, and their engineers were entirely at fault as to the manner in which to fortify the southern side with rapidity, Todtleben stepped forward and made certain proposals for placing it in a proper state of defence. His plan showed so much judgment and talent that Prince Menchikoff determined on following his advice, and gave him *carte blanche* to do whatever he liked. Todtleben undertook to fortify Sevastopol in such a manner that the garrison would be able to resist any sudden attack on the part of the Allies, and hold out the usual term of a siege, — say one month. This was all Prince Menchikoff expected, or even wished, as he hoped within a month from the time of the Allies breaking ground to be able to collect such a force as to ensure the total destruction of the invaders, by attacking them in the field.

Although the attack on Inkermann totally failed, one of its great objects was attained by the enemy; for it had the effect of preventing our assault on Sevastopol, which, though a great error on the part of the Allies, fully answered the purpose of the Russians.

We now see more clearly than ever how much to be regretted it is, that Lord Raglan's wish to assault the town after the battle of Inkermann was not carried out; but the smallness of the force under his command obliged him, sorely against his will, to give way to the objections raised by the French. The Russians failing in their attempt to raise the siege by the battle of Inkermann, turned all their energy to improving and strengthening the defences of Sevastopol, as they could not but perceive that the works of the Allies made but tardy progress, and that after the entire cessation of the first bombardment they had considerably the advantage of fire over us; besides the daily augmentation of the garrison giving them actual strength, it increased their moral courage and confidence to resist the attempts of the Allies to reduce their stronghold. Now that the severity of the winter is past, on the very first days of spring they seize upon the opportunity of extending their defences, and begin by the construction of the Ouvrages Blancs, only as a preliminary to one of far greater importance on the Mamelon Vert, as a horn-work for the better defence of the key of Sevastopol — the tower of Malakoff.

On March 12th, Omer Pasha arrived early at the English Headquarters in compliance with the wish of Lord Raglan and General Canrobert; and in the afternoon of the same day a Council of War was held, consisting of the three Commanders-in-Chief of the Allied Armies, and the two Admirals of the English and French fleets. It was then arranged, I understand, that a division of Egyptian troops (mustering about 12,000 men) now at Constantinople should immediately be brought up to Eupatoria; and on its arrival there, Omer Pasha should embark with 20,000 men, and land them at Kamiesch, for the purpose of co-operating with the Allies. This movement of the Turkish troops will take upwards of a fortnight.

On March 15th Lord Raglan, accompanied by the Staff, rode down to Balaklava in the morning, and was there the greater part of the day. On his entrance into the town, his Lordship was met by General Simpson, who had just landed, and who had mounted his horse to ride up to Headquarters to pay his respects and report his arrival to the Field-Marshal. He continued riding about with Lord Raglan all the day. The Commander-in-Chief then visited the Convalescent Hospital, which has lately been established on the heights, close to the old Genoese castle. The hospital is to consist of some 30 large huts, which have been sent out from England, especially constructed for that purpose, and, when completed, will admit of from 350 to 400 men. At the present time there is not accommodation for more than 200, about which number were there. The majority of the men looked well; and the medical officers stated that they thought it a particularly healthy locality.

The health of the army has most wonderfully improved of late; last week I understand, 500 men were discharged from the field-hospitals to return to their duty, and this week, they say, upwards of 700 have come out. A month ago even a single man going back to his regiment would have been thought quite a wonder.

There have lately been several races in the allied camps. The first 'Spring Meeting' was held on the 5th instant, in the valley of Karani, and was conducted by officers of the cavalry division and Royal Artillery; since that several others have taken place in the different camps. Yesterday there was a meeting not far from here, got up by the officers of the French cavalry, in which those of the Chasseurs d'Afrique played a conspicuous part, and today there are races in rear of the camp of the 4th Division; so one sees the sporting community here are not altogether without their favourite amusement.

General Simpson took up his residence, and commences his functions as Chief of the Staff immediately.

Sir John Burgoyne leaves the Crimea today (March 20th) and returns to England. He will be much missed by all those who have ever had anything to do with him on duty, or who have had the pleasure of his acquaintance. Lord Raglan in particular, I believe, regrets that he is obliged to return home; from the first he has been of the most valuable assistance to him, and by his sound judgment and counsel has aided him in almost every operation of the army. There are many in England who choose to underrate Sir John Burgoyne's military ability, and who call in question his engineering skill; but considering that he has the experience of upwards of fifty years of military life, I think it would be difficult, at any rate in the English army, to find one better qualified to occupy the important place Sir John has filled since the commencement of the campaign.*

The railroad is getting on with considerable rapidity; the other day Lord Raglan rode down to inspect the works. A stationary engine has been erected on the top of the high ground on which General Vinoy's brigade is camped; this engine is placed there to drag the train of waggons up the incline plane which commences at the village of Kadikoi. The length of the incline is about half a mile. The greater portion of the supplies for the army are now brought up to just this side of the stationary engine, which saves animal transport a distance of nearly three miles.

The Russian work on the Mamelon has not as yet opened fire, but has daily increased in magnitude, and, with the exception of the Malakoff, is, I believe, by far the strongest work round Sevastopol, and will, before it is captured, cost the Allies very heavy loss; for taken it must be before we can get into the town. The

---

* I may here remind the reader that it was from Sir John Burgoyne's able plan, that the celebrated flank march was so successfully carried out; that it was Sir John Burgoyne who, from the first moment of the Allies sitting down before the town, pointed out the tower of Malakoff as the key of Sevastopol; and that the general plan of attack against the town, finally adopted by the Allies, was only an enlargement of that first proposed by him.

advanced parallel connecting the English right attack with the French Inkermann attack has been greatly improved during the last few days, but nevertheless it is far from an agreeable trench to walk along during the day, as, from the rocky nature of the ground, the bottom of the trench is full of inequalities, so that frequently you are obliged to stoop or else expose your head and shoulders above the parapet; if you do, whiz, whiz, come the bullets, and you are lucky to escape untouched. Besides which, the Russians appear particularly jealous of this communication, and not unfrequently fire salvoes of six or eight gun-shells at some particular portion of the parapet, which generally succeed in making a breach or gap in it, rendering a passage along the trench past such places a service of considerable danger. For the last 10 days, the French have had nightly encounters with the enemy.

As I have recorded, the French have for some time past been endeavouring to capture the rifle-pits between their most advanced parallel and the Russian work on the Mamelon. Being unsuccessful in their attempts, they decided upon a novel expedient against works of so small a nature, viz. that of making a flying sap, by means of which they hoped to be able to take several of the enemy's rifle-pits in reverse. They had nearly effected this object; that is to say, the head of the sap was almost in line with the rifle-pits, and they had intended making a general attack upon them in the course of a day or two, when the sap should be completed. The Russians, naturally anxious to stop the progress of a work which would inevitably lead to the loss of their pits, determined on making a sortie in force, to endeavour, if possible, to destroy the French sap. Accordingly, on the evening of March 22nd, soon after dark, the enemy began collecting troops in the redoubt on the Mamelon, besides placing as many men as possible in their different rifle-pits. A large column of infantry was also posted in the Karabelnaia ravine between the Malakoff Tower and the English right attack, where they were completely under shelter from the fire of our guns. The French appear to have been to a certain extent prepared for an attack from the enemy, for they say that they saw the troops collecting soon after dark, and indeed in the earlier part of the evening the Russians commenced a very sharp fire on the French advanced trench. Our allies consequently had a considerable body of men in their trenches, I understand upwards of 8000.

It was shortly after 11 p.m. that the enemy advanced in great force, and assaulted the head of the French sap, at the same time falling upon their parallel in two different places, from both flanks of the Mamelon. Our allies, after a gallant resistance, were forced to relinquish their parallel. It was, however, but for a moment, as they were immediately led back, and drove the enemy again over the parapet. There several times did the Russians come on, and endeavour to take the French parallel; but they were always met with such steady determination and so heavy a fire from the Zouaves who occupied it, that their energy was unavailing; and, finally, after upwards of an hour's fighting, the Russians retired, having been totally unsuccessful in their attempt to destroy the French sap, and, with the exception of upsetting a few gabions at its head, did no further damage. On the other hand, our allies in their last repulse of the enemy levelled several of the rifle-pits which had caused them so much annoyance.

About the same time that the enemy commenced their attack on the French, a portion of the column stationed in the Karabelnaia ravine, between the English right attack and the Malakoff Batteries, advanced up, and meeting with, comparatively speaking, slight resistance from the few men in the parallel which connects the English and French attacks, crossed it, and then threw themselves on the extreme right of our trenches. They were here met by a detachment of the 97th Regiment, who guarded this part, under the command of Captain Vicars, whose gallantry and courage materially contributed to the repulse of the Russians. Most unfortunately for the service he was killed while in the act of charging the enemy at the head of his men, shouting out, "This way, 97th!" It is said that he knocked over two Russians before he received his death-wound.

The enemy's career was checked in the first instance by the gallant conduct of the detachment of the 97th. They were immediately reinforced by a portion of the 77th, under the direction of Major Gordon, R.E., who, with great judgment, conducted the repulse, and finally drove the Russians out of the parallel. He was unfortunately severely wounded by a musket-ball through the arm, and will for some time be unable to resume the important duties which he has, from the commencement of the siege, so ably performed.

After our troops had driven back the Russians on the right, a considerable body advanced up the Woronzoff-road ravine, and turned the *left* flank of our advanced trench of the right attack. It was here that one of the fatigue parties was at work; but on the enemy approaching, the officer of the Royal Engineers who superintended the construction of the battery, Colonel Tylden, caused the men of the 7th and 34th Regiments to be formed up by their officers, and promptly led them against the Russians, who, after a severe struggle, were driven off, but not without inflicting on us considerable loss.

The Russians also made a third attempt at about the same time on the extreme left of our left attack, and got into an unfinished battery, which was at the moment in course of construction. A working party of 60 men of the 57th Regiment immediately repulsed the enemy, but not until they had succeeded in carrying off Captain Montague, R.E., who was in the trenches directing the work. Our losses were severe; but considering the numbers in which the enemy attacked, and the amount of casualties they met with in their various sorties, they were not so heavy as might have been expected. The following will show the losses of the Allies:—

				Killed.	Wounded.	Missing.	Total.
English	Officers	..	..	3	3	2	
	Men	..	..	18	48	11	85
French	Officers	..	..	13	12	4	
	Men	..	..	169	361	83	642
						Casualties ..	727

On March 24th there was an armistice for some three hours to bury the dead on both sides; and according to the reports of those who were appointed to count the Russian bodies, it appears that over 400 were left on the ground; and from statements made since by deserters, their losses in the different sorties on the night of the 22nd amounted to from 1200 to 1500 men.

CHAPTER 12

Capture of ambuscades

IT is 12 months this day since I left England; a year of great events and a period which I shall remember above all others to the end of my life whatever else may happen.

We have lately learned from our spies that, since the fine weather, the enemy have largely increased the number of troops near Tchorgoun, and have also brought up a large force from the interior to the Mackenzie Farm Heights. The troops at the former place are stated as being from 10,000 to 12,000 in number, and those at the latter no less than 30,000, so that they could bring any morning against Balaklava or any other portion of our lines at least 40,000 men. It is an attack from these troops that has so much alarmed the French Generals.

I ought to observe that Lord Raglan is much against the Turks coming here: I understand he thinks that there may possibly be some difficulty in carrying on effective operations with three armies differently organized, each with an independent chief, and no one to command the whole. Omer Pasha considers himself senior both to Lord Raglan and General Canrobert, as he has been a Marshal for more than a year. Then, unfortunately, the French do not pay that respect to Omer Pasha that is due to his rank and command, and it requires all Lord Raglan's well-known tact to keep the Commanders-in-Chief of the French and Turkish armies on that footing of cordiality so necessary to successful co-operation. Lord Raglan has also another reason for not wishing for the Turkish troops; he thinks bringing more men to this already crowded ground, now that the hot weather is coming on, likely to promote sickness and disease.

After all these changes, one will not be surprised to hear that the French on April 4th, 1855, insisted on the day of our opening fire being put off, giving as one of their reasons that they did not wish to engage the enemy on Good Friday! This, we think, is all humbug, and a very lame excuse to gain time, so that Omer Pasha may arrive with his reinforcement before the bombardment commences. Some delay has taken place in the embarkation of the troops from Eupatoria, in consequence of the Turkish authorities not having sent up more than half the Egyptian division. Omer Pasha will therefore only bring with him 13,000 instead of 20,000 men.

Great preparations have been made for the reception of our wounded in the ensuing bombardment; there is extra accommodation for 300 patients in the regimental hospitals, and a large number of huts, capable of holding upwards of 500 men, have been prepared in rear of the 3rd and 4th Divisions; and in the Sanitarium, on the heights above Balaklava, there is room for about 200 patients. There are also five good sized steamers fitted up as hospital-ships, which will contain, with comparative ease, upwards of 600; so that at the present moment, arrangements have been made for the housing of at least 1600 wounded soldiers, and it is proposed that, should the number of our casualties require it, a regiment now in huts should be put under canvas, and consequently room would be obtained for nearly 500 more wounded. It is to be hoped that, although our losses will be far more severe than during the last bombardment, yet we shall not require so much accommodation as is already prepared. The fact of our trenches daily advancing, and also the extra fire poured upon us from the large work on the Mamelon, has much increased the number of our casualties; besides which, the enemy have joined their rifle-pits in front of our right attack, so as to make a sort of parallel, and in this they place a large number of sharpshooters who keep up an incessant fire of small arms on our men in the advanced trenches.

On April 4th and 5th, Lord Raglan went through the whole of the trenches of both attacks, and even visited some of our rifle-pits, much to the anxiety of the members of the Staff who were with him. He was accompanied everywhere by General Jones, and, to our horror, we saw them on one occasion coolly walk across the open from the 2nd to the 3rd parallel; fortunately they were not discovered by the enemy soon enough to send round shot at them, but the musket-balls came whistling about in dozens, and why neither were hit seemed wonderful. I should also tell that Lord Raglan will never allow (on ordinary occasions) any of his Staff, except one aide-de-camp, to follow him when he exposes himself in this manner.

Omer Pasha landed on April 8th, bringing with him a strong brigade of near 5000 men, having been preceded the night before by Ismael Pasha with a division of 9000 Turks. This reinforcement of near 14,000 men has been landed at Kamiesch, and is now encamped near that place; their destination is to be the high ground near the Col, as being midway between Balaklava and the heights before Inkermann, so that they will be available to be sent to either place in the event of an attack from the enemy on any portion of the rear of our position.

We kept up the same incessant bombardment all last night, and throughout April 12th. I understand that we have seven guns disabled by the fire from the town, and unfortunately the roads and trenches are in such a dreadful state that it is quite impossible to replace them. 300 men were employed for some hours last night trying to get some guns into the two unarmed, last-constructed batteries in the left attack, but they were unable to move them. The greater part of this day has been fine, and for some hours it was quite hot and sunny. This afternoon, General Bizot (Chef du Corps du Génie) was shot by a bullet through the head, fired from one of the enemy's rifle-pits, the ball entering in under his jaw and left ear, and lodging in his right cheek. He was at the time passing from the English right attack to the French Inkermann trenches, in company with General Niel. It was at first reported that General Bizot was killed; but although dangerously wounded, the doctors still hope that he may recover. The loss of his services at the present moment is a most unfortunate circumstance, and everyone feels for the poor old General, who is much respected for his undaunted courage, independently of his great military talents.

The French kept up a heavy fire of shells and rockets during the night from their Inkermann attack; we only fired at intervals, as it was found necessary to repair our trenches; besides which, we were desirous of getting some fresh guns in battery. As it was, we managed to place four 32-pounders in the six-gun battery in the advanced parallel left attack. The French had a serious affair last night on their extreme left: they have been contemplating for some time past an advance against the Russian ambuscades. These are rather more than rifle-pits, being a sort of small quarries, probably where stone or rock have been taken out for building purposes; and they are close up to the cemetery of the quarantine. The night before last the French had attempted to take this ground, but finding the enemy in force, did not actually attack. However, last night a large number of troops were told off for the purpose, and in the first instance advanced with great resolution, drove the enemy off, and immediately commenced destroying such of the ambuscades as would be useless to them, and altering the remainder to suit their own purposes. The Russians did not long leave them unmolested, for in a few minutes a column of infantry advanced, covered by a cloud of skirmishers, and opened so destructive a fire against our allies, that they speedily had to retire and abandon the work which they had commenced. The Russians, taking advantage of the confusion of the French retiring, poured into them an incessant fire, causing them very severe loss. The fusillade continued on both sides until the first dawn of day. The French admit that this affair cost them 250 casualties!

This morning the fire from the English batteries was reopened with renewed vigour, but during the first few hours we suffered some loss, especially amongst the sailors of the Naval Brigade, whose batteries in our right attack it appeared the enemy were particularly desirous of destroying, and for this purpose brought every gun they could to bear upon them. But Captain Peel, R.N., with his usual judgment, in spite of this heavy cannonade, commanded the sailors' batteries with the utmost coolness and courage, and succeeded in completely silencing the enemy's guns, which were firing at them from the Malakoff and Mamelon. Lord Raglan sent to request Sir E. Lyons for more men to fill up the casualties in the Naval Brigade, and also to enable us to open some fresh guns. In consequence Sir Edmund has promised to send up 200 men from H.M.S. *Rodney* tomorrow morning.

General Bizot is better; the ball was extracted this morning from his cheek.

On the night of April 13th, in consequence of the fatigue party losing their way in the great darkness, only one new gun was got into its place; this was a 32-pounder in the advanced six-gun battery left attack. This morning our most advanced battery right attack, armed with eight 8-inch guns, opened for the first time with wonderful effect and completely shut up the Malakoff Batteries it bore upon. The Russians, on the other hand, opened a heavy fire again from the Mamelon both on ourselves and the French. Our fire continued with vigour throughout the day, except the unlucky six-gun battery left attack, which was overpowered by the concentrated fire from the Russian Redan, Barrack, and Garden Batteries: several of our artillerymen in it were killed and wounded and one gun disabled, otherwise our casualties were few during the day.

This morning a division of Turks (9000 strong) marched from near Kamiesch to the heights above the Col and the village of Kamara, under the immediate command of Omer Pasha; five other battalions of Turks (over 4000 men) were sent by him to Balaklava to be attached to the force under Sir Colin Campbell's command. The end of the wire of the submarine electric telegraph was landed about midday near the monastery of St. George: it has come in a direct line across the Black Sea from Cape Kalagria, which is about 30 miles north of Varna. The telegraph is now laid down from England to the Crimea, with the exception of from Giurgevo to Varna; but that will be finished in less than a month. As it is, Lord Raglan can communicate with the government in London in about 30 hours. The first detachment of the 10th Hussars arrived today from Egypt, mustering 100 men and horses, exclusive of officers.

On April 14th, the English right attack and the French Inkermann attack continued to fire incessantly during the night. In our left attack we were pretty quiet, so that we might repair damages and place guns, etc. In this we were very successful, and we got eight 32-pounders into the unarmed battery in the advanced trench to the right of our left attack, and replaced the disabled guns in the six-gun battery, besides getting five 13-inch mortars in the first parallel left attack, and replacing a disabled 68-pounder right attack. The French made a successful advance last night on the left, and captured several of the enemy's ambuscades near the cemetery of the quarantine. This was not done without great loss. It had been determined by the French Generals that this ground should be captured cost what it might, as their daily losses from the Russian sharpshooters in these pits could be borne no longer. Accordingly, two columns of attack were organised: one — from their extreme left, consisting of about 800 men, was to advance, capture and hold six ambuscades near the quarantine cemetery; the other — consisting of about 500 men, was to move out of one of their advanced batteries near the centre of their trenches, and attack and hold four large ambuscades above the others. It would appear that the enemy were prepared to receive this attack of the French, as they were in great force. The two French columns advanced simultaneously; the left, after a considerable struggle, was successful, and got possession of, and held, the six ambuscades. The right column, in the first instance, was not so successful, as on their attacking the enemy's pits they were received by a most murderous and well-directed fire, which killed and wounded numbers of our allies, who were soon obliged to retire to their trenches; but immediately afterwards the supports were brought up, and a second attack was made with perfect success, though not without some hard fighting. The Russians were obliged to abandon their pits, which our allies continued to occupy during the night, and contrived by this morning to turn and connect together, so as to make a sort of new advanced trench. They had six officers killed and 11 wounded, and 207 men killed and wounded. It is impossible to estimate the Russian loss, but, from the number of dead which they left behind, it must have been considerable.

During the night of April 14th we repaired our trenches and parapets, and orders were previously sent down to reduce the fire of our artillery from 120 rounds per gun to 80 in the 24 hours. Colonel Parlby (10th Hussars) came up to report his arrival to Lord Raglan today; as senior officer he takes command of the division of cavalry in the absence of General Scarlett. General Bizot died this afternoon, although up to shortly before his death the doctors thought he would recover.

Shortly after dusk, Lord Raglan, accompanied by the Staff, rode up to the Maison d'Eau to meet General Canrobert and his Staff, to see three mines blown up between the most advanced French sap and the Russian Bastion du Mât. The object of this was to open the ground between the works of our allies and the enemy, and immediately after the explosion, men were to rush into it, and form an advanced trench; in this manner it was hoped to crown the salient angle of the Bastion du Mât, with the ulterior object of establishing a battery on it which would fire on the inner defences of the town. The explosion did not take place until 8.30 p.m., when only two out of the three mines blew up. Directly after, the Russians opened a most furious cannonade from all their batteries opposed to the French, and also some on us. They evidently thought it was an assault on the town, for five minutes after the explosion their parapets were lined with men, who kept firing peals of musketry indiscriminately towards the French; besides which, they flung showers of hand-grenades and threw numbers of small Cohorn shells at the advanced portion of the trenches. Indeed, every species of missile seemed to have been used by the Russians on this occasion. It was a magnificent scene, but our excitement was cut short by the rain, which fell in such quantity that we were all wet to the skin in a few minutes. The torrent of fire continued for about an hour, when the enemy probably found out that no assault was intended, and consequently relapsed into sullen silence.

We have learnt the effect of the explosions in front of the Bastion du Mât. Immediately after the two mines had been fired, about 300 volunteers rushed in and commenced clearing away and opening out a communication between them. This work was one of great difficulty, for, independently of the nature of the ground, which was very hard and rocky, and the intense darkness, the Russians continued pouring upon them showers of missiles of all sorts: but, in spite of their severe losses, our allies, in the most gallant manner, continued working, and succeeded to a great extent in effecting their purpose; but as no communication could be made with the trenches in so short a space of time, it was thought advisable to abandon the greater portion of the new work shortly before daylight this morning. A heavy fire was kept up throughout the night on the town from the batteries of the Allies. About 2 p.m., a shell from the enemy burst in front of the door of the magazine in the centre of our 8-gun advanced battery, right attack, and blew it up with a tremendous explosion. It for a time completely ruined the battery, the earth thrown up literally burying some of the guns and filling up seven of the embrasures. However, one gun was unhurt, and the officer of the Royal Artillery in command of the battery, Captain Dixon, immediately ordered it to be fired, and continued to reply from this single gun to the tremendous cannonade which the enemy, seeing our disaster, poured upon us. Nothing could exceed the gallantry of this officer, whose coolness and courage excited the admiration of all.* By the explosion we lost one man killed, who was in the magazine at the time (the poor creature was blown to pieces, nothing but one of his hands being found), and nine other men of the artillery wounded, but fortunately only two seriously. Several men of the infantry (guard of the trenches) were more or less injured by the falling of earth, stones, etc., blown up into the air by the explosion. Lord Raglan, who was riding up at the front at the time, and saw our misfortune, after giving directions for restoring the battery to a serviceable state, went and visited the poor men who had been hurt. This is the first occurrence of the sort that has happened to the English during the siege.

* For his distinguished conduct on this occasion Captain Dixon has received the Victoria Cross.

The 8-gun advanced battery in our right attack, and in which the magazine was blown up yesterday, was repaired during last night, and this morning opened as if nothing had happened: this is very creditable to our engineers. Orders were sent down to the batteries to reduce our fire to from 30 to 40 rounds per gun daily. This is in consequence of an arrangement which has been come to between the allied Generals that the assault of the town shall not take place for eight or 10 days, in order to give time for the French to take the Mamelon and the Ouvrages Blancs, which General Canrobert has pledged himself to do in the course of a few days.

On the night of April 18th, the Russians made two sorties on the French from the Bastion du Mât, probably with the object of preventing our allies from completing the trench and work commenced by them on the night of the 15th instant, after the explosions. They were in both instances speedily repulsed, but the loss on both sides was considerable, the enemy leaving many dead bodies behind him, and our allies having 61 casualties. The latter were particularly unfortunate yesterday, as I understand from Colonel Vico that during the last 24 hours they have had no less than 12 officers and 132 men killed and wounded!

There was a reconnaissance made early this morning under the direction of Omer Pasha, for the purpose of ascertaining the enemy's force on the Tchernaya river, as we have been led to believe from spies and others, that the greater portion of the troops had been withdrawn for the purpose of reinforcing the army on the north side of Sevastopol. Omer Pasha's force consisted of 12 battalions of Turkish infantry, a regiment of French light cavalry (Chasseurs d'Afrique), and a battery of artillery: two squadrons of the English heavy cavalry, two squadrons of the 10th Hussars and a troop of horse artillery. They proceeded shortly after daylight from the plain immediately in front of Balaklava, and, passing by the village of Kamara, advanced towards that of Tchorgoun, the Cossack videttes retiring before our skirmishers, without attempting to come in collision. At one moment a few rockets were fired by the French artillery at a picket of Russian cavalry, which speedily dispersed them, though apparently without doing them any injury. The enemy drew up what force they had on the heights above the village: it consisted of but two battalions of infantry and four guns. The object of the reconnaissance being accomplished, Omer Pasha ordered the troops to withdraw. I should have mentioned that Lord Raglan and General Canrobert with their respective Staffs were present during the latter part of the reconnaissance, but only as spectators, not wishing to interfere in any way with Omer Pasha's arrangements. He afterwards expressed to them the pride he had felt in commanding English and French troops in the field, though but on so trifling an occasion, and tendered his thanks for the compliment thus paid him. Lord Raglan ordered that the remaining three of the enemy's rifle-pits immediately in front of our right attack are to be recaptured. For this purpose, a few extra companies are sent into the trenches of that attack.

Early in the night the three Russian rifle-pits were taken at the point of the bayonet, without a shot being fired, by a portion of the 77th Regiment, supported by 200 men of the 34th Regiment. This was done at about 9.30 p.m. The Russian sharpshooters, being taken completely by surprise, never attempted any resistance, but ran away as fast as they could. About 2 a.m. the Russians came down in force to retake the pits which we occupied; our men, with great courage, but very foolishly, rushed out to meet the enemy, and immediately found themselves under an awful fire, and in presence of an overpowering force. The Russians, daunted by the determined attitude of the English troops, did not come on, but after firing a few volleys retired, leaving us in possession of the pits. But our loss was severe.

A propos of the rifle-pits, I must mention a circumstance that occurred at their capture the other night. A drummer-boy of the 77th Regiment went with his comrades in the first rush against the enemy's pits, when he saw a Russian trumpet-boy trying to clamber over the parapet in order to get away. He was immediately collared by our drummer who, being unarmed, began to pummel him in truly British fashion. The Russian boy, not understanding this mode of treatment, tried to grapple with him, but in this he signally failed, as the English boy threw him on the ground, made him a prisoner, and took his trumpet from him. He afterwards gave it to Sir G. Brown, who liberally rewarded him for it, and praised him much for his courage and daring. Lord Raglan, hearing of the circumstance, also made the boy a present.

I was sent again early this morning to take in a flag of truce, to give over some letters from Russian officers to their friends, and others to English officers, prisoners of war. I went as before to the advanced French trench on the extreme left, near the Quarantine Fort. The Russian officer who met me was a very civil, gentlemanlike man, and began by apologizing for keeping me waiting, which I had been doing for some 10 minutes. In giving him the letters for our officers who are prisoners, I asked after them; he said that none remained in Sevastopol, except Captain Montague (Royal Engineers), who is living with an aide-de-camp of the General commanding the town; he added that he was very well; and that last night he had had '*un verre de grog*' with him, and they had passed a very pleasant evening together. Before we parted we shook hands, and he expressed a wish that we should meet some day on more familiar terms.

We have at last really commenced the bombardment: on April 19th at 5.15 a.m. the guns in all the batteries, French and English, opened fire. They consist of no less than 464 pieces of ordnance: of these, 303 are in the old French attack, 109 in the English attacks, and 52 in the French Inkermann attack. It rained all through the night previous to our opening fire, and literally poured the whole of yesterday and part of last night: now it is clearing up. I think yesterday was the worst day we have had since the dreadful storm of November last. It had its advantages too; in the first place, we completely took the Russians by surprise, for they did not generally open their batteries until half an hour after us, and during that time the Allies must have thrown upwards of 2000 shot and shell into the town. In the second place, the Tchernaya river is so much swollen from the quantity of rain which has fallen, that it has overflowed its banks some distance on each side; and the portion of the valley of Balaklava on which the celebrated Light Cavalry charge took place is also partly under water, and the ground so deep as to be quite impracticable for the movement of troops, or at any rate for cavalry and artillery. Consequently we may consider our rear at present to be almost unassailable by the enemy.

At the commencement of the day our artillerymen were allowed to fire at will, though towards the middle of the day, when the enemy's fire had greatly diminished, orders were given not to exceed the rate of 120 rounds per gun in the 24 hours. We have between 500 and 600 rounds per gun in all the English batteries, and from 600 to 800 rounds per gun in our artillery parks, besides as much more at

Balaklava ready to be brought up to the front should it be required. Our batteries have continued blazing away ever since, and have done great execution, many of the Russian batteries being in the most complete ruin, and, with the exception of one or two, they none of them fire above one shot to five of ours. This weather is dreadfully trying to those in the trenches; and, as an instance, I may mention that in one of the batteries which I visited in our right attack, the artillerymen serving the guns were standing almost up to their knees in water; unfortunately there was no help for it, as from the nature of the ground at this point it was impossible to drain the battery.

In spite of the weather the men all appear in the highest spirits, and are most anxious to be allowed to attack the town. I fear at present there will be little chance of that, as I understand already that General Canrobert does not think sufficient impression has been made to warrant an assault. It appears that he has received instructions from the Emperor Napoleon not to assault unless perfectly certain of the result not only being in our favour, but also not to attempt it if the sacrifice of life should be great, as His Majesty is anxious for operations in the field against the enemy to be commenced immediately. Lord Raglan takes quite a different view; he is for assaulting the town without delay, as he thinks that the longer it is postponed the more difficult it will be to accomplish; for as the season advances reinforcements will be daily arriving to the Russians, and he doubts the feasibility of carrying on with energy operations in the field as well as continuing a siege of such gigantic dimensions. One drawback at the present moment to a general attack on Sevastopol would be, that in consequence of the badness of the weather the allied fleets could not in safety go near enough to the Russian sea batteries. Not that it is intended for the ships again to engage the forts, but merely as a diversion in our favour, as it would oblige the Russians to keep manned the sea defences, and they would consequently have fewer artillerymen to serve the guns in the works against the Allies. Nevertheless, we may consider the commencement of this bombardment to be satisfactory.

CHAPTER 13

General Canrobert resigns

AT the Council of War held in the afternoon of May 1st, 1855, Lord Raglan managed, after much talking, to persuade General Canrobert of the great advantages to be derived by immediately taking Kertch, so that at length he gave way. It was decided that the French force under General d'Autemarre should consist of 11 battalions of infantry and two batteries of artillery; in all about 8500 men. We were to send the 42nd, 71st, and 93rd Regiments, four companies of the Rifle Brigade, two companies of sappers and miners, 700 royal marines, one battery of artillery, and one troop (50 horses) of light cavalry; in all about 3000 men. Three weeks provisions for the troops were embarked, and a sufficient number of baggage-animals for the transport of stores, ammunition, and tents. The entire force was under the order of Sir George Brown. I should have mentioned that General Canrobert had been the first to propose that Sir George Brown should take command of the expedition, a very high compliment to him; and further, he had selected General d'Autemarre, as he knew he would most cordially co-operate in any undertaking with the English General. I need scarcely remark that Lord Raglan was equally desirous that the chief command of the expedition should be intrusted to a man of whom he had so high an opinion as Sir George Brown.

On the afternoon of the 3rd, everything being in readiness, the expedition sailed from Kamiesch Bay and Balaklava Harbour, and, taking a northerly direction, steered past Sevastopol. This was done in order to mislead the enemy, and, if the feint succeeded with them as well as it did in the allied camps, the Russians must have been put entirely on the wrong scent. It is needless to say that every endeavour had been made to keep the destination of the expedition secret; but like all secrets known to several people, it had got pretty generally believed that it was to go to Kertch. In consequence of this northerly movement of the fleet on its departure, it was bandied about in the camps that Odessa was to be attacked, and on the way the fleet was to pick up a large force of Turks at Eupatoria. The French actually published a memorandum to that effect! So far all went well, and we were looking forward to the laurels to be gained by the force under Sir George, and hoped at last that we were really going to do something of importance. Our wishes were not destined to be fulfilled.

Shortly after 10 p.m. the same evening (not six hours after the sailing of the expedition), General Canrobert came to Lord Raglan and told him, that he must recall the French troops, as he had received a peremptory order from the Emperor to concentrate all his forces with the object of attacking the enemy in the field, and therefore he did not feel justified in allowing any troops to depart, especially the fleet which was to transport the reinforcements from Constantinople to the Crimea. Lord Raglan used every argument he could think of to induce General Canrobert not to recall the French troops, and tried to convince him that, as the Emperor was in total ignorance, when he wrote those orders, that the expedition to Kertch was about to sail, the despatch could not refer to the present circumstances. Lord Raglan ended in convincing General Canrobert, sorely against his will, and he went away, apparently with the full intention of abiding by Lord Raglan's advice. However, two hours more had not elapsed before General Trochu, chief of General Canrobert's personal Staff, arrived at the English Headquarters, and requested an interview with Lord Raglan. He then stated to his Lordship that he had been sent by the French Commander-in-Chief to say that, on again reading over the Emperor's instructions, he felt himself obliged to recall the French fleet and troops. Such being the case, Lord Raglan had no other course to pursue but again to give in to the wishes of General Canrobert, and sat up the whole night writing despatches to Sir Edmund Lyons and Sir George Brown, informing them of the reasons for the recall of the expedition ; but at the same time, I understand, he gave the latter full power to go on without the French, if he thought there was a good chance of success, and that he (Lord Raglan) would take the full responsibility. This despatch was entrusted to Lieutenant Maxse, R.N. (Naval aide-de-camp to Lord Raglan), who started early yesterday morning (4th) for the rendezvous where it was known the expedition was to muster previous to entering the Straits of Kertch. I can scarcely describe the indignation we all feel towards the French, which, though not quite just, I am sure is very natural ; and one will not be surprised that Lord Raglan feels how utterly impracticable it is to carry on a joint command with a man for whom it is impossible he can entertain that feeling of confidence so necessary to successful co-operation. At the same time I must add, that Lord Raglan continues on the same friendly terms with the French Commander-in-Chief as before.

And now, after having abused our allies pretty roundly, I must relate an affair they had the other night, that did them great credit, for the gallant manner in which it was done, and the courage displayed on the occasion. Ever since the fire of the Allies has been slackened, indeed, I may almost say suspended (as we never fire except when any number of the enemy make their appearance), the Russians have been most assiduous in the construction of new rifle-pits on a larger scale than any made in the earlier part of the siege. These our allies call ambuscades, and several of them have been made during the last week in front of the Bastion du Mât and the Bastion Centrale, and have caused our allies very serious loss every day, since they have been occupied by the enemy's sharpshooters. These the French have several times attacked, but, although frequently successful in turning the enemy out, they have never been able to hold them a sufficient time, either to destroy or turn them in their own favour. The loss, however, caused by the nightly encounters with the enemy for the possession of these pits, decided General Canrobert at length to give orders for a grand attack in force ; and for this purpose a very large number of men were sent into the trenches on the left, on the evening of the 1st instant. I should also say, that what made these pits more formidable than any others that had yet been constructed, was the fact that they were connected together by a trench, and consequently were capable of giving one another support; besides, it was difficult to say where the enemy would stop, if once allowed to obtain a firm footing on ground in advance of their original works.

The French troops, which consisted of upwards of 10,000 men, were disposed into three columns, two of which were to attack the flanks, and the third the centre of the line of the enemy's ambuscades. Soon after 10 p.m. the troops advanced, and, as had been before arranged, carried the work at the point of the bayonet. This was not done without considerable fighting; the Russians made every effort to hold their ground, but our allies finally overcame them and drove them back towards the town, having captured a number of prisoners, and nine small mortars.

Directly the enemy became aware that their troops had been driven out of the work, they opened a tremendous cannonade on the French, who now occupied it. This cannonade caused the French dreadful loss, but in spite of it they continued to hold the ground, turned the ambuscades in their own favour, and commenced a trench to connect them with their works. The Russians attempted no less than three times to retake the ground they had lost, but our allies, with the greatest endurance and bravery, maintained and held it until morning.

I understand that this affair cost the French 10 officers and 270 men killed and wounded. They continued to work throughout the following morning, and had got the whole line of ambuscade turned, and a good communication made with their trenches. Early in the afternoon the Russians made a sortie from the town, to endeavour, if possible, to recapture their work, and, taking the French in the first instance completely by surprise, got once more into the ambuscades, and for a moment possessed them; but the French supports coming up, they were obliged to retire, leaving behind them many killed and wounded. The losses of our allies were very severe, for, in the first rush of the enemy, numbers were bayoneted and shot before they could offer any resistance. It is stated that they had 23 officers killed and wounded and upwards of 600 men hors de combat; making a total of upwards of 900 casualties for the possession of these ambuscades. The advantage gained by our allies is considerable; a great blow has been struck against the enemy, and the French have advanced a portion of their siege-works 100 yards nearer the town.

On May 3rd, the enemy sent in a flag of truce proposing a suspension of arms for a sufficient period to bury the dead. This of course was agreed to by General Canrobert, and accordingly on the same day flags of truce were put up, and the last rites paid to the brave men who had fallen on both sides. The Russian loss must have been very great, as the French state they gave over 150 bodies found in and about the contested work.

The expedition from Kertch returned safe on May 5th, the officers and men of both army and navy very much disgusted at being recalled. General Canrobert has now succeeded in making himself unpopular in both armies and both fleets. We were all in great hopes that the speedy arrival of the Emperor Napoleon would put an end to the indecision shown by General Canrobert, but we are to be disappointed here too, as we know now, without doubt, that His Majesty has given up the idea of visiting the Crimea.

Omer Pasha has offered to place 14,000 of his best troops at Lord Raglan's disposal, for the purpose of forming part of a fresh expedition against Kertch, a proof of how fully Omer Pasha coincides in all Lord Raglan's plans. On the same day (May 8th) General La Marmora, Commander-in-Chief of the Sardinian Contingent, arrived in a steam-frigate at Balaklava, and the following morning he came up to the English Headquarters, to announce his arrival and pay his respects to Lord Raglan. He has brought with him 5000 infantry, and 9000 more are now at Constantinople ready to come up to the Crimea, forming the greater portion of the force, all of which may be expected here in the course of 10 days more. Those that have arrived are not landed, by Lord Raglan's particular request, as the weather is so bad that it would be most trying to fresh troops to camp out.

General La Marmora is a tall, fine-looking man, with the air and bearing of one of great determination, but at the same time with most courteous manners. Lord Raglan is most favourably impressed with him, and feels confident that he will most ably assist him in anything he may propose.

Our cavalry force is looking up, for, independent of about 500 horses that have arrived as drafts for the different regiments in the Crimea, the whole of the 10th Hussars are now here and nearly all the 12th Lancers. We have now nearly 1800 effective horses in the cavalry division. The present state of the English army is — *effective*, 26,000 infantry, 4800 artillery, 1800 cavalry. Then we expect during this month drafts for the infantry amounting to about 6500 men, for the artillery 1500, and for the cavalry 500, so that, with the Sardinian Contingent of 15,000 men, I hope that before very long Lord Raglan will have under his immediate command between 50,000 and 60,000 effective troops. The health of the army daily improves; numbers of men every week come out of hospital and return to their duty. I am sorry to say that the cholera is reported to have broken out in Constaninople with increased virulence; we have had a few bad cases of it in the English army here the last week or ten days, but not to any great extent. The French have had it more or less the whole winter, and have lost many men from this dreadful scourge. Directly all the Sardinian troops have landed, we intend to extend our position in order to gain fresh ground to encamp the troops. It is proposed to take up as our line of defence the Tchernaya river from the ruins of Inkermann to the village of Tchorgoun, and then from there the line will turn back to Balaklava, occupying all the high ground between the villages of Tchorgoun and Kamara. Another advantage of this movement will be that we shall gain the fresh water of the river; and although there is a very tolerable supply from the numerous springs on the plateau before Sevastopol, still, from the enormous quantity of dead animal matter which has been buried on that ground, it is possible that the water there, to a certain extent, may have become tainted. Besides this, we shall be able to clear Balaklava and its vicinity of almost all the troops now stationed there, for, if it was allowed to remain in its present crowded state, fever and disease would probably ensue.

I have not mentioned that Miss Nightingale, to whom the army is so much indebted, came up here a short time ago to see the hospitals at Balaklava and in the camps: it is heartening to hear that she was surprised to find them in so good a state after having read all the abuse of them in the English journals. She has visited also

Right: Florence Nightingale, who gave it "as her opinion that in every respect the English camp hospitals were better provided than those of our allies".

Florence Nightingale
May 14/56

her own signature

several of the French ambulances, and gives it as her opinion that in every respect the English camp hospitals were better provided than those of our allies. She is accompanied by Mr. and Mrs. Bracebridge and M. Soyer: the former, kind, benevolent people, who have attended Miss Nightingale throughout her mission of mercy; and the latter is the celebrated *chef*, who has already been of great use to the army by making admirable improvements and suggestions in the camp cookery.

As regards the siege there is but little to tell. For the last three nights the enemy have been endeavouring to overthrow our advanced works, and the week before they attempted the same thing. On the night of the 5th instant, they attacked our advanced parallel, right attack, and, coming on with great impetuosity, they succeeded in the first instance in penetrating into our trenches, but were shortly dislodged by some of the 30th and 49th Regiments, who defended this portion of them. About the same time an officer of the 4th Regiment, Captain Arnold, was taken prisoner, after being severely wounded when posting his advanced sentries in front of the left attack. I regret to say, besides losing the services of the above-mentioned officer, several men were killed and wounded in the repulse of the enemy. Their loss was apparently far more considerable than ours, as they left a number of their dead just outside our parapets. On the night of the 9th instant, they made two sorties on the right attack, but were each time met with great determination by the English troops and driven back with severe loss. On the ensuing night they made another sortie for the same purpose, under cover of a tremendous cannonade from all their batteries, but, in spite of this, our sentries having given warning of their approach, the guard of the trenches was moved down and opened so destructive a fire upon the enemy's approaching column that they at once retired, leaving several dead behind. Last night they attempted the same thing, only on our left attack; they ascended the Woronzoff-road ravine in two columns, and came on with so much resolution and courage that the head of one column got into a portion of our advanced parallel, but were immediately driven out by the men of the 68th, who formed the guard of the trenches at this point. This was not done without some loss: an officer of the 68th, Captain Edwards, was killed, as well as five men of the same corps, besides a considerable number wounded.

I will now give as clearly and accurately as I can, the *proposed* movements of the allied armies during the ensuing summer. But first of all I must record that the English and French Governments (chiefly, I believe, at the instigation of the Emperor Napoleon) have suggested this plan, which they have ordered to be carried into effect, if the Commanders-in-Chief of the allied armies think it practicable. They propose virtually to discontinue the siege, merely holding our trenches with a sufficient force to prevent the possibility of the enemy taking them, and to commence operations in the field, which, if successful, would prevent all supplies and reinforcements from reaching Sevastopol, and consequently the Russians would not be able to hold the town, except for a limited period; or at any rate, finding their communication cut off from the interior, they would be more likely to be overcome whenever the Allies might think proper to assault the town.

The plan suggested is as follows:—that the allied forces should be divided into three distinct armies: the *first*, the army before Sevastopol to consist of 40,000 French and 20,000 Turks, with a small English force to garrison Balaklava (say 3000 men): the *second*, a force of 30,000 English, 15,000 Sardinians, and 20,000

Turks, to be an army to operate against the enemy in the field; the *third*, composed of the main body of the French army, or about 60,000 men, to be landed somewhere on the south coast, probably Aluschta.*

The *first*, under General Pélissier, was to guard the trenches and our present position before Sevastopol.

The movements of the two armies in the field are to be determined according to circumstances. The *second*, under the command of Lord Raglan, was to place itself in the valley of Baidar, and thus be in communication with the *first* before Sevastopol. The *third*, under the command of General Canrobert, was to land, if circumstances would permit, at Aluschta, and after carrying the mountain pass of Ayan was to advance on Simferopol. On the completion of this movement, which it is taken for granted would be successful, Lord Raglan's army was to assault the Mackenzie Heights; having gained which, it was either to march on Batchi-Serai with the ulterior object of making a junction with General Canrobert's army; or else it was to turn along the heights above Inkermann, and, taking in reverse the defences of the north side, complete the investment of Sevastopol. A large force of Turks was still to remain at Eupatoria to be available as might be required, and it was to be left to Omer Pasha to place himself wherever he thought his presence was most desirable. I understand the Emperor's plan was much to this effect, although there is little difference in the numbers and disposition of the three proposed armies.

One perceives from this plan that it is always supposed that the Allies are successful in every operation, and no allowance is made for the contingency of failure and disaster. All this was fully discussed at the Council of War sitting on May 12th. I have good reason to believe that Lord Raglan altogether objects to the propositions above-mentioned from first to last, as he conceives, as indeed has been his opinion for some time past, that the town ought to be assaulted without delay; but to this General Canrobert and the principal French Generals will not agree. One will observe in the plan in question that it is proposed that the besieging army should consist of only 40,000 French and 20,000 Turks. It is much to be doubted whether this force would be able to resist any determined and sudden attack of the enemy on the rear of our position, and at the same time properly defend the allied trenches. Lord Raglan, I understand, positively refuses to give up the English siege-attacks to the Turks, as he has learned from past experience how little dependence can be placed upon our Mahometan allies; and he does not choose to risk even the possibility of English guns being again captured by the enemy, when under the protection of the Turks, and held up hereafter to the world at large as trophies from the English. The French, with only 40,000 men, would not be able to under-take so extensive a line of works.

Since the Council of War, on the 12th instant, a very long conference was held between Lord Raglan, General Canrobert, and Omer Pasha, at which these plans, and especially the Emperor's proposals, were particularly discussed, and General Canrobert used every endeavour to persuade Lord Raglan to adopt, in conjunction

* The numbers above include only infantry and artillery. The cavalry force will consist, it is hoped, of about 14,000 horses; of these 6000 French, 5000 Turks, and 3000 English and Sardinian.

Overleaf: Troops on reconnaisance watch a field battery opening up on the heights while the Sardinian cavalry chase the Russians in the valley below in front of the Mackenzie Range.

with him, a plan of operations similar to that proposed, as I have narrated above. But nothing would induce Lord Raglan to give way on this point, as he felt so strongly the importance of measures being taken for the immediate capture of Sevastopol, and he considered that perhaps, after all, the greatest objection to the proposal of forming the allied forces into three great armies was, that there would be no one chief to direct the whole, and in such complicated movements as those under consideration it would be almost inviting failure for the armies to be acting under independent commanders. General Canrobert, in order to overcome this objection, with laudable self-denial which will always be remembered to his credit, tendered to Lord Raglan the command-in-chief of the whole, as far as he (General Canrobert) was himself concerned; and further, begged Omer Pasha to do the same. Lord Raglan, I believe, hesitated to accept so great a responsibility without more consideration, and gave General Canrobert to understand that, should he accept what had been so nobly offered to him, he should feel it his duty to require one of two things: either that, in the first place, in the event of undertaking operations against the enemy in the field, the French should occupy what are now the English trenches; or, in the second place, should it be determined to continue the siege on its present footing, that he should desire the immediate assault and capture of the Mamelon Vert (and consequently the Ouvrages Blancs) only as a preliminary to a grand attack on Sevastopol itself after the expiration of a few days. To this General Canrobert would not give his sanction, as he stated that the daily losses now incurred by the French army engaged in the siege operations were so great that it was impossible to expect such sacrifices as would necessarily be entailed on the French troops.

Thus, unfortunately, the allied Commanders-in-Chief could come to no satisfactory agreement, and that earnest and happy wish to co-operate which had animated them earlier has now received a check, the results of which are difficult to anticipate. I am given to understand that the only movement Lord Raglan advocates against the enemy in the field (besides the capture of Kertch) at the present time, would be one from Eupatoria against Batchi-Serai, which would thus cut off the communication between Sevastopol and the interior; a corresponding movement to be made at the same time by a portion of the army before Sevastopol against the Mackenzie Heights, and so completely isolate the Russian force on the north side and in the town. Objections were raised by the French Generals to this, on account of the scarcity of water from Eupatoria to the interior, and the difficulty of supplying a large army with that greatest necessary of life; besides which, they maintain that the Mackenzie Heights are unassailable. As regards their first objection, I see no reason why a large force should not be landed near the Alma river, and, following the neighbourhood of its course, attack the town of Batchi-Serai.

As to any opposition that might be made on the part of the Russians, it would be the thing most to be desired, as the force landed would be of such strength as to ensure success against any numbers the enemy might bring against it, and, after one general action in favour of the Allies, the chances are its march on Batchi-Serai would be further unopposed. As to the impossibility of attacking the Mackenzie Heights, this is a matter of opinion. It is a position of great natural strength, but I believe it might be attacked with every probability of success, if undertaken with judgment and determination. Such are the plans and proposals that have been discussed by the allied Generals during the last few days, but, as one will observe, nothing definite has been settled.

A great change has taken place this morning (May 19th), no less than that General Canrobert has resigned, and General Pélissier reigns in his stead! I understand from an officer of the État-Major that three days ago General Canrobert sent a telegraphic message to the Minister of War, begging him to lay his resignation before the Emperor on the score of ill-health, and recommending General Pélissier as his successor. It appears that the Emperor's reply accepting the resignation of General Canrobert and the appointment of General Pélissier to the command-in-chief of the French army, was received last night in a telegraphic message.

Early this morning, General Pélissier came to the English Headquarters to announce to Lord Raglan in person the change that had taken place. After breakfasting together, they remained in conference for some hours. General Pélissier informed Lord Raglan that he perfectly agreed in his views as to the proper manner of carrying on the war, which had been communicated to him by General Canrobert. He thought no time should be lost in taking immediate steps for the capture of Kertch, and also announced his intention of attacking the Ouvrages Blancs, to be directly followed, if not at the same time, by an attack on the Mamelon Vert; as he considers that, above all, the prosecution of the siege for the speedy reduction of Sevastopol is of the first importance.

Probably several days will elapse before arrangements can be made to carry all this into effect, as General Pélissier requires a little time before he will be settled in his new command. He also informed Lord Raglan that General Canrobert, at his own request, was going to take command of the 1st Division of the French army, which he had held up to the time that he succeeded Marshal St. Arnaud as General-in-Chief. General Pélissier said that by desire of the Emperor he had offered him the command of the 1st Corps, But General Canrobert had refused this, and had begged to be allowed to return to his old division. It would be useless to deny that Lord Raglan is very glad of this change, as General Pélissier's known firmness and determination give him great hopes, that all that he says he will perform, will be successfully carried out. Early this afternoon, General Canrobert came to take leave of Lord Raglan on quitting his command. He was attended only by two aides-de-camp and an escort of four Hussars, a great contrast to the brilliant Staff and numerous cortège who had before this always accompanied him. The Field-Marshal received him, if possible, with even more than his usual courtesy, as he could not but feel admiration for one who had shown so much self-denial and forgetfulness of his own interests, when they clashed with his duty to his country; and he was particularly anxious not in any way to wound his feelings by any apparent difference in the respect he had always shown him as General-in-Chief of the French army. General Canrobert told Lord Raglan that he was extremely glad to be succeeded by General Pélissier, as he knew him to have the greatest respect for his (Lord Raglan's) judgment, and also that he agreed, even to detail, with him in his proposals for the progress of the campaign. He then thanked his Lordship for the kindness he had invariably received at his hands, and assured him that he

Overleaf: Sardinian review by General Canrobert. The Bersaglieri are in the left foreground and General Pélissier's arrival can be seen in the centre.

should always remember with the greatest pleasure and satisfaction his connexion with him, in spite of their differences of opinion. In taking his leave, the French General was a good deal overcome, and Lord Raglan could not but feel much touched at parting with one, with whom he has been for many months so intimately associated, and he much admires the liberal spirit which has prompted General Canrobert to tender his resignation, and the manner in which it has been done.

On May 17th Lord Raglan went through all our trenches, accompanied by General La Marmora and a numerous Staff. As usual, he visited the most advanced parallels and took the General, who was not a little astonished at his Lordship's coolness, into two of our rifle-pits. I understand Lord Raglan likes him very much, as he is a most willing, obliging man, and perfectly ready to fall in with the Field-Marshal's views. We all like what we have seen of the Sardinians. The officers are gentlemanlike men, very clean and smart in their dress, and most friendly in their manner. The soldiers are for the most part very nice-looking troops; their uniform remarkably well made, and in drill, I think, equal to the British soldiers. If their soldier-like demeanour is any criterion of what they will be in presence of the enemy, we may congratulate ourselves on having received a most valuable reinforcement. All the troops of the Sardinian Contingent that have landed are encamped near the village of Karani, beyond the English cavalry division. Their ambulance waggons particularly attracted my attention; they are light easy carriages, I should think not half the weight of those of the English, and certainly far more comfortable, the seats being all padded, etc. They have also ambulance carriages for the especial use of the officers, which are fitted up with great attention to comfort. Fancy the outcry the British public would make if there were special ambulances for the officers in our army! and yet, I believe, ours is the only exception in the armies of Europe. We have for some time past been receiving large reinforcements to the Royal Artillery, and before another month we shall be able to bring 96 guns into the field—the largest number that have ever been employed at one time with an English army on service.

There was a grand Council of War on May 20th at which all the allied Generals attended (Omer Pasha having come from Eupatoria expressly for it). It was for the purpose of arranging the expedition to Kertch. It was settled that the French should send 7500 men, and three batteries of artillery, the Turks 5000 men, and one battery of artillery, and the English 3800 men, one battery of artillery, and a troop of cavalry. General Pélissier himself proposed that Sir George Brown should take the command-in-chief of the troops, General d'Autemarre to command the French, and Redschid Pasha the Turks. The force is to consist of 16,300 men, with 30 pieces of artillery. This has been thought necessary, as it is not improbable that the Russians may by this time have heard through the spies that we had attempted an expedition the other day, and therefore they may have sent more troops into the neighbourhood of Kertch.

Yesterday, last night, and today, the troops have been embarking, and it is intended that the expedition shall sail this evening, and they hope to be off Kertch ready to land on the morning of the 24th. It is possible that Theodosia may be attacked and a landing effected there first, as a feint to blind the enemy, but this is only to be done if Sir George Brown considers it advisable on arriving off there, and it will depend upon a variety of circumstances. Meantime, whilst this expedition against Kertch is going on, I hope we shall not be idle here. It is proposed again shortly to open our fire, and, after a day or two's bombarding, the French will attack the Ouvrages Blancs and the Mamelon Vert, and the English what are called the Quarries. This last place I have never before mentioned, as until quite lately it has been unimportant. It is nothing more nor less than a considerable excavation in the ground, which has apparently been made to obtain gravel. This, the Russians usually occupy in the daytime with about 250 men, but at night probably there may be twice or three times that number. They have constructed a loopholed parapet along its edge, behind which their sharpshooters keep up a perpetual fire against our trenches, and it is not possible for us to advance farther towards the Redan until this is captured, as it would take any new forward parallel in reverse.

It is situated about midway between the English right attack and the Redan, the Woronzoff-road and Karabelnaia ravines being on its flanks. It is hoped that, if we are successful in our attack, we shall be able to push forward flying saps towards the Malakoff Redoubt from the Mamelon, and towards the Redan from the English right attack, and by this means be near enough to make a final rush on their two great works of defence and carry them. The town will then be at our feet, and the fall of Sevastopol inevitable. It is not anticipated that there will be any difficulty in holding the town while the Russians still possess the northern side of the harbour, though, no doubt, they would at first make the place too hot for large bodies of troops to move about during the day, or perhaps to garrison it with any considerable force. But if once in our possession, I believe we could easily hold it with 5000 men against any attempt the enemy might make from the northern side. It would only be necessary to have strong guards down by the water's edge, to prevent any sudden night attack, which they might make more with the object of annoying us than with any idea of recapturing the place. I ought to apologise for being thus premature in my remarks, especially as, in the opinion of many, Sevastopol will never fall into the hands of the Allies. You may well say to me the old saw — "Do not count on your chickens before they are hatched."

Sir Edmund Lyons, being anxious, partly with a view of misleading the enemy, to make a reconnaissance along the coast as far as Yalta, ordered a steamer to be in readiness for that purpose on the same day. I obtained leave to go with it, chiefly as I wished to see over again some of the haunts I had visited previously to the war. Sir Edmund Lyons was unable to go, in consequence of the Council of War at Headquarters, sitting for the purpose of making the arrangements for the expedition which is to sail tonight.

We started at about 9 a.m. from Kazatch Bay, in the screw despatch-boat *Telegraph*, and half an hour later steamed past the harbour of Balaklava. The day was magnificent, the water smooth as glass, so that we could coast along quite close in-shore, at times within a stone's throw. You never saw anything more beautiful than the scenery from Cape Aiya to Yalta. It seemed so strange to be gazing on the scenes I had visited scarcely three and a half years ago, but under such different circumstances. I recognised all the spots I had visited in the autumn of 1851. First, the pass of Phoros, where the great south road crosses the mountain ridge, and, entering the valley of Baidar, follows its course until it reaches the village of Kamara, and so to Sevastopol. Next we passed the château of Prince Demidoff, Kastropolo by name; an ugly enough house, but beautifully situated close down to the shore. A short distance further on, we came in sight of Prince Woronzoff's magnificent residence of Alupka, the beauty of which grew upon us as we approached. So much has been heard and said of this place, that it naturally excited the curiosity of all on board. The steamer was run as close to the land as was considered safe, that we might all get as good a view as possible of the beautiful structure and the lovely garden by which it is surrounded. Everything appeared exactly as when I had last seen it: the gardens as beautifully kept; the greatest profusion of flowers, whose fragrance we were near enough to enjoy; nothing seemed to indicate the absence of its owner, except that the window blinds were all drawn down. You can hardly fancy a more lovely situation; a magnificent mountain range (Mount Ai Petros) rising immediately behind the palace, which is itself imbedded in a bank of wood of the richest foliage; while in front lies the garden in a series of terraces, balustraded with Carrara marble, and studded with the prettiest little oriental fountains and statues, many of the latter the workmanship of Canova. Even when staying there, I do not think I was so much struck with its beauty as on this second visit. We remained gazing at the scene of peaceful grandeur before us, and were contrasting it with the din and tumult that daily surrounded us before Sevastopol, when we observed six Russian soldiers creep from behind some bushes, and almost immediately raise their muskets and fire a volley at us. I don't believe they were loaded, as no one heard the whistling of bullets or saw anything strike the water after the discharge. A foolish piece of bravado on the part of the Russians, as, although we were not in a ship of war, still there were two carronades on deck, with plenty of ammunition ready in case of emergency; so that, if we had chosen to take this as an insult, we could have been revenged without any trouble. However, we were all too accustomed to be fired at to care about a few paltry shot, which caused a little laughter, and only made us look with greater eagerness through our glasses, to watch the movements of the worthies who thought to frighten us.

The expedition to Kertch sailed on the evening of May 22nd from Kazatch Bay, and arrived off Theodosia on the morning of the 23rd, where they remained the whole day, so as to mislead the Russians into the belief that a landing was to be made there. Lord Raglan received intelligence of their safe arrival as far as this place, and also that they intended to leave that night and sail for the Straits of Kertch, and it is hoped that yesterday the landing was effected; we cannot receive intelligence until tomorrow evening.

General Pélissier, on succeeding to the command-in-chief of the French army, determined at once to attack the enemy's new works, and ordered General De Salles (the officer who had succeeded him in the command of the 1st Corps d'Armée) to make the necessary arrangements for so doing. Accordingly, it was settled that on the night of the 22nd, the attack should be made. It consisted of two columns of infantry, the left on the ambuscades on the top of the Quarantine Bay, the right on the upper end of the Cemetery. The left column was composed of four battalions of infantry, and the right, of three battalions of infantry and two battalions of the

Right: Lord Raglan visited in a dream by the Duke of Wellington on whose Staff he had served. During that campaign his arm was amputated, and his cool remark to the surgeon became legendary. "Here, bring that arm back, there is a ring my wife gave me on that finger".

180

Voltigeurs de la Garde: the latter were to be held in reserve. The command of the attack devolved on General Paté, who soon after 9 p.m. gave the signal to advance.

The troops rushed on with the greatest bravery and determination, and in a very short time carried the ambuscades, driving the enemy out of them. They did not remain in undisputed possession many minutes; the Russians soon appeared in great force, and evidently determined not to give up the ambuscades without a further struggle. They advanced towards the French troops with great solidity and steadiness, and then charged with the bayonet; and now commenced another of the bloody struggles which this war has witnessed. Portions of the ambuscades were taken and retaken perpetually, and it was difficult to say, when both sides fought so magnificently, which was the bravest. Once, indeed, the French were for a time overpowered, and had to retreat to their trenches, but only to reform and once more charge the enemy.

The French had been unable during a sanguinary struggle to turn the works in their own favour, but nevertheless managed so far to destroy them that they could not be occupied during the ensuing day by the enemy. The conduct of the French troops on this occasion cannot be too highly extolled: the Voltigeurs of the Garde displayed the greatest bravery, and earned for themselves a name worthy to be classed with the Old Garde of Napoleon I. The French losses were, however, frightful; it is said the Voltigeurs alone had 27 officers and upwards of 600 men killed and wounded. General Péllissier determined, that as they had not been able to complete the work which had been ordered (viz. turning the Russian ambuscades in their own favour), that the following night another attack should be made by a

Picture drawn by a fellow artist of Sardinian troops arriving at their Headquarters.

Sardinian Head Quarters Karlton

Engraving of General La Marmora, Commander-in-Chief of the Sardinian Contingent.

fresh division of infantry, under the command of General Levaillant; and, *at their own request*, by the remainder of the Voltigeurs of the Garde, who had so distinguished themselves the night before.

The second attack was made with the same impetuosity as the first; our brave allies were successful everywhere; the Russians, although again in considerable force, were driven off, followed by a continuous discharge of artillery from the French batteries. The Corps du Génie set to work, and before morning had succeeded in turning the newly captured ambuscades; and, in spite of the perpetual fire the Russians poured upon them, they obtained good cover, besides connecting the ambuscades with their advanced trenches.

Yesterday morning (25th) General Osten Sacken requested, through a flag of truce, a suspension of arms to bury the dead. This was granted, and for near five hours friend and foe mingled together, exchanging bodies of their fallen comrades.

The 24th inst. being Her Majesty's birthday, Lord Raglan ordered a review of the cavalry division, two troops of horse artillery, and the two new heavy batteries Lord Raglan and the whole of the Staff attended in full uniform; General Pélissier

Left: The Duc de Vallombrosa, redolent of Paris and civilisation, briefly visits the Crimea.
Right: Russian deserter, a half-wild specimen from the interior, who wanted to be sent back.

and Omer Pasha, followed by their brilliant Staffs, were also present. General La Marmora was unable to attend: After the review, the allied Generals partook of a luncheon at the English Headquarters, at which General Pélissier made a speech and proposed the health of *"la Reine Victoria"*. In the evening Lord Raglan gave a dinner to his Generals of division and heads of departments. The English troops by his Lordship's order all received an extra ration of rum to drink the Queen's health.

I mentioned that it was in contemplation, after the arrival of the Sardinian troops, to extend our position to the Tchernaya river, etc. Accordingly, yesterday morning at 2 a.m. the divisions under Generals Canrobert and Brunet (about 14,000 men), the whole of the French cavalry (about 2000 horses), and five batteries of artillery, moved down from the heights in rear of the plateau to the plain of Balaklava. A portion of the cavalry and a few chasseurs crossed the

Tchernaya by the Tractir Bridge, and drove off the enemy's pickets in the immediate neighbourhood. The French then encamped themselves along this side of the Tchernaya River. They were supported by two strong divisions of Turks, under command of Omer Pasha (about 16,000 men), who took up a position on the scene of the celebrated English Light Cavalry charge immediately in rear of the French.

The greater portion of the Sardinian troops, about 8000 men, under General La Marmora, marched from their camp at Karani across the plain of Balaklava, and camped themselves on the most advantageous ground from the village of Kamara to that of Tchorgoun. They were assisted in this by Sir Colin Campbell, who caused the Royal Marines on the eastern heights of Balaklava to move on to the next ridge of hills, and thus overlooked the village of Kamara and a portion of the valley of Baidar; while two regiments of cavalry (10th Hussars and 12th Lancers), under command of Colonel Parlby, went in advance of the Sardinian troops, reconnoitered the country, and patrolled the Woronzoff road for a considerable distance in the direction of Baidar.

The Russian troops at Tchorgoun and in the neighbourhood made no resistance, but quietly withdrew before our skirmishers. The French cavalry took a Russian picket near Tractir Bridge by surprise, and made some 15 men prisoners. We have gained a large quantity of ground, besides the immense advantage of having the fresh water of the Tchernaya, and yet this important movement was made without the least opposition on the part of the enemy.

Soon after General Canrobert had taken up his new position by the Tchernaya river, Lord Raglan paid him a visit there. They rode all about the ground, and conversed together for two or three hours. General Canrobert was much pleased at his Lordship's attention; and when taking leave of him, said, with a voice full of emotion, "Ah! milord, you are very good to me, for you visit me in adversity, and treat me in the same manner as when I was in prosperity; that is not the case with most men."

CHAPTER 14

Assaults on enemy positions

AS regards the progress of the siege of Sevastopol, we are supposed to be waiting for darker nights, as at present the moon shines with such brightness, that it is quite impossible for the men to work in the advanced trenches. As an instance of how light it is in this climate at night, I may mention that the last mail from England arrived very late in the evening at Headquarters. On June 5th, 1855, I got my letters between 10 and 11 p.m., and read them by moonlight! This, in England, one would hardly think credible.

The weather continues magnificently, but I regret to say that the cholera, if anything, has rather increased than diminished. Every day we hear of men cut off in the prime of life by this dreadful disease, and almost without a moment's warning. The regiments that have lately arrived are those that suffer most. The 10th Hussars and 12th Lancers have both lost a number of men, as also have several infantry regiments, who have only been a short time here. Our Sardinian allies have, I am sorry to say, suffered considerably. Everything has been done that the medical men can think of to try and check the malady, but nothing seems to be of any use. They are camped on fresh, healthy ground, with plenty of excellent water, plenty of firewood, good wholesome rations, including fresh meat and bread, and with but little duty to perform; in short, the treatment of cholera is an enigma, of which our medical men have not yet discovered the solution.

Admiral Boxer (the Port-Admiral of Balaklava) died of it last night. Poor man! he felt very much the abuse that has been heaped upon him by the English newspapers, and that made him very restless, and, no doubt, to a certain extent, accelerated his death.

The General After-Order of yesterday, describing the Kertch expedition: is worth quoting here.*

* *General After-Order, June 4th, 1855.* — The Field-Marshal announces to the army the further gallant exploits of the Allies (with the Kertch expedition), which this time have chiefly been accomplished by the ships of the French and English navies. Berdiansk has been destroyed, with four war-steamers. Arabat, a fortress mounting 30 guns, after resisting an hour and a half, had its magazine blown up by the fire of our ships. Genit-Chesk refused to capitulate, and was set fire to by shells. Ninety ships in its harbour were destroyed, with corn and stores.

In these operations, the loss to the enemy during four days has amounted to four war-steamers, 246 merchant-vessels, and corn and magazines. Upwards of 100 guns have been taken.

It is estimated that four months' rations for 100,000 men of the Russian army have been destroyed.

On the Circassian coast, the enemy evacuated Soujak-Kaleh on May 28th, after destroying all the principal buildings and 60 guns and six mortars.

The fort on the road between Soujak-Kaleh and Anapa is also evacuated.

At the commencement of the month it was agreed between the Commanders-in-Chief of the English and French armies that immediate steps should be taken for the capture of the Ouvrages Blancs and Mamelon Vert by the French, and the Quarries by the English. They each, therefore, gave directions to their respective Generals of Engineers to prepare notes of their proposals to carry this object into effect; these notes were exchanged, and comments made upon them by the said Generals. General Niel was much opposed to an attack being made against the works above mentioned for the present, as he considered it too hazardous; and proposed that first of all a movement should be executed against the enemy on the Mackenzie Heights for the purpose of making a diversion: that would draw troops from the north side, and consequently limit the reinforcements that would be available to be sent into the town. On the other hand, General Jones thought that the time had arrived for the assault of the works; he so far agreed with General Niel that it would be judicious to make a movement against the Mackenzie Heights as a diversion, but wished it to be simultaneous with the attack on the Mamelon, etc. It was to discuss these propositions that a Council of War was held at the French Headquarters, consisting of the principal officers of Engineers and Artillery of the English and French armies.

General Pélissier was also present, and made a speech to the officers in which he stated that he was aware that those whom he then addressed would be very diligent in devising various schemes for the reduction of Sevastopol, but he begged to inform them that on the 7th instant the Mamelon Vert, the Ouvrages Blancs, and the Quarries must be taken, adding, "Lord Raglan and I have decided it;"—and he therefore wished to impress upon them, that they were there only for the purpose of arranging and settling the best means of carrying this decision into execution. I understand that here General Bosquet took upon himself to dissent altogether from the views of the Commander-in-Chief, but was immediately stopped by General Pélissier, who begged to remind him of what he had just said—that the attack was *decided* upon. General Bosquet made no further remark.* General Niel then got up, having in his hand a long written statement, which he proceeded to read as follows: "In operations of this kind it is necessary to commence at the beginning. Now to commence with the left." General Pélissier here interrupted him, and pointing to the map said, "We will suppose the left side not to exist; we will speak as if there was no left. I know you are all gentlemen of genius and science, and could give me good advice if I asked it. But I do not want it. The entire responsibility belongs to Lord Raglan and to me. I have announced to you our determination: the Mamelon Vert, the Ouvrages Blancs, and the Quarries are to be taken on June 7th. Now, if any of you have suggestions to make as to the means of accomplishing this end, pray state them." One may imagine after this no one was bold enough

---

* It may be as well to state, for the information of the reader, that three of the highest Generals on the French Staff were always against an assault on the town, and invariably advocated operations in the field. The Generals alluded to were Bosquet, commanding the *2nd Corps d'Armée*; Niel, *Chef du Corps du Génie*; and Martimprey, *Chef d'Etat Major*.

Overleaf: An evening attack on the Mamelon Vert. General Pélissier is in the right hand foreground. The reserve under General Brunet is retaking the work and passing on to the Malakoff—a part branching off to support the right.

to oppose himself to General Pélissier's wishes, and the French Generals for the first time were astonished to find that they had a man of spirit and determination as their chief, whose will was law.

General Pélissier is a great contrast to his predecessor: he is a man who cannot bear being dictated to, and one who speedily makes up his mind and loses no time in carrying out his object with decision. At the same time, he has the greatest respect for Lord Raglan's judgment, and since he has assumed his present high command he has consulted his Lordship continually, even in trifling matters connected solely with the French army.

I never mentioned before that, immediately after the French took up the line of the Tchernaya, General Canrobert, who had been given the command of the troops at this point, begged to be relieved and to be replaced by General Morris, who, after all, was of senior rank as General. General Pélissier acceded to this request, and accordingly General Morris now commands the two French divisions of infantry, and the whole of their cavalry and artillery, posted by the Tchernaya.

The only movement worth recording that we have made since my last letter was a reconnaissance by the French along the valley of Baidar. It consisted of the whole of the French cavalry and General Canrobert's division of infantry. They met with no opposition, none of the enemy's troops appearing but a few Cossacks. The reconnaissance returned before nightfall.

The assault on the Mamelon Vert and other works proved most successful. I will now give a general outline of the operations of the last three days, together with some of the details of the attack. The Allies opened their fire at 3 p.m. on the 6th instant, against the beleaguered town. The English batteries consisted of 155 guns and mortars,* all of heavy calibre, probably the most powerful ordnance ever used before at a siege. All the batteries of the French Inkermann attack likewise opened (upwards of 100 guns and mortars), but their old attack between the English left and the sea fired but little, as they are very short of ammunition; besides which, many of the guns are much worn. So, in fact, the cannonade upon the town generally was not so heavy as when we opened in April last, but from the English attacks far more severe, as our guns are advanced nearer the enemy's works, and many are of heavier metal, besides there being a greater number of them. We apparently took the Russians by surprise, for they did not answer from their batteries for some minutes. This cannonade and bombardment has been kept up ever since, and will not be discontinued till a general assault is made upon the town, and, it is hoped, with success. The effect of our fire was such that, by midday of June 7th, the Russian batteries wore almost silenced, that is to say, we were throwing 20, and in some instances 30, shot to one from them. But this was not accomplished without a heavy loss to us, and on the morning of that day a powder-magazine was blown up by a Russian shell in one of our most advanced batteries, which for some time completely ruined it.

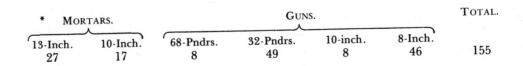

* MORTARS.		GUNS.				TOTAL.
13-Inch.	10-Inch.	68-Pndrs.	32-Pndrs.	10-inch.	8-Inch.	
27	17	8	49	8	46	155

190

The details of the attack on the Mamelon Vert, the Ouvrages Blancs, and the Quarries had been arranged at the Council of War a few days before. The arrangements for the English assault were as follows:—Two parties of 200 men each, placed in the advanced trench, right attack, were to turn the flanks of the Quarries after capturing which, they were to advance towards the Redan as far as practicable, and then, lying down, keep up a heavy fire of musketry upon the embrasures of the enemy's batteries in their front. This they were to do, to cover the work of 800 men, who were, immediately on the Quarries being taken, to enter and commence operations to turn that work in our favour, and make a trench to connect it with our most advanced parallel. Besides this, there were two bodies of 500 men each ready to support in case of need, and also two regiments were to be placed in reserve in the Woronzoff-road ravine, between our two attacks. There was to be the usual guard of the trenches and the artillerymen serving the guns, amounting to about 3000 men; so that in all we probably should have about 6000 men present for the operation, the whole to be under the command of the general officer of the trenches, right attack, on duty for the day.

The French attacks on the Mamelon and the Ouvrages Blancs were to be on a far greater scale. One should first understand that the French Inkermann attack is divided obliquely by the Careening Bay ravine, so that, in point of fact, one may say that there are two attacks, although they are not generally known as such. Four entire divisions of the 2nd Corps d'Armée were told off for the purpose. On the right of the ravine, General Mayran's division was to assault the Ouvrages Blancs, supported by General Dulac. On the left of the ravine, General Camou's division was to attack the Mamelon, supported by General Brunet's. There were to be two battalions of the Imperial Guard in reserve, and also a division of Turks under the command of Osman Pasha, but these last were to be at a considerable distance in rear—in fact, on the ground before Inkermann. Besides all this, there were to be the usual guard of the trenches (about 3000 men) and the artillerymen (about 1000), so that in all our allies were to have present at least 34,000 men.

It was about 5.30 p.m. when Lord Raglan, accompanied by the whole of the Staff, left Headquarters and rode up to Cathcart's Hill, in front of the 4th Division. On his arrival in the camps, his Lordship was greeted with the most tremendous cheers; all the men, turning out of their huts and tents, crowded round the Staff, and made the whole plateau resound with their loud huzzas. Nothing could exceed the spirits of the troops. This excitement had indeed commenced the day before, for on Lord Raglan passing through the camps on the 6th instant, to see the opening of our fire, he was vociferously cheered by the men. General Pélissier also came in for his share of popularity with the British soldiers, for, on returning from Fort Victoria on that evening, he was received with loud plaudits by the Light Division, which was taken up in succession by each of the English divisional camps through which he rode. I understand from his Staff that he was much touched with this proof of popularity, and, with tears in his eyes, he turned to an aide-de-camp and said, "With troops in such high spirits as these we cannot but succeed." What made General Pélissier feel this the more was the fact that he is fully aware he is not liked in the French army. Not that they do not think him a good General, but he is looked upon as rather disregarding the lives of his troops, and one who never changes his mind, he is more feared than liked.

But to return to where we left Lord Raglan on Cathcart's Hill, on the afternoon of June 7th. Lord Raglan and the Staff dismounted, and, leaving their horses there, proceeded on foot to a knoll just in rear of the right of Chapman's battery, as from that point the best general view could be obtained of the French and English trenches, and the enemy's works to be captured; and which, although an exposed place, was at the time, comparatively speaking, safe, as the fire from the town was so much silenced. A flag-staff had been erected half an hour previously at this spot, that the Commander-in-Chief might signalise to the general officer in the advanced trenches for the assault of the Quarries. This was Colonel Shirley, 88th Regiment, who, as senior officer, acted as a Brigadier-General in the Light Division. The attack was to be begun by the French, as some guns in the Mamelon completely enfiladed the Quarries, and consequently it would not be tenable until the Mamelon was taken. We waited in anxious expectation for near half an hour, when the signal of three rockets, fired from the Victoria Redoubt, in which General Pélissier was stationed, was given. It was then 6.45 p.m. In two or three minutes we saw the Zouaves rushing up the side of the Mamelon towards the work, in a cloud of skirmishers. They formed the advance of the left column of attack, and consequently were more under our immediate observation. Beyond them was a regiment of the Line, and again, on the further side, the Mamelon was assaulted by the Tirailleurs Indigènes. These three regiments formed one brigade of General Camou's division. Nothing could be more magnificent than the advance of the troops. The garrison of the Mamelon, who had kept themselves as much under cover as possible, for protection from the awful fire which had, since early dawn, been poured upon them from the batteries of the Allies, now that they were relieved from the heavy cannonade and bombardment, sallied forth to defend their work from the assault of the French. Their efforts were of no avail, nothing could stop the impetuosity of the Zouaves; regardless alike of danger and death, these gallant men rushed on, and, with a rapidity quite astonishing, descended the ditch and clambered up the high parapet of the redoubt, and, though the first who entered the work met with a soldier's death, they were speedily avenged by their comrades who followed them. A footing once obtained in the angle of the redoubt, the Mamelon was lost to the Russians, for the French troops now poured in everywhere along the face of the work, and in the course of a quarter of an hour the whole of the assaulting column, consisting of General Camou's division (from 4000 to 5000 men), were in and about the Mamelon Redoubt.

During this attack a desperate struggle had been going on at the Ouvrages Blancs. As soon as the signal of three rockets for the advance of the troops was seen, the two brigades of General Mayran's division advanced, each in column, against the two works known as the Ouvrages Blancs, but, before reaching the objects of their attack, suffered very severely from the heavy fire poured upon them from the batteries of the town. The first was assaulted in the most determined manner, and carried by the French troops with but little loss, the garrison being driven out and retiring into the work in their rear, much the strongest of the two, and which as yet

Left above: A ravine of Sevastopol after the explosion on the Mamelon Vert.
Left below: From this signal post it was intended that, as soon as the Malakoff was secure, a signal was to be given by rockets for the attack on the Bastion Centrale and Bastion Mât. Owing to the high wind, the rockets were not seen for a long time.

had not been reached by the column of French destined to assault it. They had not however long to wait: the French pushed on with great steadiness in spite of the heavy fire of musketry, shot, and shell hurled upon them at every step of their advance. The garrison fought manfully, but nothing could withstand the ardour of our allies: led by their officers right up to the work, a large portion engaged the enemy with a tremendous musketry fire, while others jumped into the ditch, and scrambled up the outward face of the parapet. A desperate hand-to-hand combat ensued, in which the French soon gained the mastery; once in the work, its fate was decided. Those of its garrison who were not killed or wounded were driven out, and retreated to a small work which had been constructed early in May in rear of those mentioned, which was situated at the point of land which runs out between Careening Bay and the harbour. This redoubt, though of but little importance to the enemy as an offensive work (except as a *place d'armes* for collecting troops for the support of the Ouvrages Blancs), was nevertheless a most dangerous one to attack, as it was completely commanded by a heavy battery in the town, and also by several others on the north side of the harbour. But in spite of these difficulties, the French, flushed by their success, advanced from the work they had last captured, and succeeded in penetrating into it, the garrison retiring down the steep slope between it and Careening Bay. The enemy in the town, seeing that their own men had abandoned the work, immediately poured a heavy fire upon it, which, causing the French considerable loss, they very wisely evacuated it, after spiking the few guns it contained.

Seeing the success which had attended the assaults on the Ouvrages Blancs, General Dulac, commanding the supporting division, sent forward one of his brigades as a reinforcement; and two battalions going down the ravine towards Careening Bay came upon the Russian garrison of the captured works retiring towards the defences of the town, round the head of the bay. The latter, being taken by surprise on the sudden appearance of the two French battalions, fled precipitately, and our allies, rushing down upon them, succeeded in making 12 officers and 280 men prisoners.

I have thus related the most important events of the French attack; we must now return to the exploits of our own men. Immediately on Lord Raglan perceiving that the Mamelon was penetrated by General Camou's division, he ordered the signal to be hoisted for the advance of the British troops against the Quarries. The storming party of the English, consisting of men of the 7th Fusileers, 31st, 34th, and 88th Regiments, under the immediate command of Lieutenant-Colonel Campbell (90th Regiment) instantly rushed out from the flanks of the advanced trench, and took the Quarries at the point of the bayonet, without firing a shot; so suddenly was this movement executed, that the enemy, although evidently expecting an attack, were seized with a panic, and bolted towards the Redan, leaving behind them between 70 and 80 men, who were bayoneted in the work: only three Russians were made prisoners. The working party of 800 men was immediately brought up and set to work to connect the Quarries with our advanced trenches, and also to throw up a parapet on the side of the Quarries towards the Russians. The workmen were covered by the men of the storming party, who advanced towards the Redan, and, lying down, kept up a well-directed fire into the embrasures of the Russian batteries. I need scarcely mention that all this time, from the very commencement, a heavy cannonade had been kept up from the trenches of the Allies against the batteries of the enemy, especially those of the Malakoff and Redan.

Shortly after all this, when we began to fancy that the Allies were well established in the captured works, a heavy column of Russians sallied out of the town near what is called the 'Little Redan', situated about midway between the Malakoff and the harbour. They advanced as if with the intention of retaking the Mamelon, and the Zouaves, excited by the success that had attended them, very foolishly rushed out to attack the enemy. This they did with such impetuosity, that the column was driven back to the works of the town in such confusion and disorder that many of the men got into the ditch and scrambled over their own parapets in preference to waiting for their turn so as to retire through the sallyport. The Zouaves continued close on the enemy, and attempted to follow them into the body of the place, but the Russian artillerymen, disregarding the lives of their own men mixed up with the French, fired into the mass with shell and grape-shot from a flanking battery near the edge of the harbour. The most horrible carnage now ensued, and the Zouaves, after having endeavoured with rash bravery to penetrate the lines of the enemy both at the sallyport and also over the ditch and parapet between it and the Malakoff, were finally compelled to retire towards the Mamelon, after having lost an immense number of men.

Just as they began to retire, a sort of panic seized the troops occupying the Mamelon; someone had found a burning fuse sticking in the ground, and therefore supposed that it was connected with a mine to blow up the work. This report spread amongst the men, a panic seized them, and nothing their officers could say or do would prevent their abandoning the Mamelon; so the whole of the troops rushed out, to the number of 3500 men, and when the Zouaves re-entered the Mamelon from their unfortunate attempt to penetrate the works of the town, they found it almost evacuated, and, being informed of the reason, caught the panic, and, dashing through the redoubt, ran out at the other side, and retired towards their own trenches. The Russians, on the Zouaves first retiring, sallied out again in considerable force, and, following them into the Mamelon, found it deserted, and immediately occupied it. Fortunately, as all the guns had been spiked, they were unable to use them against the Allies, and had therefore to depend solely upon their small arms. Their possession of the Mamelon did not last long, for a portion of General Camou's division, with the whole of General Brunet's, advanced against the work and carried it in the most gallant manner. The Russians fought admirably, and were not driven out until immense numbers had been killed; then finding themselves outnumbered and entirely overmatched, they retired out of the rear of the Mamelon, and re-entered the works of the town, near the Little Redan. Their retreat was made in good order, unfollowed by the French, who had now learned prudence; but a heavy fire was poured upon them as they retired, which must have cost them severe loss.

On the Russians retaking the Mamelon, a large body of men was sent out by them from the rear of the Redan to attack the Quarries, but it was entirely unsuccessful; and although it cost us the lives of many brave men, scarce any of the enemy returned, as the large majority was killed or wounded by the tremendous fire of the troops that occupied it, and also from the guns of our batteries.

It was now quite dark, and, with the exception of the cannonade which continued from the trenches of the Allies, nothing of importance took place for two or three hours. Lord Raglan and the Staff returned to Headquarters shortly after midnight. Between that time and the dawn of day on the ensuing morning no less than four attacks were made by the enemy on the Quarries, but they never got possession of them for a single moment, and by daylight very tolerable cover had been obtained by the indefatigable exertions of our working parties.

The French were not unmolested, for the enemy kept up a heavy fire from the north side against the Ouvrages Blancs, and during the latter part of the night a large party of workmen, supported by a body of infantry, turned the head of Careening Bay, and re-entered the small redoubt, which the French had not been able to occupy. The object of the enemy now was merely to destroy and dismantle it, which was accordingly done before daylight. They then returned to the town.

On the morning of June 9th the enemy sent in a flag of truce to the Mamelon, proposing a suspension of hostilities to bury the dead, and it was settled that after midday all firing should cease on both sides. I accordingly rode down on a pony to our look-out station in front of the Light Division, then dismounted and walked down the Karabelnaia ravine, finally emerging between the Mamelon and the Malakoff Tower. The flags of truce had been flying some time; the line of sentries on both sides had been posted, and the fatigue parties of the Russians and the Allies were carrying to and fro the bodies of the gallant men who had fallen on the 7th. The ground of the scene of contest presented the same horrible appearances as the battlefields of Alma and Inkermann. Mutilated corpses and bodies covered with ghastly wounds met the eye all around. The pale, upturned, happy faces of some, apparently in peaceful slumber, marked the instantaneous death which they had met; the outstretched arms, as if imploring aid, in others—the dreadful contortions of those who had suffered agonizing deaths—were to be seen in both friend and foe, as they lay close to each other. One battlefield is generally like another, the same features mark all; and as I have before given some idea of them, I will spare now the relation of further horrors.

Strolling about the ground, I got into conversation with a young Russian officer, who was very civil and polite in what he said, and appeared to regard the capture of the Mamelon and other works as of but little importance. While I was conversing with him, a tall handsome man, still in the prime of life, passed by, attended by an orderly on foot. His uniform was like that of the officer with whom I was talking, except that he had a broad gold strap upon his shoulders: his cap also had a certain quantity of lace upon it. As he passed by, my friend drew himself up and saluted, and, when he had gone on, I said to him, "Is that an officer of high rank?" to which he replied, "Yes, it is General Todtleben." Being anxious, if possible, to speak to one who had made so great a name for himself, I shortly took leave of my friend, and walked on to where I saw General Todtleben with two French officers, and, joining the party, we were soon engaged in conversation. He appeared to treat the capture of the Mamelon with perfect indifference, and said that it had cost them the lives of so many men to construct and hold it, that its value was questionable; adding, significantly, to the French officers, "You will find that to be the case too." He also intimated that we were no nearer taking the place than before. However, it was not said with an air of confidence, only I suppose he felt himself bound to appear cheerful on the occasion. He is a man of very gentlemanlike address, with handsome features, and his bearing seems to betoken great resolution and firmness. I shortly afterwards returned to Headquarters not a little pleased at having conversed with General Todtleben, the man who has most distinguished himself in the Russian army during the war.

I must record a curious fact, showing how necessary it is for a General commanding an army in the field to use his own discretion, even when contrary to the orders that he may receive from home. The responsibility is of course great, but his reliance on his own judgment should be greater. The instance was as follows:—Shortly before General Pélissier left the French Headquarters to witness the attack against the enemy's works on the afternoon of the 7th instant, he received a telegraphic message from the Emperor Napoleon, ordering him on no account to assault the Mamelon, as His Majesty considered that it would be attended with defeat and disaster. General Pélissier quietly put the telegram in his pocket, and shortly afterwards mounted his horse and rode off to witness the capture of the Mamelon, etc. When all was over, and he had returned to camp, he showed it in triumph to some officers of his personal Staff—a great contrast to General Canrobert's conduct when he received the order for the recall of the Kertch expedition.

I have just heard that Lord Raglan proposed to General Pélissier that the assault on the Malakoff and Redan batteries should be made the morning after the capture of the Mamelon, etc.; but it was thought best that a Council of War, consisting of

General Sir James Simpson was Chief of Staff and, on Lord Raglan's death, was appointed Commander-in-Chief of the British army.

the Generals of Engineers and Artillery of the English and French armies should assemble to discuss the matter. I understand that the English Generals were in favour of an immediate assault, but were overruled by the French, who proposed that certain batteries should be constructed on the Mamelon and Ouvrages Blancs to subdue more completely the enemy's fire from the Malakoff and ships in harbour. These batteries are to be completed in about a week's time. This plan having been decided upon, the English also are to erect fresh batteries against the Redan. In consequence of these arrangements, the fire from our guns has been ordered to be reduced, after the suspension of hostilities of this day, from 100 to 20 rounds in the 24 hours.

The following is an approximate return of the casualties of the Allies during June 7th and 8th: —

		Killed.	Wounded.	Total.
English	Officers	6	30	492
	Men	25	431	
French	Officers		90	2,790
	Men		2,700	
				3,282

The Russian losses are variously stated: judging from the reports of prisoners, their casualties were quite as great inside as outside their works. I understand the French declare that they gave over today between 700 and 800 Russian bodies, which had fallen in and about the Mamelon and Ouvrages Blancs, besides which, they could see heaps of slain being removed outside the sallyport, near the Little Redan. Their loss is estimated at 6000 casualties, but this may possibly be an exaggeration.* I should mention that the French gained 73 guns altogether in the different works of the enemy they captured on the 7th instant; of these 52 were in the Mamelon. They took 14 officers and 460 men prisoners, of whom two officers and 180 men were wounded.

The fall of Anapa was curious; as, if the Russians had not evacuated it, the Allies would *not* have attacked it. Several days ago General Pélissier came to Lord Raglan and told him that he had received a positive order from the Emperor by telegraph, *'not to allow the French troops to land at Anapa, but to recall them immediately to before Sevastopol'*. General Pélissier was quite as much disgusted as Lord Raglan at having the arrangements they had made overthrown by the Emperor, but there was no help for it, and a steamer was accordingly despatched with orders for the French troops to return immediately to Kamiesch. The same morning that this steamer arrived at Kertch, another came in with the intelligence that the enemy had evacuated Anapa, after having destroyed the principal public building and all the military stores and guns, and that the town was then occupied by the Circassians. As the recall of the French part of the expedition was kept a secret, what I have just reported will probably not be generally known. Orders have now been sent for the expedition, naval and military, to return here; with the exception of the small

---

* The *Invalide Russe*, in recounting the capture of the Mamelon and other works, places their loss at about half this, viz. 100 officers, and 2800 men killed and wounded.

198

English and French force left to garrison Kertch and Yenikale, besides a brigade of Turks.

In the meantime, matters are going on as regards the siege much in the same way as before the taking of the Mamelon. The French are constructing heavy batteries on the Mamelon and Ouvrages Blancs, to fire against the Malakoff Tower, the Little Redan, and the ships in harbour. The English are sapping up from the Quarries towards the Great Redan, and have already got 100 yards in advance of them. Our casualties have been considerable of recent weeks, but our near approach to the works of the town naturally causes us greater loss than heretofore. Our allies have suffered very considerably in the last captured works from the enemy. I understand that since their occupation of the Mamelon they have lost daily in it alone 100 men, chiefly from the salvoes of shells which the Russians perpetually pour upon them from mortar batteries in rear of the Malakoff. In the Ouvrages Blancs their losses have likewise been severe, caused by the fire from the enemy's batteries on the north side of the harbour.

Omer Pasha, for some reason or other, has taken offence, and says he has not been treated with confidence by the allied Generals, and that they only employ his troops to do the dirty work. Unfortunately General Pélissier, to all appearance, treats his (Omer Pasha's) opinion with the greatest contempt, and, I understand, at the conferences never listens to a word he says. Omer Pasha has in consequence written to the Turkish Government demanding to be allowed to send in his resignation. His want of cordiality towards Lord Raglan has been occasioned by hearing of the proposed Turkish Contingent, of which he not unnaturally supposes Lord Raglan to be the originator. He says, and I think with justice, that it will tend to demoralize his army, as the English propose to give the troops of the Turkish Contingent higher pay than his get, and that of course they will receive it regularly; whereas his men at this moment are ten months in arrears of pay! This he thinks will make his troops discontented with their present position.

I am sorry to say the cholera has been, and still is, very bad among the Sardinians. Four days ago they lost in 24 hours four officers and 76 men, all of whom died of cholera. The last three days it has decreased; yesterday they lost one officer and 47 men. Among the officers was a brother of General La Marmora, who commanded one of their divisions. In the English army, I am glad to say, the cholera is diminishing rapidly, and it appears in a milder form, as many men taken with it recover.

For state of army Vide Appendix B

CHAPTER 15

Death of Lord Raglan

IT has been settled that we shall open fire tomorrow morning at daybreak, and that on Monday, June 18th, 1855, at 6 a.m. an assault is to take place. The allied fleets came back yesterday morning from the expedition to Kertch, having completed one of the most successful, though bloodless operations in the annals of war. I record here a General Order, which gives a summary of the latest successes of the expedition.*

I believe it is intended that at the moment of our assaulting the town, the ships of the Line of the allied fleets are to make a demonstration against the sea defences of Sevastopol, but they are not to engage them, only to threaten; in the hope of keeping the marine batteries manned, and thus employ a large force of artillery-men, who would probably otherwise be engaged fighting in the land defences against the allied troops.

The general plan of assault is, I understand, to be as follows (going from west to east on the map). I will divide the position of the allied trenches into four parts, viz.: — 1st. French left attack. 2nd. English left attack. 3rd. English right attack. 4th. French right or Inkermann attack. The assault from the French left attack is to consist of three distinct columns of a division each; one on the left, to attack the Quarantine Batteries, one in the centre to attack the Bastion Centrale, and one on the right, to attack the Bastion du Mât; the whole to be under the direction of the General commanding the 1st Corps d'Armée, General de Salles. As the Woronzoff-road ravine runs across the front of the English left attack, and between it and the defences of the town, no column of attack is to advance from there. From the English right attack, there will be two columns of assault of 400 men each; the left column is to advance from the left of our attack against the west face of the Redan, under the command of Sir John Campbell: the right column, to advance from the right of our attack, against the east face of the Redan, under the command of Colonel Yea (7th Fusileers). Besides the above, General Eyre's brigade (3rd Division) is to go down the ravine, between the English left attack and the old French attack, and make a demonstration against the Russian works at the end of

---

* *Extract from the General Orders, 14th June, 1855*: — The naval operations against Taganrog, Marianopol, and Geisk, which took place on the 3rd, 5th and 6th instant, have been perfectly success-ful. The public buildings, and numerous magazines of provisions, have been burnt, thereby causing immense loss of supplies to the enemy.

The fortress of Anapa was abandoned and destroyed by the enemy on the 5th instant: 30,000 sacks of flour were destroyed in the neighbourhood of Arabat on the 9th instant.

the Man-of War harbour: General Barnard's brigade (3rd Division) is to be posted in the same ravine, to be ready to give support if necessary to the left column of assault. There are to be also large supports in our rear parallels, to be brought up as required. The whole of the assault is to be under the command of Sir George Brown. The assault from the French right or Inkermann attack will also consist of three columns of a division each; the left column, under the command of General D'Autemarre, to advance along the Karabelnaia ravine round the Mamelon, and assault the battery Gervais and west face of the Malakoff: the centre column, under the command of General Brunet, to advance from the trenches and Mamelon Redoubt, and assault the east face of the Malakoff, the little Redan, and the curtain that connects them both: the right column, under the command of General Mayran, to advance along the Careening Bay ravine, and attack the enemy's batteries next the harbour.

The whole of the French assault is to be under the immediate command of General Regnaud de Saint-Jean-d'Angély there are also to be supports and reserves in each of the different attacks. I hear that in the French left attack, 15,000 men will be held in reserve; English attacks, 10,000 French Inkermann attack, a division of the Garde Impériale, 10,000 strong, to be placed in rear of the Victoria Redoubt, so as to be available for any column that may require reinforcements. There is also to be a division of 10,000 Turks to be placed on the field of Inkermann. The garrison of Sevastopol is calculated, at the present moment, to consist of from 45,000 to 50,000 men. I believe it is in contemplation, the morning of the attack, to make a demonstration in the direction of the Mackenzie Farm Heights for the purpose of directing the attention of the Russian troops in that quarter. This operation is, it is said, to be under the direction of General Bosquet, who was removed from the command of the 2nd Corps d'Armée and French Inkermann attack by General Pélissier, only yesterday; his place being, for the present, occupied by General Regnaud de Saint-Jean-d'Angély. This change has greatly annoyed General Bosquet, who considers that he has been very ill-treated by the General-in-Chief of the French army; but at the same time, it is but just to General Pélissier to state, that on every occasion that he has proposed any offensive movement against the town, General Bosquet has always objected, and I understand, not infrequently, in very strong terms, besides predicting all sorts of disasters and defeat. Such being the case, General Pélissier felt that a man who had no confidence in the success of the operations was very unfit to be in command of them.

I should record that several steam-frigates and sloops of war of the allied fleets are to engage the sea-batteries of Sevastopol during the two nights previous to the assault, and at the same time, a number of the launches of the line-of-battle ships are to throw rockets into the town, so as to harass the enemy.

In endeavouring to give an account of the proceedings of June 18th, one must not be surprised if it is somewhat confused, as were the whole of yesterday's doings from beginning to end—nothing but confusion and mismanagement. I will also try to give the apparent reasons for our late repulse. I have given the general arrangements without detail, proposed for the distribution of the troops for the assault. On the afternoon of that day, General Pélissier came to Lord Raglan, and told him that he had been informed by General de Salles, that there was a strong feeling among the officers of Engineers and Artillery of their left siege attack, that none of their assaults there would be successful; and that he (General Pélissier) thought them unimportant, as the Malakoff was doubtless the key of the town. He proposed therefore that these three assaults should not take place, unless the others on the Redan and Malakoff were perfectly successful. To this, I believe, Lord Raglan objected, but seeing that General Pélissier had himself no confidence in the success of these attacks, he gave way. Eventually it was settled that a demonstration only should be made from the French left attack, at the same time as the assaults from the English right, and French Inkermann attacks, but that in the event of these two last being successful, the French left should afterwards assault. The English arrangements for the assault of the Redan were also somewhat changed, and a 3rd column of 400 men was to attack the salient angle of the Redan, in the event of those on the flanks succeeding. The head of each column was to be covered by parties of the Rifle Brigade, who were to advance in skirmishing order, and getting as near the Redan as practicable, were to endeavour to pick off the enemy's gunners. Parties of sailors (50 men each) were told off to carry scaling ladders under the direction of Captain Peel, R.N., and others of soldiers (60 men each) to carry wool-bags. An officer of the Royal Engineers was also to go with their parties to direct where the scaling ladders and wool-bags were to be placed. Each column was to be accompanied by an officer and 20 men of the Royal Artillery to spike the enemy's guns, immediately on the work being carried, or turn them against the enemy according to circumstances. *The English were not to advance until after the French had got possession of the Malakoff Tower*. This was all settled on the afternoon and evenings of Saturday (16th), and all Sunday the necessary arrangements were being made, and every detail gone into with the Generals of division and brigade. The whole of the 1st Division was brought up from Balaklava, and camped on the plateau in rear of the 4th Division.

At daylight (17th), all the batteries of the allies opened once more a most furious cannonade, which was continued incessantly throughout the day, to all appearance with the greatest success, as the enemy scarcely answered us at all. At night, our horizontal fire ceased, but the vertical fire from all our mortars was continued, and bombs and shells were showered incessantly into the Malakoff and Redan. One reason for the cessation of our cannonade during the night was to allow, under cover of the darkness, the assaulting columns, supports, etc., to be moved into the trenches, and arranged well under the shelter of our parapet, and consequently hid from the enemy. Six o'clock on Monday morning (18th) was the time fixed for the assault to be made, which at this time of year would be nearly three hours after daybreak: and that, if possible, a heavier fire than ever was to have been poured against the enemy's defences from early morning, until the signal for the advance of our columns was given. Such were the arrangements made between the allied Commanders-in-Chief.

About 8.30 p.m. on Sunday (17th), an aide-de-camp from General Pélissier arrived at Headquarters with a despatch, informing Lord Raglan that a Council of War had just been held of the French Generals of Engineers and Artillery, in consequence of an intimation which he (General Pélissier) had received from General Regnaud de Saint-Jean-d'Angély, stating that it was found, upon trial, quite impossible to place the columns of French infantry for the assault in their trenches, without their being seen by the enemy. He proposed that the assault should take place 'au point du jour', as the Russians would not have time to make preparations to defend the place before the columns of assault would be down upon them; whereas, if they waited until 6 a.m. the enemy, during the three previous hours of daylight, would be certain to discover the presence of the troops, and would naturally suppose that so large a mass of men would not be so placed, without a grand attack being about to take place. The enemy would therefore make every arrangement in their power to counteract the efforts of the allies. General Pélissier stated that the council had discussed the merits and demerits of the case, and had come to the conclusion that it would certainly be best to assault at daybreak, and that he (General Pélissier), though he much regretted changing the plan of operation at so late an hour, thought so also.

Lord Raglan was excessively annoyed at receiving this despatch, and said that, altering the arrangements at the last moment was quite enough to imperil the success of the undertaking. He had all along thought the numbers of the French assaulting columns unnecessarily large: indeed, as the best proof of this, I need only state that they were no less than 15 times the strength of the British; our columns consisting of 400 men each and the French of 6000 each! Certainly, they had far more to attack than we had, but still the proportion of troops in their favour was 10 times as many as ours. Indecision at such a moment as this would have been fatal to the operations; Lord Raglan therefore agreed to accede to General Pélissier's wishes, but, at the same time, expressed his opinion that the change was most unwise, and he feared that much confusion would ensue. Lord Raglan had then to issue fresh instructions to Sir George Brown and the different general officers connected with the attack; and it was not until past midnight that his Lordship was able to retire for an hour's rest.

Shortly after 2 a.m. (18th), Lord Raglan and the Staff (consisting in all of upwards of 30 officers) left Headquarters. It was so dark that we could only go at a foot's pace. In about half-an-hour, we had reached the commencement of our trenches, right attack; that is to say, the first parallel or Gordon's Battery. We all then dismounted, and proceeding along the trenches on foot, arrived a little before 3 a.m. in the mortar battery third parallel, which spot had been selected by Lord Raglan as commanding a good view of the Quarries and Redan, and also of the Mamelon and Malakoff works; and from its very forward position (being but a few yards in rear of the quarries) was convenient for sending orders, etc. In other respects, it was anything but a spot in which the Commander-in-Chief should have been stationed, as it was exactly where the cross-fire from the Malakoff and Redan met, and thus rendered it perhaps one of the most dangerous places in the whole of the trenches. Indeed, before we had been there many minutes, as some of the troops were filing past, more than one remarked upon the unsafe spot Lord Raglan had chosen for himself, but his Lordship, although told of it, thought that his position was the best for observing the assault, and consequently declined moving to any other place. We soon found out its danger, as directly the assault commenced a continuous shower of shot, shell, and grape came crashing just over our heads, knocking over portions of the parapet which was low and weak.

General Pélissier had stationed himself in what the French call 'la batterie Lancaster', which is, in fact, the English old five-gun battery, and in which we had four 95-cwt. guns (68-pounders) and one Lancaster. The signal for the advance of the French assaulting columns was to be given by General Pélissier, from that place; it was to consist of three firework rockets.

While we were waiting for the signal of assault, the anxious moments seemed to drag along, and no wonder, considering how much depended on the issue of another hour. All was still, save the occasional booming of distant guns; for in our own trenches and those of the French next to us, not a shot was fired, though occasional heavy shell was still thrown from our rear-mortar batteries into the Redan and Malakoff. The suspense, though of but short duration, was most trying: the darkness, still so considerable that the forms of the men lining the trenches looked like spectres as we traced their dim outline against the black sky, added much to the feeling of awe which would come over one as the thought crossed one's mind of the approaching struggle, and the brave men who must fall to rise no more before our aim could be accomplished. The idea of an unsuccessful attack never even suggested itself. We had not been in the mortar battery more than 10 minutes, it being still quite dark, before we heard a heavy musketry fire going on upon the extreme right of the French Inkermann attack, apparently about the head of Careening Bay. This increased in rapidity, and in a few moments the roaring of shot and shell was mingled with it, and it seemed as if a pitched battle was raging. We were all at a loss to imagine what it could be, as the signal had not been given, and we therefore concluded that the French could not have advanced as yet. It was generally supposed that it was a sortie from the garrison, who had chosen for us this very inopportune moment to attack the French lines. It soon became apparent that, whatever it was, the whole of the Russian garrison was roused by it, for we could hear the beating of drums and the sounding of trumpets in every direction, inside what we thought the doomed city. As it afterwards appeared, it was the right French column assaulting the enemy's works between the Little Redan and the Harbour Batteries. This was commanded by General Mayran, who had mistaken an ordinary rocket for the signal of assault, although warned by several of his Staff that he was in error.

It was still quite dark, and the men leading the column got confused and went directly towards a Russian battery, instead of keeping down the Careening Bay ravine, and then following the edge of the harbour, which would have brought them eventually on the flank of the battery. The enemy's sentries and guards were driven in by the advance of the French column, which very foolishly began to fire upon them, and thus showed the artillerymen in the Russian batteries where they were. They then opened a tremendous fire of shot, shell, and grape upon the French, who were thrown into great confusion by the dreadful slaughter which ensued. General Mayran was himself mortally wounded and was carried to the rear. The troops, losing all confidence, began to retire, followed up by a murderous cannonade both from the Russian batteries, and also from some of the ships in harbour which fired up Careening Bay ravine.

It appears that General Pélissier did not arrive in the position he had selected for himself (in the Lancaster Battery) until 10 minutes after the advance of General Mayran's division, and he expressed his astonishment with considerable warmth, as to who had given the signal. General Regnaud de St.-Jean-d'Angély, who was also stationed there, and who had witnessed the advance, was as much at a loss to understand how it had happened. However, although it was scarcely daylight,

General Pélissier thought it advisable to make the signal for the general assault, and, accordingly, a moment after three rockets flew into the air and burst into a bouquet of fireworks. (I looked at my watch by the light of a portfire, it was exactly seven minutes after 3 a.m.) Immediately the two columns under Generals d'Autemarre and Brunet commenced their advance. The former moved on with rapidity round the left of the Mamelon and up the Karabelnaia ravine towards the battery Gervais to the west of the Malakoff; but the enemy having been put completely on the *qui vive*, by the premature attack of General Mayran's column, immediately discovered the other columns advancing and opened upon them a most tremendous fire of grape, which in a few minutes knocked over dozens of men.

Day now broke, and the first streaks of light showed us General d'Autemarre's column advancing under an awful fire towards the battery Gervais. The Russians redoubled their efforts, and now added the fire of musketry to that of their heavy guns. The head of General Brunet's column had some difficulty in moving out of the trenches; in fact, the signal for attack was given at least 20 minutes sooner than had been expected, and consequently the French officers had not completed the proper placement of their men, so at the very commencement of their advance, they were more or less in disorder and confusion. Before many minutes, this was greatly increased by the unfortunate death of General Brunet himself, who was shot by a musket ball through the body. The command of this column then developed upon General Lafont de Villiers. This change in command caused some little delay, and when the troops moved forward to their difficult task, they were met by an overpowering cross-fire from the east face of the Malakoff and the Little Redan. Nevertheless they still pushed on, and almost reached the ditch in front of the curtain connecting the two last named works together. Here they were received by volleys of musketry, fired by masses of the Russian infantry behind the parapets, and to whom, in return, they could do but little harm. After a desperate struggle they were compelled to retire to their trenches, having left on the ground heaps of bodies of their fallen comrades, but I believe they managed to carry off the greater portion of their wounded.

Immediately on General Pélissier being informed of the mistake and consequent disaster of General Mayran's column, he ordered down to their assistance four battalions of the division of the Garde Impériale, which was in reserve. These troops, on arriving in the lower part of Careening Bay ravine, found the column in a very disordered state, but on receiving this great reinforcement, an assault was again organized under the command of General de Failly (who had succeeded General Mayran, after he had been carried to the rear), but unfortunately with the same result as before; the leading troops being swept away at any fresh discharge from the enemy's batteries. The assault by this column was therefore most reluctantly abandoned, and they retired up the ravine towards their own trenches, carrying with them their wounded, and covered by the battalions of the Garde under General Mellinet.

To return now to General d'Autemarre's division, on the left column of assault. Their progress towards the point of attack was necessarily slow from the frightful fire which they encountered. Nevertheless, in the course of a few minutes, a great mass of men had arrived at the ditch before the battery Gervais; their formation had been much broken by their severe losses, and they presented more the appearance of a hurried crowd, than a regularly formed body of troops. But this was of less importance, as all were animated by the same desire of penetrating into the enemy's work. A rattling fire of musketry was now going on between the Russian troops behind their parapets and the French column, which caused the latter especially, very considerable loss, and added much to the confusion.

In a few minutes more, we had the satisfaction of seeing some of the French clambering over the parapet of the enemy's battery, and they were immediately followed by many others. After penetrating the work, the French found themselves in the Karabelnaia suburb; the houses of which were mere hovels, mostly without roofs, but their low stone walls made admirable cover for troops; and on the Russian infantry and artillery being driven out of the battery Gervais by the entrance of our allies, they fled to these houses, and kept up a heavy fire, which greatly checked the progress of the French. The officer commanding the most advanced companies, and who had led the assaulting column throughout, Commandant Garnier, so disposed his troops, that, as far as possible, they should be under cover from the guns of the Malakoff and the fire of the Russian infantry, while he despatched repeated requests for reinforcements to be sent up.

We must now leave our allies, and turn to the advanced mortar battery where Lord Raglan and the Staff were assembled. But first, I must record the conditions on which our troops were to advance against the Redan, viz.: that the English were not to assault, until the French got possession of the Malakoff. That they never did, although they penetrated the battery Gervais on its flank. It had now been daylight some little time, and Lord Raglan, on seeing and admiring the gallant efforts the French were making, felt that he would hardly be doing them justice if he were not to second their endeavours by ordering our assault on the Redan, which would necessarily take off a portion of the enemy's fire from our allies, and thus make a diversion in their favour. Accordingly, he gave the order for the signal of two rockets for the advance of our two flanking columns to be made. Immediately after we saw the parties of Rifles leaving our trenches and running up towards the abattis round the Redan, followed directly by a number of sailors carrying scaling ladders (led in the most gallant manner by Captain Peel, R.N.), and the soldiers told off to carry woolsacks. The artillerymen to spike the guns also rushed forward; but of these, scarce one-third returned untouched, the rest all being killed or wounded. They were quickly followed by a storming party, consisting of 400 men of the 34th Regiment, under the command of Captain Gwilt, senior effective officer of that corps, supported by a portion of the 33rd, commanded by Lieutenant-Colonel Johnstone.

The troops moved out of the trench in anything but good order: they had been arranged along it about three deep, and immediately the signal was given, had to clamber over the parapet, and thus started in some sort of confusion. The Russians were quite prepared for their appearance, for they instantly opened a most tremendous fire of grape and musketry. Colonel Johnstone was almost immediately struck down, and had his arm shattered, and Captain Gwilt was also severely wounded. Seeing their leaders fall, the men naturally got dispirited, and the torrent of grape-shot which swept through and through them visibly diminished the thin line of British troops. They began to waver; Colonel Yea, perceiving the state of affairs, saw there was nothing for it but to endeavour to form them up in some sort of way, and lead them to the attack. This he did by voice and gesture, and then putting himself at their head, gallantly led the way towards the Redan. He was some yards in advance of his column, when a charge of grape-shot struck him in the body and head, and he fell to the ground, pointing out with his sword the direction the troops were to take. Thus gloriously died, at the head of his men, one of the bravest and best officers in the British army.

So many officers had now been killed and wounded that no orders were given: the men became completely disheartened and commenced firing against the Russians, who swarmed in hundreds on the parapet of the Redan, displaying great bravery in the manner in which they exposed themselves in repelling the advance of our men. The fire from the Russians, if anything, increased, and the British troops, after in vain endeavouring to make further advance, were compelled to retire to our trenches.

I have only described the right column of attack, because it was immediately in front of where the Staff were stationed, and we could see them so much better than the other column. There is but little to tell different in the assault of the left column. The same confusion occurred at the first movement of advance from the same causes; Colonel Shadforth (57th Regiment), who led the storming party, was shot dead before he was many yards out of our trench. Upon seeing this, Major-General Sir John Campbell immediately went forward to lead the stormers himself. The men, struck by his noble devotion, rallied directly and followed Sir John up towards the west face of the Redan, but on arriving close to the abattis, he met with the same fate which, almost at the same time, attended Colonel Yea, and he fell dead, while in the act of cheering on his men. The officer next in seniority was Colonel Lord West (21st Regiment), who took the command and used his best endeavours to form the stormers up for another effort, but it was too late now: the men reduced to half their numbers could not be properly got together. All hope of success was for the present at an end; there was nothing to be done but to retire to the trenches and organize a fresh attack.

I cannot describe the feeling of disappointment which came over all, as we saw that the gallant efforts of our troops had been unavailing. Lord Raglan, who maintained his usual coolness and decision in spite of the reverses with which we had met, immediately ordered General Dacres (Commanding Royal Artillery) to give directions for every gun and mortar to open, in both attacks, that could be brought to bear either on the Redan or Malakoff. This was promptly executed, and in five minutes we had the satisfaction of seeing and hearing our shot and shell fly roaring through the air, carrying death and destruction to our enemies.

I should record that from the moment of the first advance of the British troops, and when the enemy opened their terrible fire of grape-shot, etc., we found our situation in the mortar battery anything but pleasant, as these dreadful missiles came about us like hail, and, considering the danger we were in, it was wonderful that any escaped alive. Lord Raglan desired everyone, both officers and men, to sit down, so as to keep as much under cover as possible, and not attract the attention of the enemy by looking over the parapet. But his Lordship and General Jones, from the first moment that we came into the battery until after our troops had retired, leant over and watched the assault of our allies first and afterwards our own. It was strange to observe the countenances of these two veterans; perfectly calm and collected, they talked earnestly to one another, but without any excitement being apparent in voice or gesture, disregarding alike the heavy round shot and minié ball, which every moment flew close past them. Shortly after the first advance of our troops, General Jones, while leaning over the parapet conversing with Lord Raglan, was struck on the forehead by a grape-shot, which knocked him backwards — we all thought dead; he was caught when falling by one of his aides-de-camp, and gently laid down on the ground. It was a pitiful sight to see the poor old General, with a frightful gash across his forehead, his face covered with blood, which came streaming down from the wound. To the great delight of all, upon being given some water, he appeared to revive, and a medical officer being in attendance, his wound was dressed and a bandage placed round his head. He shortly after took his place again by Lord Raglan's side, who, when he ascertained that General Jones was not mortally wounded, had returned to watch the progress of the attack. An officer of the 88th Regiment, Captain Brown, was standing among the Staff and talking to some of us, when a round shot came and took his arm clean off, the limb flying several yards from him, and nearly striking General Airey, who was on the other side of the trench, on the chest. An artillery-man, who was with us to discharge the signal rockets, had his head smashed by some grape-shot, and a sapper, who was also there with signal flags (in case they were required), was killed by a round shot going through his chest: the poor fellow was literally knocked to pieces. Enough of these horrible details.

In the meantime, when Commandant Garnier's messenger reached General d'Autemarre, he, having no more reinforcements at hand, sent back to General Pélissier, informing him of the state of affairs at the battery Gervais. General Pélissier, on hearing this, ordered the Zouaves of the Garde to move down without delay to reinforce Commandant Garnier. But all this took a long time to accomplish. In the first place, the French Commander-in-Chief was upwards of a mile as the crow flies from General d'Autemarre's position, so that a messenger having to pass along crowded trenches, the way perpetually blocked up by wounded men being carried to the rear, would be at least half an hour in reaching the Lancaster Battery. Then again, from there General Pélissier had to send back to the general officer commanding the Garde in rear of the Victoria Redoubt, which would also take some little time. Altogether it was upwards of an hour from the time General d'Autemarre despatched his messenger, to the time when the Zouaves of the Garde began their march. They had not proceeded any distance before intelligence reached General Pélissier that the English assault had been unsuccessful, and also that the French in the battery Gervais had been forced to retire. He therefore gave orders to halt the Zouaves until he had communicated with Lord Raglan. He then desired General Regnaud de Saint-Jean-d'Angély to make arrangements for a fresh attack, which he did, by sending instructions to that effect to General d'Autemarre, who, in consequence of the death of General Brunet and the mortal wound of General Mayran, was now senior officer in the trenches. The French Commander-in-Chief then despatched General Rose with this information to Lord Raglan, and expressed a hope that he would agree with him, and organize a fresh attack from our trenches; in which case the French troops should again assault the Malakoff as soon as possible, and in the event of their being successful he hoped the English would attack the Redan, as before arranged.

208

But to return once more to the English trenches. Our batteries had, during this time, been keeping up a rapid and well-directed fire against the enemy's works, and in the course of three-quarters of an hour from the time they opened, the enemy's guns were almost silenced; this showed what an error it was, not having the three hours bombardment previous to the assault, as Lord Raglan had so earnestly desired, and to which the French, at the eleventh hour, would not agree. As to their idea, that the enemy, with a garrison of 45,000 men in Sevastopol, would be unprepared, or taken by surprise by our attacking them at daylight, it seems to me simply absurd, and our experience with the Russians up to the present time ought pretty well to have shown us how much on the alert they always are. Besides, it is an established rule with all armies in the field, in presence of an enemy or a besieged town, that the troops are invariably all under arms an hour or more before daylight, as that hour is supposed to be dangerous, and one cannot be aware as to what movement the enemy may have made during the night.

But this is a digression. When Lord Raglan saw that the enemy's fire was once again completely subdued by the cannonade and bombardment we had brought to bear upon them, he resolved, with the concurrence of General Pélissier, that a fresh attack should be made, and for this purpose, he gave directions to Sir George Brown to order down the supports, and have them placed in the advanced trenches in the same manner as the last, ready for an assault. He then despatched Colonel Vico to General Pélissier to inform him of the arrangements he had made, and proposing that another attack on the Malakoff and Redan should take place after a few hours longer bombardment, which would not unlikely put the Russians off their guard, and more completely silence their batteries; besides giving time for the removal of the wounded out of the advanced trenches, and also for replacing those troops, that had already been engaged, with fresh bodies of men.

Well, Lord Raglan waited for a long time for General Pélissier's answer, and at last General Rose arrived with the message from the French Commander-in-Chief. It appeared that he had met Colonel Vico just at the entrance of our trenches, so that the two messages of the allied Generals had crossed. Lord Raglan, fearing that there might be some mistake, as his and General Pélissier's ideas of the best time to assault were rather at variance, thought it best to go and settle the question himself. Accordingly, he proceeded, accompanied by his Staff, to the rear of our trenches. Passing along the trenches on our return was anything but a movement of rapidity: the approaches were quite choked with the supports and fresh troops coming down, and were perpetually blocked up by the poor wounded fellows, officers and men, who were being borne to the rear on litters. It was shortly after 7 a.m when Lord Raglan arrived at the Lancaster Battery, where he found General Pélissier, General Regnaud de Saint-Jean-d'Angély, and the French Generals of Engineers and Artillery. The two Commanders-in-Chief retired, and had a long consultation together; I understand General Pélissier was perfectly ready to fall in with Lord Raglan's views. But before they had fully arranged their plans, a message arrived from General d'Autemarre to his Commander-in-Chief, to the effect, that he feared it was quite impossible to assault again, as the French losses had been so great, and the troops were so dispirited that he doubted the result being successful; and adding, that in his opinion, it would only be taking the troops to be uselessly slaughtered. General Pélissier was a good deal puzzled what to do, but very properly thinking that, in this instance, General d'Autemarre's opinion, as regards the temper of his troops, was superior to his own, he deemed it impossible to attack, and appealed to Lord Raglan for his advice. I understand that his Lordship gave it, that much as he wished for an immediate repetition of the assault, it would be absurd attempting it, if the French troops were really as dispirited as General d'Autemarre appeared to consider. In this dilemma, General Pélissier decided that the risk was too great, and consequently the proposed attack was abandoned.

Thus ended the unfortunate assault of the Allies on the Malakoff and Redan on the 18th of June. I believe its failure was chiefly owing to two causes: the first and greatest, that a cannonade and bombardment of two or three hours' duration did not take place on the Malakoff and Redan previous to the assault, as it would be perfectly impossible for any large body of troops to exist in those works, exposed to the tremendous fire the Allies could bring to bear upon them. The second cause, a fatal one also, was General Mayran attacking before the proper time, and consequently giving the enemy an opportunity of repelling, as it were, the different columns of attack in detail, and likewise hurrying, as I have described, the movements of the other columns, especially as regards the division of General Brunet. In operations of this nature, simultaneous movement is absolutely necessary to ensure success. Had the three assaulting columns of our allies advanced at the same moment, I believe the day might have been successful; but the enemy had time to repulse the attack of General Mayran before called upon to drive back that of General Brunet.

Another error which was committed on this day, but one which we cannot but admire from the motives which actuated it, and the bravery it called forth, was the fact of the general officers commanding each column taking the post of leaders of a storming party. Out of the five general officers who commanded each column four met with a glorious but untimely death, by which sad catastrophe, in each instance, their men were thrown more or less into confusion, and the commands devolved on officers who, although possibly equally brave and zealous, were probably not so well informed of the arrangements for the attack. The names of these gallant Generals were: General Mayran, mortally wounded; General Brunet, killed; Colonel Yea (Acting-Brigadier-General), killed; and Major-General Sir John Campbell, killed.

After a protracted conference with General Pélissier, Lord Raglan returned to the English Headquarters, visiting on his way the different divisional camp hospitals, cheering, with his kind manner and sympathizing words, many a poor fellow who was suffering from the torture of his wounds. He arrived back at Headquarters about midday, and there found that his despatches and letters from England had just arrived. One of the first letters he opened announced to him the death of his last surviving sister, a blow which, to his kind heart and warm affections, was even more severe than the disasters of the day.

I now report on the attack of General Eyre's column against the enemy at the end of the Man-of-War harbour. It appears, that about an hour previous to the signal of assault, General Eyre started down the ravine, between the English left attack and the old French trenches, with his column, consisting of about 2000 men of the 9th, 18th, 28th, 38th, and 44th Regiments. They arrived at the extremity of our works a little before 3 a.m.; General Eyre then halted the column and made his arrangements for the assault. Volunteers from each regiment, to the number of about 200, formed an advance guard under Major Fielden of the 44th Regiment (who distinguished himself throughout the day). These were supported by three battalions; on the right the 44th and 38 Regiments, and on the left the 18th Regiment; the two remaining battalions of the 9th and 28th Regiments being kept in rear as a reserve.

A body of French infantry had also been told off to co-operate on the left with the English troops. The troops were then ordered to advance. The first obstacles in their way were two ambuscades, occupied by small parties of the enemy; these were immediately captured without any loss to the allied troops, the English taking the one in their front and the French the other on the left. Our allies then contented themselves with the assistance they had given us and advanced no further, the officer commanding them intimating that he had instructions not to proceed beyond that point. Immediately after this, the English troops marched on the cemetery on their front, which had always, up to this time, been occupied by a strong body of the enemy.

As it was not yet daylight, it was impossible to estimate their force, but from the flashes of their muskets when they fired first on our advancing column, it would seem that they were in considerable numbers. However, they made but little stand and our men got possession and occupied the cemetery with but little loss, the Russians retiring to some houses on either side of the ravine, in rear of the cemetery. General Eyre ordered those houses to be attacked, which was immediately done. The 18th Regiment advanced, drove out the enemy and occupied the houses on the left, which were immediately under what are known as the Garden Batteries to the left rear of the Bastion du Mât: the houses on the right were taken and occupied by the 44th Regiment, and the 38th was pushed forward and took some houses in their front, from whence they commanded and took in reverse a portion of the Strand Battery, which is at the extremity of the Man-of-War Creek, and sweeps with its guns the ravine our troops occupied.

On the enemy being driven out of the houses above-mentioned, they retired to the town defences on each flank of the ravine, those on the right going to the Barrack Batteries and those on the left to the Garden Batteries. The enemy then opened a heavy fire from their guns, together with a sharp musketry fusillade; against the latter, our men were well sheltered, but against the former, the thin walls of the houses they occupied were but of slight protection. This cannonade cut up our troops dreadfully: several houses were knocked down and others set fire to by the shells. We continued to occupy them despite our losses, and the steady and well-directed fire against the Russian infantry caused them to discontinue their fusillade, and the accuracy of our aim at the embrasures of the enemy's batteries silenced many of their guns and must have caused them numerous casualties among their artillerymen; but the enemy placed several of their ships of war so that their guns could be brought to bear upon the ground our troops had acquired, and the heavy shot and shell which pitched perpetually among them cost us many valuable lives. Against this, our men were helpless. General Eyre could not attempt any further advance until he knew of the success of the attack on the Malakoff and Redan; indeed, as it was, he had exceeded his orders, as it had only been the intention of Lord Raglan that a demonstration should be made to occupy the attention of the enemy at this part of their defences, during the grand assaults from the English and French trenches; and in the event of these assaults being successful, General Eyre was then to convert his feint attack into a real one. He was not aware of the checks with which our efforts had been met till about 9 a.m.; he then sent an officer to inform Lord Raglan of his position, and begged to know what he was to do. Lord Raglan immediately communicated with General Pélissier, and after explaining to him what had taken place, said that, as the new ground now occupied by our troops was of far more importance to the French old attack than to the English left he hoped that he would take it off his hands and occupy it with French troops. General Pélissier at once saw the importance of keeping possession at any rate of a portion of the acquired ground, and agreed to occupy it with some of his troops if his General of Engineers, upon examining the ground, found it practicable. He then gave directions to General Niel to send an officer to examine the ground. Upon this, Lord Raglan despatched an officer with this information to General Eyre, but at the same time, ordered him to retire if not relieved by the French at nightfall.

Throughout the day, the troops had to continue under, at times, a most galling fire from the enemy's batteries and from the ships, which fired up the Man-of-War Creek from the Great Harbour, causing us very severe loss both in officers and men. General Eyre was himself during the morning severely wounded on the head, but with great resolution and courage continued to command the troops till 5 p.m., when feeling the effects of his wound, he resigned to the next senior officer, Colonel Adams (28th Regiment). During the afternoon, a French officer of Engineers visited the ground, and said it was of importance that it should be held by the Allies, and told General Eyre that a considerable body of French troops should be sent to relieve the English immediately. Nevertheless, no relief ever arrived, and therefore at nightfall, in compliance with the order of Lord Raglan, Colonel Adams gave directions for the troops to retire: leaving only a strong picket in the cemetery, so that the ground might be re-occupied, if thought advisable the following morning. The retreat was made without molestation from the enemy, and in such order and regularity that they were able to carry to the rear all our wounded, many of whom it had not been possible to remove during the day. The loss of this column, like those on the Redan, was very severe: no less than 31 officers and 531 men being killed and wounded.

Thus concluded the operations of this eventful day. Much of it we must look upon with regret and sorrow: — with regret, that our efforts were unavailing; with sorrow, for the noble lives that were lost. But our honour remains untarnished: England may still be proud of her soldiers: officers and men, from the first General to the last joined recruit, alike showed their bravery and devotion to their country.

This day (19th), the melancholy task of collecting and burying the dead has been taking place. I have just returned from seeing the suspension of arms, which was demanded this morning by a flag of truce by the allied Generals from the Russians. It did not begin until 2 p.m., when parties from both sides moved out of the advanced works and commenced their sad duty. For some hours previous, no firing had gone on: all seemed impressed with the loss which had been occasioned yesterday. I have described so often the horrors of a battlefield that I will spare the infliction now: the wounds were perhaps more horrible than before, from the amount of grape-shot that had been used by the enemy in repelling the advance of the troops. I believe only two or three English wounded were found, the others having been withdrawn during the night. Our allies, whose attack was so much more extended, found great numbers of their poor countrymen, who had been struck down so near the enemy's works that they could not be carried off. Who shall describe the protracted agony and suffering many of these brave men endured, during the long 30 hours from the time of their receiving their wounds! Perhaps I was most struck by the mangled remains of those two noble officers, Sir John Campbell and Colonel Yea, which lay further advanced than any other red coats, close under the abattis of the Redan!

As before, I got into conversation with some Russian officers: they all appeared more cold and reserved in their manner than on former occasions, and seemed, I thought, more melancholy than either the English or French. One young Russian cadet, with whom I was talking, in reply to a remark of mine as to our losses, said, with great bitterness of manner, and a voice choked with emotion, "Losses! You do not know what the word means! You should see our batteries; and dead lie there in heaps and heaps! Troops cannot live under such a fire of hell as you poured upon us!" In fact, I am more convinced than ever, that, had the assault taken place at 6 a.m. yesterday, after three hours cannonade and bombardment, Sevastopol would now be in the hands of the Allies.

It is impossible for me to estimate accurately either our own or the French losses, as the return at present has not been made out; but I fear the English approximate near 1500, and those of our allies to between 3000 and 4000.

I regret to say that the allied fleets have also had some losses in the last two nights attacks against the sea-defences of the town; Captain Lyons of H.M.S. *Miranda* was severely wounded on the night of the 17th, by the bursting of a shell. He has been sent down to the naval hospital at Therapia for recovery. In consequence of the non-success of our assault on the Malakoff and Redan, the attack on Mackenzie's Heights by the force under General Bosquet's command did not take place, but on the morning of the 17th, the Turkish and Sardinian troops under Omer Pasha and General La Marmora crossed the Tchernaya, and now occupy a position on the high ground in front of Tchorgoun. The enemy have not attempted to molest them.

We are beginning to recover a little from the 'bitter pill' we had to swallow on Monday last (18th), but still everyone is more or less out of spirits. Lord Raglan is perhaps the most cheerful of anyone, considering how much he has had lately to worry and annoy him: but at the same time, I fear that it has affected his health: he looks far from well, and has grown very much aged latterly. Added to our other misfortunes, several of our best Generals are incapacitated from ill-health, and are obliged temporarily to resign their commands. Sir George Brown and General Codrington have gone on board ship at Kamiesch sick; General Estcourt has been dangerously ill during the last two days at Headquarters with cholera, and is even

Overleaf: A truce for burying the dead. Both sides often sent a flag of truce to obtain permission to remove their dead and to ascertain what prisoners had been taken. The Malakoff is on the left, the Mamelon on the right.

214

now in a very precarious state; General Pennefather has been so ill with dysentery, that the medical men have ordered him to leave for England immediately, as the only chance for his recovery. General Buller also was obliged to leave in consequence of fever a short time back. Generals Jones and Eyre are, as you know, both wounded, and although going on most favourably and able to carry on their respective commands, are not fit as yet to resume their more active duties. So altogether we are very short of general officers. General Mayran died yesterday from the effects of the dreadful wounds he received on the 18th instant.

I have omitted to record that we re-occupied on the 19th instant the ground which General Eyre's column took the morning before, but which they abandoned in the evening, leaving only a picket in the cemetery. On the morning of the 19th, the engineer officer of the left attack, whose duty it was to report every morning any fresh circumstance or movement on the part of the enemy, that might come under his observation, remarked that the ground above alluded to was still unoccupied by the enemy. This information he instantly sent up to Headquarters, and orders were then given by Lord Raglan that the picket should be immediately strengthened and sentries posed across the newly acquired ground. This was all done. Lord Raglan also communicated the circumstance to General Pélissier, and it was arranged between them, that a force of English and French troops should be sent down there in the course of the day; instructions were given to the commanding officers of the Royal Engineers and the Corps du Génie to erect such works as might be thought desirable, both to strengthen the ground, and connect it with the English and French trenches on both sides of the ravine. Accordingly, the same evening (19th), a strong force of English and French were sent down there, and commenced the works ordered to be constructed; since which time they have been completed, and now present a formidable appearance. They have cost us a considerable number of men, from their nearness to some of the enemy's batteries: nevertheless, the ground is of great importance to the Allies, as indeed is proved by the jealousy with which the Russians regard our occupation of it.

For some reason with which I am unacquainted (it is said because the French Commander-in-Chief is not pleased with the arrangements of General Regnaud de Saint-Jean-d'Angély on the 18th instant), General Pélissier ordered General Bosquet on the 20th instant, to take up again the command of the 2nd Corps d'Armée and the French Inkermann attack. The French troops on the Tchernaya are now under the immediate orders of General Herbillon, and General Regnaud de Saint-Jean-d'Angély has returned to his old command of the Garde Impériale and Corps de Réserve.

As regards the siege-works, we are running forward a sap towards the Great Redan, more with the object of forming an advanced musketry-trench than with the idea of crowning the work. The French are making two other saps from the Mamelon and the trenches to its right, towards the Malakoff and Little Redan. They are also working nearer to the Bastion du Mât and the Bastion Centrale in their old attack. Our engineers say that it will be at least three weeks before these saps, and the works connected with them, will be completed. The Russians appear also to be employing themselves strengthening their line of defence: it is said they have commenced the erection of a Star Fort in the Karabelnaia suburb, which, when finished, is completely to command the Redan and Malakoff. This would be

216

Attack on the Bastion Centrale by troops under the command of General de Salles. The men could not get into the Centrale and came back into the trenches. The General did his best to urge them on, tearing off the epaulettes of the young soldiers who sought sanctuary . . . and telling them: "Vous n'etre pas Francais!" One poor lad of a conscript got so indignant at this that he screamed out: "Ah, je ne suis pas Francais, a moi les braves!"—and clambered back into the breach.

a work of such magnitude, and requiring so great a quantity of material and labour, that I doubt the truth of the report.

Very little firing has been going on from the guns on either side since the flag of truce on the 19th, but our daily losses are still considerable, from the nearness of our trenches to the enemy's works, and the rattle of musketry never ceases day or night. Our allies suffer severely from the occupation of the Mamelon, as the Russians at intervals throw into it salvoes of heavy shells from some large mortars in rear of the Malakoff.

The last few days we have had a great number of deserters from Sevastopol, who one and all declare that, had we assaulted the town again on the 18th, it would have fallen an easy conquest into our hands. Their troops were so disheartened by the heavy losses they met with from the cannonade opened by us on them imme- diately after the assault, when their masses of infantry were collected in heavy columns in rear of the Redan and Malakoff. They also tell us that immense numbers of men ran down to the water's edge during this heavy fire, and such was their panic, that they actually fought for the possession of boats and rafts, etc. (which were there for the removal of the wounded), in order that they might cross over to the north side of the harbour. They say that Prince Gortschakoff, in order to check this feeling as much as possible, has relieved the greater part of the garrison with fresh troops on the north side, and that on the arrival of reinforcements, the entire garrison will be changed. Their accounts of their losses on the 18th of June vary considerably; some say 5000, others 10,000.*

The casualties of the Allies are as follows: —

				Killed.	Wounded.	Total.
English	Officers	..	..	22	78	
	Men	..	..	244	1209	
				266	1287	1553
French	Officers	..	..	37	96	
	Men	..	..	1274	1644	
				1311	1740	3051

Total of the Allies killed and wounded .. 4604

General Estcourt's death on Sunday, the 24th, had thrown a gloom over all. He was buried yesterday morning early, in the little cemetery at the end of the vineyard at Headquarters, and all connected with the general Staff attended, to show their last respect to one who was beloved by all who knew him. He had been nursed through his painful illness, and his last hours soothed, by the tender care of his wife and sister, who some little time ago came up from Constantinople to pay him a visit. The night before his death, Lord Raglan, although himself far from well, from an attack of dysentery, went to take leave of the poor General, who was an old and dear friend of his. His death has been a great shock to him. He had intended to have been present at his funeral, and got up for that purpose, but he found the trial too much for him, and for the first time his wonted composure left him, and he was quite overcome with grief. In the afternoon, after the burial, Lord Raglan went and visited the grave.

I understand that Lord Raglan has recommended Colonel Pakenham to the Minister of War, to be the new Adjutant-General to this army. Colonel Pakenham has been acting under General Estcourt since the commencement of the war.

Lord Raglan's sudden death at his Headquarters before Sevastopol is indeed a severe and heavy blow. It is quite impossible to describe the sorrow and grief the death of our beloved chief has caused to all and each one at the English

* According to Prince Gortschakoff's despatch, as published in the *Invalide Russe*, the losses of the garrison of Sevastopol during June 17th and 18th were as follows: —

	Killed.	Wounded.	Total Casualties
Officers	16	153	
Men	781	4826	
	797	4979	5776

Headquarters. It was so awfully sudden and unexpected!—even now, we cannot realize it. Lord Raglan's distress at General Estcourt's loss had much added to his indisposition. Still, no one thought for a moment that it was anything to be alarmed about. It was on the afternoon of Tuesday last (26th), that after writing all the morning his numerous despatches and letters, he felt so unwell that he was advised by Dr. Prendergast, his medical attendant, to lie down, which he accordingly did. He did not feel equal to appearing at his dinner-table in the evening, but the doctor's report was favourable. It was deemed advisable that someone should sit up with him; accordingly, two of his personal Staff relieved one another in their watch over him. On Wednesday morning (27th), Lord Raglan not being any better, it was thought necessary to telegraph to England that he was ill. Another message was again sent on the evening of that day, giving a better account. On Wednesday night, two other members of his personal Staff sat up with him, during the greater part of which he slept tranquilly. On the morning of Thursday (28th), a consultation was held upon his case by his personal medical attendant and two of the principal surgeons of the army, and they decided that a telegraphic message should be sent to England, to the effect, that Lord Raglan was *much* better. Just as the Military Secretary was going to send it off, Dr. Prendergast, who apparently did not take so sanguine a view of the case, strongly urged that it should be altered to, 'Lord Raglan has passed a tranquil night, and is no worse this morning', or words to that effect. I should record that Dr. Prendergast was constantly with his Lordship, and was unremitting in his attentions to him, sleeping, the two nights of his illness, in his clothes, in a room next to Lord Raglan's. It was not until about 3.30 p.m. that Lord Raglan's servant went to fetch Dr. Prendergast, who had left him a few moments before, saying that he thought his Lordship worse. The Doctor found him very low, and complaining of pains, but did not anticipate any immediate danger till 4.30 p.m., when a sudden change came over him, and he saw he was sinking. He then sent to Colonel Steele, and said that he thought a telegraphic message to that effect should be sent home. Soon after 5 p.m., it was generally known at Headquarters that Lord Raglan was dying, about which time he became insensible, and so continued to the last. All was over at 8.35 p.m. The whole of his personal Staff were with him when he died; also his nephew, Colonel Somerset (Rifle Brigade), Generals Simpson and Airey, and Colonel Lord George Paget. The principal Chaplain to the Forces went into his bedroom shortly before his death, and read the Service, and after, when all was over, a prayer was offered up by him, in which all most earnestly joined. Nothing could have been quieter or more peaceful than his death-bed—so calm, and without an effort. It was scarcely possible to tell the moment when his spirit fled to rest. I need not record the grief; it can better be imagined than described.

His death has created a profound sensation in the army; now that he is gone, everyone finds out what a loss they have sustained. Our allies, especially the French, have shown great sympathy with us on this sad occasion. The Commanders-in-Chief of each army, and the Admirals of the Allied Fleets, came up to Headquarters on the morning of the 29th instant, to take a farewell look at their late colleague. All seemed deeply impressed by the event. It was a touching

Overleaf: Departure of the cortege for Lord Raglan's funeral

Canrobert   Omar Pasha Simpson

departure of the C

Pelissier   La marmora

e for Lord Raglans funeral

sight to see these old warriors who had so often looked death in the face unmoved, shedding tears of regret over the body of our beloved Commander. General Pélissier stood by the bedside for upwards of an hour, crying like a child.* General Canrobert also testified the most profound grief on seeing the remains of him for whom he entertains a sincere affection. It has since been decided, in compliance with the wish of the late Field-Marshal's relatives, that his body shall be taken home to England for interment. It is to be removed on Tuesday (July 3rd) to Kazatch Bay, and from there conveyed in the *Caradoc* steamer (Commander Derriman) to England, and will be accompanied home by the five aides-de-camp and the Doctor. It is interesting to record the last General Order given to the army, by Lord Raglan, on the morning of the day of his death, in reference to the assault of the 18th of June : —

General Order.

28th June, 1855.

The Field-Marshal has the satisfaction of publishing to the army the following extract of a telegraphic despatch, from Lord Panmure, dated 22nd June : —

'I have Her Majesty's commands to express her grief that so much bravery should not have been rewarded with merited success ; and to assure her brave troops that Her Majesty's confidence in them is entire.'

I record now the announcement to the army of Lord Raglan's death by General Simpson.

Morning General Orders.

29th June, 1855.

No. I. It becomes my most painful duty to announce to the army the death of its beloved commander, Field-Marshal Lord Raglan, G.C.B., which melancholy event took place last night about nine o'clock.

No. II. In the absence of Lieutenant-General Sir George Brown, the command of the forces devolves on me, being the next senior officer present, until further orders from England.

No. III. Generals of Division and Heads of Departments will be pleased to conduct the respective duties as heretofore.

(Signed)   JAMES SIMPSON.
Lieutenant-General.

Sir George Brown leaves for England this day, his health having completely given way before the accumulation of trials which he has lately had to go through, augmented by the grief he feels at the loss of Lord Raglan.

On July 3rd, the late Field-Marshal's remains were removed from Headquarters to Kazatch Bay, and then transferred on board H.M.S. *Caradoc* for conveyance to England. A procession was formed at Headquarters at 4 p.m., and moved down to the harbour between a double rank of infantry, on each side of the road. From the English to the French Headquarters the line was formed by British troops, consisting of 50 men and three officers from every regiment out here — a distance of about a mile ; from the French Headquarters to Kazatch Bay by the French troops, consisting of a portion of the 1st Corps d'Armée and the Garde Impériale — a distance of nearly six miles. A guard of honour of the Grenadier Guards was formed up in the courtyard, opposite the principal door of the house, and presented arms as the coffin was brought out. A salute of 19 guns was fired by two

* As another instance of the affection and respect entertained by the French Commander-in-Chief for the late Lord Raglan, it may be stated, that General Pélissier placed on the coffin enclosing the remains a wreath of *immortelles*, requesting it might never be removed. It is needless to add that this desire was fulfilled.

Lord Raglan's body arrives at Kazatch Bay for conveyance to England on the steamer Caradoc.

field-batteries of the Royal Artillery, stationed on the hill opposite Headquarters, when the cortège moved off. The united bands of three regiments of the Line at the same time played the 'Dead March in Saul'. The escort was composed of four squadrons of British cavalry, two of which formed the advance and two the rear of the procession; two squadrons of Sardinian cavalry, eight squadrons of French cavalry, two troops of French horse-artillery, and a field-battery of the English artillery. The coffin was placed on a platform fixed upon a 9-pounder gun, drawn by eight horses of Captain Thomas's troop of horse artillery; at the wheels of the gun-carriage and limber were the four Commanders-in-Chief of the allied armies, viz. General Simpson, General La Marmora, General Pélissier, and Omer Pasha. After them was led the favourite charger of the late Field-Marshal, followed by his relatives and personal Staff. Every general officer of the allied armies who was not absent on account of duty or health, joined in the procession. An immense number of officers of the British army also accompanied the mournful cortège. On the way down, the French had placed at intervals batteries of artillery, which fired salutes as the procession passed by. They also had several of their regimental bands, which played some sacred music. Arriving at Kazatch Bay, the coffin was received at the English wharf by Admirals Bruat and Stewart (Sir Edmond Lyons did not feel equal to attending the sad ceremony), and numbers of naval officers, both English and French. It was then placed in the launch of the *Royal Albert*, which was towed by one of her large boats, and moved slowly off to H.M.S. *Caradoc* (which had been painted entirely black), while two batteries on shore boomed their last adieu of 19 guns.* The *Caradoc* immediately got under steam, and half-an-hour later started from Kazatch Bay, with the touching signal *Farewell* flying at her mast-head.

* A curious circumstance was remarked, whether by accident or design I cannot say. During the whole time the procession lasted, not a shot was fired from any of the Russian batteries, and consequently none from us. Might it not have been an act of courtesy on the part of Prince Gortschakoff to the remains of his old friend FitzRoy Somerset?

223

The General Orders of July 2nd contain translations of the French and Sardinian Orders on the death of Lord Raglan. That issued by General Pélissier has excited particular admiration. It is couched in the most happy terms, and is calculated to please everybody; 'for it is *not unworthy of the subject*, and more cannot be said in its praise'.

Morning General Order.

July 2nd, 1855.

The Lieutenant-General commanding the Forces hastens to publish to the army the following telegraphic despatch, received last night from the Minister for War, dated June 30th: —

I conveyed your sad intelligence to the Queen. Her Majesty received it with profound grief. Inform the army that Her Majesty has learnt, with the deepest sorrow, this great misfortune which has befallen the army in the loss of its late distinguished Commander-in-Chief.

The country has been deprived of a brave and accomplished soldier, a true and devoted patriot, and an honourable and disinterested subject.

General After-Order.

July 2nd, 1855.

The Lieutenant-General commanding the Forces has the satisfaction of publishing to the troops the following translation of a General Order issued by General Pélissier, Commander-in-Chief of the French army, on the occasion of the death of the late Field-Marshal Lord Raglan, G.C.B.: —

(TRANSLATION.)

Army of the East. — No. 15, General Order.

Death has suddenly taken away while in full exercise of his command the Field-Marshal Lord Raglan, and has plunged the British in mourning.

We all share the regret of our brave Allies. Those who knew Lord Raglan, who know the history of his life—so noble, so pure, so replete with service rendered to his country—those who witnessed his fearless demeanour at Alma and Inkermann, who recall the calm and stoic greatness of his character throughout this rude and memorable campaign, every generous heart indeed, will deplore the loss of such a man. The sentiments here expressed by the General-in-Chief are those of the whole army. He has himself been cruelly struck by this unlooked-for blow.

The public grief only increases his sorrow at being for ever separated from a companion-in-arms whose genial spirit he loved, whose virtues he admired, and from whom he has always received the most loyal and hearty co-operation.

(Signed)   A. PELISSIER,

Commander-in-Chief.

Headquarters before Sevastopol, June 29th, 1855.

By Order,

(Signed)   E. DE MARTIMPREY,

Lieut.-Gen., Chief of the Staff.

It is also gratifying to the Lieutenant-General to publish the following translation of a General Order issued by General La Marmora, Commander-in-Chief of the Sardinian army in the Crimea: —

(TRANSLATION.)

Headquarters, Sardinian Army, Kadikoi, 29th June, 1855.

Order of the Day.

Soldiers. — Yesterday, after a short illness, died Field-Marshal Lord Raglan, the illustrious Commander-in-Chief of the English army here. His long career, the important services he has rendered his country, his heroical courage, and the exemplary constancy with which, together with his army, he endured the hard trials and privations of a winter campaign, have made his loss a great calamity. He esteemed highly this our King's army, and did much to minister to its wants; let us unite therefore with our brave Allies in deploring his death, and venerating his memory.

(Signed)   LA MARMORA,

Commanding-in-Chief.

It will afford satisfaction to the army to be informed of the sympathy of our Allies in the heavy loss we have sustained by the death of our great Commander.

By order,

(Signed)   W. L. PAKENHAM,

Left: General Pélissier and General Simpson

Lieut.-Col., Assist. Adj.-Gen.

CHAPTER 16

The fall of Sevastopol

ON the evening of July 1st, 1855, a telegraphic message arrived from Lord Panmure, at the English Headquarters, announcing to General Simpson that he was to continue in command of the army; but it was not until the 21st that he received the official notification of the fact. Upon this, General Simpson issued an Order to the army, which, from its simple language and modest expression, deserves to be recorded:—

General After-Order.

July 21st, 1855.

Lieutenant-General Simpson announces to the army that he has had the honour to receive from Her Majesty the Queen the appointment of Commander-in-Chief of the army in the Crimea. The Lieutenant-General, though deeply impressed with the responsibilities of the position in which he is placed, is most proud of the high and distinguished honour, and of the confidence thus reposed in him by his Sovereign.

It will be the Lieutenant-General's duty to endeavour to follow in the steps of his great predecessor, and he feels confident of the support of the Generals and of the Officers and soldiers in maintaining unimpaired the honour and discipline of this noble army.

(Signed)   JAMES SIMPSON.

Lieutenant-General Commanding.

Another General Order, published about that time by the new English Commander-in-Chief, is well worthy of notice, as expressing Her Majesty's sentiments on receiving the intelligence of the death of the late Lord Raglan. It was as follows:—

General After-Order.

July 18th, 1855.

Her Majesty the Queen has been pleased to command me to express to the army Her Majesty's deep and heartfelt grief at the loss of our gallant and excellent commander Lord Raglan, which has cast a gloom over the whole service.

Her Majesty further desires to assure her army of her earnest hope and confident trust that all will continue to do their duty, as they have hitherto so nobly done; and that Her Majesty will ever be as proud of her army as she has been, though their brave chief, who has so often led them to victory and glory, has been taken from them.

(Signed)   JAMES SIMPSON,

Lieutenant-General Commanding.

During the month of July the cholera still continued in the allied camps, though, apparently, the epidemic was of a lighter character than before, as the ratio of deaths to the admissions into hospital for treatment was not above half what it had been in the same month of 1854. The English Headquarters seemed to have a sort of fatality connected with it, for on July 10th and 11th two more victims were added to those who had lately fallen before this fearful scourge. They were Lieut.-Colonel Vico, French Commissioner attached to the English Headquarters, and Mr. Calvert, head of the Intelligence Department, or Secret Service of the army. Both were much liked by all the officers who associated with them — both were a great loss to the army. Colonel Vico had been indefatigable in his duties in keeping up the perpetual communications held between the English and French Headquarters ever since September 19th, 1854, when the first French Commissioner attached to Lord Raglan's Staff was taken prisoner near the Bulganak River. Lord Raglan had the highest opinion of him, and had more than once brought him before the notice of the English Minister of War, for the valuable assistance he had given him on every occasion. Mr. Calvert also had rendered many important services. He had formed a corps of guides, consisting mostly of Tartar chiefs, and had established communications with the principal towns in the Crimea. Much valuable information was obtained through his judicious arrangements, and latterly no body of troops of the enemy's army could move, or even shift their camps, without intelligence of the fact being immediately transmitted to the English Headquarters. His loss was one not easily replaced.

About this time two important changes took place in the English forces in the East, viz. Sir Stephen Lushington, who had been lately promoted to the rank of Admiral and K.C.B., being relieved from his command of the Naval Brigade engaged in the siege operations; and the Commissary-General of the army, Mr. Filder, being obliged to relinquish his important post in consequence of his ill-health, which rendered it desirable that he should return to England. The former was succeeded by Captain Hon. Henry Keppel, R.N., and the latter by Commissary-General Sir George Maclean.

Towards the close of the month General Canrobert was recalled to France by the Emperor Napoleon, chiefly, it was supposed, on account of his great popularity with the French troops, while General Pélissier was more disliked than ever, since the failure on June 18th; and it was thought beneficial to the service that the former should leave the Crimea, so that no comparisons should be made between him and his Commander-in-Chief.

During the month of July slow progress was made by the English towards the Redan; their advanced batteries were more heavily armed, the parapets strengthened and improved, and the trenches in every way rendered more capable of containing bodies of troops, under cover from the enemy's fire. The French also continued to approach the salient points of the enemy's line of defence. A parallel, with advanced trenches and numerous approaches from their old works, was made in front of the Mamelon against the Malakoff, and against the Little Redan. Their

Overleaf: Unfinished sketch on the banks of the Tchernaya during the races. The Russians were not allowed to cross, but they gathered on the river banks where the allied mob crowded to stare at them. Tobacco, knives, whips, etc., were thrown across and the races all but neglected. General Pélissier's stand is on the Mamelon which was crowded with people, flags and tents.

Greek Legion
unfinished sketch of the banks of the Tchema

The Russians were not allowed by their own authorit
when the allied mob crowded to stare at them or ex
across from side to side   and the races themselv
which was crowded with people, flags, tents &—   all

during the races

across but they gathered on the banks of the river

civilities — tobacco, knives, whips &. were thrown

but neglected — Pelissiers stand is on the mamelon

seemed poured out that day in the valley of the Tchernaia

trenches on the extreme right were much extended, from what had been the Ouvrages Blancs, towards the battery next the harbour of Sevastopol, which commanded Careening Bay. On the left the French continued to advance their siege-works; the salient angle of the Bastion du Mât was almost touched by the head of their sap. Another was made towards the Bastion Centrale, and by the beginning of August was within a few yards of the ditch in front of it. They greatly improved their trenches on the extreme left opposite the works of the Quarantine, and erected new batteries to subdue their fire.

During the whole of this time the losses of the Allies were very great, indeed probably greater than those incurred by the garrison of Sevastopol; for although but few heavy guns were fired on either side, the discharge of small arms was incessant. The French admitted at this period a daily loss of upwards of 100 men in the Mamelon alone, and their casualties amounted to no less than from 1200 to 1500 weekly, while, during the same interval of time, the English suffered in their small attacks a loss of upwards of 250 men. Certainly, some of these were caused by the numerous sorties made almost nightly by the garrison; but they rarely came out in large force, as, from the trenches of the Allies being by this time so close to the works of the town, no body of troops could leave them without being instantly discovered by the men on duty in the advanced parallels of the Allies. From their small numbers, they rarely effected any serious damage, and always lost a number of men when compelled to retire before the fire of the guards of the trenches.

This state of things continued until the middle of August, when the Russians, who for a long time had been preparing for the purpose, made a desperate attack on the rear of the allied position, which they confidently hoped would be successful, and thus compel the French and English commanders to raise the siege. The plan of attack arranged by Prince Gortschakoff showed the same cleverness as that of the battle of Inkermann by Prince Menschikoff; but, like it, failed in execution.

Before entering into the Russian plans, it may be as well to state the position occupied by the Allies. Three divisions of French infantry, those of Generals Herbillon, Camou, and Faucheux* together with three batteries of artillery, occupied the Fediukine Heights: these are some high ground situated on the left bank of the Tchernaya river, extending from the base of the plateau before Sevastopol to Tractir Bridge, and, in point of fact, separating the valley of Balaklava and the Tchernaya river. Further on, still on the left bank of the river, is some high ground, extending from near Tractir to opposite the village of Tchorgoun, known as Mount Hasfort. Here it was that the greater portion of the Sardinian army was posted, consisting of about 12,000 men and four batteries of artillery. Beyond them again were a portion of the Turkish troops, besides a large body of them being in reserve in rear of the Sardinian position. In the valley of Baidar was also stationed a mixed force of French and English cavalry and Turkish infantry, under General d'Allonville. The French had in reserve four regiments of Chasseurs d'Afrique and five troops of horse artillery, under the command of General Morris, stationed in rear of the Fediukine Heights. The larger portion of

* General Camou's division had been sent down to the Tchernaya a day or two after the taking of the Mamelon Vert, in which it had suffered so severely, and that of General Faucheux (who had succeeded on the death of General Mayran to the command of the division) had also been sent down shortly after the attack on June 18th, on which occasion it was almost cut to pieces. Consequently these two divisions were of small numerical strength.

the English cavalry, under the command of Lieut.-General Hon. Sir James Scarlett, still occupied the valleys of Kadikoi and Karani. These were brought up in reserve during the course of the battle, but took no active part in the engagement. The French force *engaged* consisted only of the three divisions of infantry placed on the Fediukine Heights, amounting to about 18,000 men and 42 guns. The Sardinian force engaged consisted only of one division of infantry, about 6000 men, and 18 guns.

The Russian force was divided into two portions, the right wing under command of aide-de-camp General Read, consisting of the 7th and 12th Divisions of infantry; and the left under Lieut.-General Liprandi, consisting of the 5th and 17th Divisions. Two other divisions of infantry were held in reserve, as was a large mass of cavalry; but these, from the nature of the ground, did not take any part in the battle. Their artillery consisted of 160 guns, the greater portion of which were brought into action. The Russians had in all 60,000 men, but of these not above 35,000 were engaged with the Allies.

It would appear that the object of the enemy was in the first instance to drive in the Sardinian outposts on the heights above Tchorgoun, on the right bank of the river, and then, establishing there a portion of their powerful artillery, to open on the Hasfort Heights opposite; under cover of these guns, General Liprandi's corps was then to advance down the valley of Schouliou, and, passing through Tchorgoun, attack the Sardinian position. General Read's corps was at the same time to advance from the foot of the Mackenzie Farm Heights towards the Fediukine Heights, and the Sardinians likewise fortified those of Hasfort. The brigade of this plan been carried out, and the Sardinian troops driven from the Hasfort heights, the enemy would then have gained a position which completely commanded the French camp on the Fediukine Heights, and would have compelled them to withdraw from that ground. What further movements the Russians would have made, it is impossible to say; but had their object been so far attained, they would at any rate have cut off the allied troops in the valley of Baidar from the main body of the armies on the plateau before Sevastopol. It has also been stated that, in the event of the Russian attack being successful, a sortie on an enormous scale would have been made from Sevastopol on the allied trenches. It is said that 40,000 men of the garrison were told off for this purpose.

It was on the evening of August 15th, that General Herbillon (who, as senior officer, had command of the French troops by the Tchernaya) received a despatch from General d'Allonville in the valley of Baidar, informing him that the Russian troops in that neighbourhood had been marching the whole day in the direction of the Mackenzie Farm Heights. General Herbillon does not appear to have been alarmed by this information, though he communicated it to General La Marmora, who thought it of so much importance that he kept the greater portion of his force under arms throughout the night. It should be stated that, for some time before, an attack by the enemy had been expected on a portion of the rear of the allied position. So much was this the case, that (in consequence of a report made by spies in the French service on August 12th, that an attack was to be made on the following day) all the troops along the Tchernaya were got under arms before daylight on the 13th; but finding that no movement was made by the Russians, the allied Generals considered that they had been falsely informed, and consequently perhaps relaxed some of their previous vigilance.

During the whole of the night of the 15th the Russian masses moved down from the Mackenzie Farm Heights to the stations appointed to them, and at the first break of day on the morning of August 16th the Sardinian outposts were driven in from off the heights on the right side of the Tchernaya, and had to retire over the river to their supports. This movement was favoured by a thick mist which hung over the low ground in the neighbourhood of the Tchernaya, and directly the firing commenced added not a little to its density. Simultaneously with the above, the main portion of the corps of General Liprandi pushed rapidly down the valley of Schouliou, and advanced on the village of Tchorgoun, taking by surprise the Sardinian picket, some few of whom were made prisoners. Immediately on the Sardinian outposts being driven in, the Russians placed their artillery on the commanding ground they had just taken, and opened fire upon the heights of Hasfort opposite. In the meantime, the remainder of General Liprandi's corps had assembled behind the village of Tchorgoun, and only waited for an order from Prince Gortschakoff to advance. General Read's corps was formed up in order of battle just out of gunshot of the Fediukine Heights, and a large number of guns were placed in advance of the troops on the most advantageous ground available. These opened at the break of day; and the first intimation the French received of the near neighbourhood of the enemy was their having round shot come bounding through their camp. All was hurry and confusion; the troops were, however, instantly turned out and got under arms.

The Russian Commander-in-Chief had stationed himself on the captured heights with his artillery, and from there made a careful reconnaissance of the allied position. From Prince Gortschakoff's account, it would appear that he had just decided to order the advance of the troops under General Liprandi, when he was startled by hearing a violent platoon firing from his right wing under General Read. In fact, he had attacked the Fediukine Heights with his two divisions. Prince Gortschakoff then states, 'It is impossible for me to explain the motive which determined that General (Read) to make the attack contrary to the adopted plan, without having received my orders to do so; for, very soon afterwards, he himself and the chief of his Staff (Major-General de Weimarn) were killed'. Thus, at the onset of the battle, the Russians appear to have made a fatal mistake.

General Herbillon had scarce got the French troops under arms, before the head of the 12th Russian Division rushed forward and captured the tête-du-pont, which had been thrown up some time before by the French to cover the bridge on the right bank of the river. The picket of infantry which occupied it could make but feeble resistance to the numbers that came against it. They fought as long as they were able, but were finally made prisoners by the enemy. Having captured the tête-du-pont, the troops then crossed the Tchernaya in heavy masses, some moving over the stone bridge, but by far the larger portion marching through the bed of the river, which at this part was nowhere more than knee-deep.

The French by this time had brought up some of their guns and opened a heavy fire upon the enemy, but were replied to with equal vigour by the Russian artillery covering the passage of their troops. They continued their advance in good order; but, before they could actually attack the Fediukine Heights, they had to surmount an obstacle far more difficult than the river; this was the aqueduct, which carried water into Sevastopol for the use of the docks, at a level of only a few feet above the

Above: The nymph of the Tchernaya. The Tartars claimed that a lady wandered about the valley at night and was seen towards morning to enter a tree trunk from which a serpent issued. Below: A dead Zouave inside the Malakoff. He had evidently arranged himself to die gracefully, a gladiatorial habit copied by the French troops from the Arabs.

bed of the Tchernaya. This aqueduct, although of but small dimensions (being not more than four feet deep and eight feet broad), from the fact of its banks being perfectly perpendicular, completely broke the formation of the Russian troops and caused considerable delay to the rear ranks, while those in front were scrambling up the bank on the further side, and this under a most galling fire from the French artillery. There was a bridge over this aqueduct, but, comparatively speaking, but few could cross over so narrow a space, especially as it was defended with great obstinacy by a French regiment, which had hastily been brought forward for that purpose. It, however, was forced to give way in a short time, as the enemy's numbers increased, and whole sections of men got over the aqueduct, and would consequently have taken the defenders of the bridge in flank and reverse. These obstacles being overcome, the Russians, with the greatest bravery, rushed on and endeavoured to take the western portion of the heights at the point of the bayonet. But the French infantry by this time were formed up along the crest of the hill, and poured so heavy a fire upon the advancing Russians, that it abruptly stopped their onward career. They then commenced a heavy musketry fire in answer to that of the French. This fusillade, which caused great loss on both sides, continued for upwards of half an hour, the Russians accumulating their men immediately in their rear, ready to take any opportunity for a more determined attack to gain the high ground in their front.

Immediately on the capture of the tête-du-pont, the 7th Russian Division was ordered to advance on their right, and, moving rapidly forward, crossed the Tchernaya and aqueduct somewhat lower down, and, shortly after, the 12th Division. They were met by a heavy fire from General Camou's division, which was drawn up to obstruct their further progress. Notwithstanding this, with great gallantry and determination the enemy pushed forward, though but slowly, and advanced half-way up the centre of the Fediukine Heights; but beyond that they were not able to penetrate, for the French troops at this moment were ordered to charge, and, headed by the gallant Zouaves, rushed down the hill with the utmost courage and impetuosity, literally overthrowing the advanced ranks of the Russian infantry. Some desperate fighting now ensued, but the enemy received so severe a check that they recoiled, and the French, still pressing on them, drove them back to the aqueduct. The scene of confusion was now past all description; the little canal was regularly choked with dead, wounded, and retreating men. Finally, the majority re-crossed the aqueduct, and, as the French soldiers were prudently not allowed to follow their example, the enemy somewhat re-formed and opened a heavy musketry fire on their opponents from the other side.

Directly after the successful charge of General Camou's division, the troops under General Faucheux were ordered to advance and do likewise, supported by a portion of General Herbillon's division. The troops moved on with great bravery, and drove the Russians back over the aqueduct. Both sides then contented themselves with pouring a heavy fire of musketry at one another. This continued for a considerable interval of time, when the Russians received a great reinforcement by the arrival of a portion of General Liprandi's corps, consisting of the 5th Division. For, upon Prince Gortschakoff seeing, at the commencement of the action, the great error General Read had made by beginning his attack against the Fediukine Heights before he had received orders to do so, he at once perceived the importance, indeed necessity, of supporting him, and abandoning for the present the attack against Mount Hasfort. He consequently gave orders that the 5th Division, belonging to General Liprandi's corps, should move round and support the columns of General Read. The distance was considerable, so that it was not until after the first repulse that they arrived at the scene of action. Prince Gortschakoff then ordered one brigade of the remaining division (17th) of General Liprandi's corps to be prepared to attack the Allies about midway between the village of Tchorgoun and Tractir Bridge; in fact, to advance up the opening into the valley of Balaklava, situated between Mount Hasfort and the most eastern Mamelon of the Fediukine Heights. A fresh general attack was then organized; the portion of the 17th Division crossed the Tchernaya and aqueduct with great resolution at the place indicated, and attempted to penetrate into the valley of Balaklava; seeing this endeavour on the part of the enemy, General La Marmora sent one of his divisions to stop their progress, and General Herbillon despatched reinforcements to the portion of General Faucheux's division that protected the high ground next to Mount Hasfort, down the side of which the Sardinian troops were already advancing on the enemy. A desperate conflict here ensued, in which the Sardinians, on this the first opportunity they had had during the war, displayed the greatest courage, and fought in a manner which fully established their reputation in the allied armies as being admirable troops. They finally drove the Russians headlong back over the aqueduct, and, following them up at the point of the bayonet, compelled them to recross the Tchernaya in the greatest confusion and disorder, making some prisoners. They inflicted very serious loss on the enemy, though that they sustained themselves was, comparatively speaking, trifling. They met with one sad misfortune; General Montevecchio was mortally wounded when leading on his brigade in their first advance against the Russians.

The attack made by the 7th and 12th Russian Divisions, supported by the 5th, on the Fediukine Heights, had also been totally unsuccessful; the enemy, although they again recrossed the aqueduct, never got further than the base of the heights, as the French poured down upon them with irresistible fury, which completely stopped any further advance. The same dreadful scene of bloodshed and death occurred as the Russians recrossed, for the last time, the aqueduct, never stopping until they had gained the further side of the Tchernaya river. Their loss at this time was greatly augmented by the tremendous fire of artillery which was brought to bear upon them. Seven French batteries were in full play, and, added to these, there had just before arrived one of the new heavy batteries of the English Royal Artillery, which, placed on the high ground occupied by the Sardinian troops, opened with most murderous effect upon the flank of the retiring Russian columns, the shot and shell ploughing through their ranks and mowing down their men by whole sections. General Pélissier had arrived in time to witness this last repulse of the Russians by the French and Sardinian troops; he had brought up with him very large reinforcements, consisting of the divisions of Generals Levaillant and Dulac, and the greater part of the Garde Impériale.

The Russian infantry, after they had retired over the Tchernaya, formed up again in order of battle, with a large force of cavalry on their right, just out of

Overleaf: The great breakfast given by General Lüders to the allied Generals.

souvenir of the great breakfast given by Gene...

horse shoe table

General Lüders   Marechal Pélissier

General Lamarmora   Sir W. Codrington

General MacMahon   the sturgeon   General Martinpr...

     General Wi...

ers to the 'allied Generals after the review on Mackenzie heights
the hetman of
the Cossacks

gunshot of the field-artillery of the Allies, and remained for a considerable space of time inactive, though their guns, which they still placed well to their front, kept up a heavy cannonade against the troops on the Tchernaya. They were replied to; but the duel of artillery apparently did not effect much on either side during this portion of the day. At first it was expected that the enemy intended to renew their attack; but, after waiting for upwards of two hours, they commenced their retreat towards the Mackenzie Farm Heights, their rear still covered by their artillery, while their flanks were protected by the heavy masses of cavalry. General La Marmora, on seeing the retreat of the Russians, immediately pushed forward a portion of his troops, re-occupied the village of Tchorgoun, and placed his outposts and pickets on the heights above it, which they had been compelled to abandon in the morning.

Some have questioned the propriety of General Pélissier not pursuing the Russians in their retreat; but, considering the enormous weight of artillery that covered the rear of the enemy, and which, as it retreated further towards Mackenzie Farm, always got the advantage of higher ground, it is not to be wondered at that General Pélissier should not wish to expose his troops to serious loss, only for the sake of possibly capturing a few of the enemy's guns.

About midday the last of the Russian troops regained the plateau of Mackenzie Farm Heights, and then commenced the laborious duty of collecting the wounded. The Russians, with great want of humanity, kept firing on the French fatigue parties employed in this duty, from their batteries on the edge of the heights, between Mackenzie Farm and Inkermann, which completely overlooked a portion of the plain.

Thus terminated the battle of the Tchernaya, one alike glorious to the French and Sardinians, while it was most disastrous to the Russians. From all accounts their losses appear to have been enormous: three Generals killed and seven wounded; 24 officers killed and 78 wounded; 3329 men killed and 4700 wounded. Of these the French took into their ambulances, from those found lying on the field, 38 officers and 1626 men. The French lost 19 officers killed and 61 wounded; 172 men killed, 146 missing, and 1163 wounded. The Sardinians lost 65 killed and 135 wounded, officers and men. So the total losses in the battle were as follows:—

Russian casualties	..	..	..	..	..	8141
Allied ditto	..	..	..	..	..	1761
						9902

It took two days for the French to bury the dead on the Tchernaya.

On the 17th General Pélissier wrote a letter to Prince Gortschakoff, expostulating with him for allowing the Russian batteries to fire upon his men who were employed in collecting the wounded and burying the dead, and informing him that, if he wished, he might send parties to bury his own dead. This offer Prince Gortschakoff accepted, and on the following day no less than 2000 unarmed infantry, under the protection of a herd of Cossacks, came down for the purpose. Prince Gortschakoff, in his reply, stated that the Mackenzie batteries did not open upon the burying parties, until the French sharpshooters had fired upon some of the Russians who were endeavouring to carry off their wounded.

It was generally reported in England, after the battle of the Tchernaya, and many letters were written in the public journals to the effect, that the English

1. Soupe à la Tortue
   Chti vert, à la russe.
2. Coulebiaka & Rasteguai.
3. Rosbif, sauce aux truffes.
   Boujénina, sauce-piquante aux oignons.
4. Esturgeon, à la Russe.
5. Salmi de gibier, aux truffes & champignons.
6. Légumes, différents.
   Pouding au sabaion
7. Veau, perdreaux, canards, bécasses,
   cailles et ortolans.
   Salade, concombres, champignons marinés
8. Moskovik et gelée aux framboises.

   Fruits.
Thé, Café
   Liqueurs & Cognac.

The Menu of the breakfast given by General Lüders "stolen" from the table and kept as a souvenir.

surgeons did not render any assistance to the French medical department, whose field-hospitals were naturally in a very crowded state after the bloody action on August 16th. This was a great libel upon the English surgeons, for at the close of the engagement several of them, of their own accord, went to the scene of contest, and moreover Dr. Hall (head of the medical department) sent out a number of surgeons to attend especially to the Russian wounded. Nothing could exceed the untiring exertions of these gentlemen; as on all similar occasions, they practised their humane though dreadful task with the greatest consideration for the sufferings of the unfortunate men they attended. The medical department, like every other branch of the service, has been at different times much abused in the English newspapers. Doubtless there have been exceptional cases; but more than once these have arisen through the misconduct of civilians who have been attached temporarily to the medical staff of the army. As an instance of this, it may be mentioned that a letter appeared in *The Times* newspaper, written from the camp on June 20th, describing the unprovided state of the hospitals and the want of care shown by the military surgeons to the wounded after the unfortunate repulse of June 18th. This letter was of so false and scandalous a nature, that a court of inquiry was ordered to investigate the matter. It was proved utterly untrue, and the man who wrote it, named Bakewell, who had been attached temporarily to the medical staff, was most properly turned out of the service.*

During the remainder of the month of August the allied Generals were in constant apprehension of another attack, of even more formidable nature than the last on the Tchernaya. This was originated by information they received from spies and others, that very large reinforcements had joined the enemy on the plateau of Mackenzie—it was said, two entire divisions of Grenadiers who had lately arrived from Russia, mustering about 24,000 men. It was therefore thought advisable to strengthen the allied position in the neighbourhood of the Tchernaya. The French accordingly constructed considerable earthworks and batteries on the Fediukine Heights, and the Sardinians likewise fortified those of Hasfort. The brigade of Highlanders was sent down from the front by General Simpson, and encamped near the ruined village of Kamara, so as to support the right of the Sardinians, and also more completely to enclose the valley of Balaklava.

---

* The following order was issued by General Simpson on the subject : —
General Order, 3rd August, 1855. — A letter having appeared in *The Times* newspaper, dated Camp before Sevastopol, June 20th, containing charges of the gravest nature against medical officers of this army, a court of inquiry was directed to examine into the truth of the allegations set forth in it.

The officers composing this court, after the most minute and patient investigation into the whole of the circumstances connected with the treatment of the wounded on June 18th, declare that this letter is 'calculated grossly to mislead the public, and to cast blame on those to whom praise was justly due'. In this opinion the Commander of the Forces concurs, after a careful perusal of the evidence. It appears that Acting-Assistant-Surgeon Bakewell is the author of this letter. He is therefore informed that his further services are dispensed with, and his name is struck off the strength of the army from this date.

Zouaves invited to a party. Above left: "Wonder what this is here . . . is it a plant? A beast . . . no, it's a salad." Above right: One of the Zouaves finds that three of his companions are having to turn in endless circles at the double. Below right: "Is that all you have to carry? Where are we going sergeant?" "You are going to a superb country . . .".

Zouaveries N° 1

Qu'est ce que c'est donc que cette plante là?
C'est il bête! c'est de la salade —

Le Zouave Abdel Kader Ben Bonichon, invité par trois de ses alliés à passer la soirée au camp Anglais trouve ses malheureux amis décrivant des cercles infinis au pas gymnastique — Le sergent lui fait comprendre que cela doit durer quinze jours comme cela — Bonichon s'adresse à un officier pour savoir s'il n'y aurait aucun arrangement possible avec le gouvernement Britannique —

rien que ça sur le dos et puis un fagot par homme! où's que nous allons donc sergent?

vous allez dans la Dobrrz-uska Jeune homme, pays superbe où's qu'il n'y a que des grenouilles il vous y faudra manger votre merle et le gouvernement vous fait porter du bois pour le rôtir

As regards the siege, after the battle of the Tchernaya, it advanced slowly but surely. A portion of the French sap against the Malakoff had at that time arrived within 80 yards of the ditch; but it was found impossible to proceed farther until certain guns which bore upon it were silenced, as they each day destroyed the work of the previous night. For this purpose it was decided that, as some of the advanced English batteries could bring a flanking fire to bear upon these guns in the Malakoff, they should open on the 17th. Accordingly on the morning of that day the greater portion of the English batteries opened once more upon the town. As the English were totally unassisted by the French, who, through some blunder, appear not to have been prepared, the Russians were enabled to concentrate their fire on the English advanced trenches, and caused us severe loss in officers and men. Two valuable officers, Hammett and Oldfield, both of whom had distin- guished themselves, were killed on that day; the former was a Commander in the Royal Navy and had charge of one of the sailors' batteries, and the latter was a Captain in the Royal Artillery. But, in spite of our losses, the object of the fire was attained, for the guns which bore on the French sap were completely silenced, and they were consequently enabled to proceed with their work during the ensuing night and following day.

It was not until the beginning of August that the engineers discovered that the Russians were constructing a regular bridge across the harbour from Fort Nicholas, on the south side, to near Fort Michael, on the north. For some months previous something of the sort had been suspected, but no one imagined that so gigantic a work could have been executed in the manner it was. After the failure of the enemy on August 16th against the rear of the allied position, they appear to have been indefatigable in their exertions to get the bridge completed, and by the 27th it was practicable for the passage of troops, carts, etc.

It was during the night of the 27th that an unfortunate catastrophe occurred to the French. Their magazine in the centre of the Mamelon was blown up by a shell from the enemy: no less than 15,000 pounds of gunpowder were exploded, and upwards of 150 French soldiers were killed and wounded by it. A few English soldiers in the nearest trenches were also injured by the falling of beams, etc., which were thrown into the air. Considering the number of troops the French had in the neighbourhood of the Mamelon, it is wonderful that their loss was not greater. The English batteries immediately opened fire on the Malakoff and Redan, so as to anticipate any sortie or attack the Russians might make, on seeing the confusion into which the French were naturally thrown by the terrific explosion. This misfortune delayed the assault of the town a few days, as the immense quantity of ammunition which had been destroyed had to be replaced before the batteries re- opened their final bombardment. It was impossible to wait much longer; and indeed there was no object to be gained by so doing. The French had now pushed the head of their sap, so that it actually touched the abattis round the Malakoff, and they were not more than 30 paces from its ditch. Besides this, they could distinctly hear the Russian miners at work, and consequently anticipated that no great length of time would elapse before these mines would be exploded against them. The English had advanced their trenches as far as practicable towards the Redan: they were now 196 yards from its salient angle; closer than that it was impossible to go for two reasons—first, that in any nearer approach they would have been completely enfiladed by the fire from the Malakoff; secondly, that the rocky nature of the ground made it a work of the greatest difficulty, if not impossibility. Besides these reasons, the Russians had commenced the construction of a more complete inner line of defence, and had already placed a certain number of guns in their new works, so that altogether it was decided that a speedy assault was imperative.* Accordingly, on September 3rd, a grand Council of War of the allied Generals was held at the French Headquarters to decide upon the final plan of attack on Sevastopol. On this occasion, unlike any former, Generals Bosquet and Niel were most anxious for the assault to take place immediately; whereas the French Commander-in-Chief appeared rather to dread the responsibility, and wished to delay it for a few days, until the arrival of a large number of mortars and a quantity of ammunition which were shortly expected from France. It should be mentioned that the French ammunition was so exhausted that they had only sufficient for five days *slow* firing. The English were better off; they had sufficient for ten days *quick* firing in their batteries and artillery parks.

The arrangements for the assault were as follows:—from the French left attack there were to be two objects of assault, the Bastion Centrale and the Bastion du Mât; the former was to be attacked by the division of General Levaillant, which, if successful, was immediately to be followed by the division of General d'Autemarre, which was to attack the Bastion du Mât on its right flank and rear. A brigade of Sardinians under General Cialdini were to be held in reserve. These two assaults were under the orders of General de Salles, commanding the 1st Corps d'Armée. The signal of assault was to be the French flag floating above the Malakoff, so that it was not to take place until that formidable work had been captured. The English assault, as before, was to be only from the right attack; it was to consist of one column of 1000 men to attack the salient angle of the Redan. It was to be preceded by 100 men of the Rifle Brigade and 100 men of the 3rd Regiment (Buffs), to pick off the enemy's gunners, and 320 men carrying scaling ladders. These were to be taken in equal numbers from the Light and 2nd Divisions, which were to form the staple of the troops in the advanced trenches. They were to be under the command of Lieut.-General Sir William Codrington and Lieut.-General Markham. The Highland Division, under Lieut.-General Sir Colin Campbell, was to be placed in the rear trenches of the right attack in reserve (having been brought up for that purpose from their camp at Kamara). The 1st Division, under Lieut.-General Lord Rokeby,

---

* It may be as well here to state that the English force of all arms in the Crimea on the 1st of September amounted to 48,024 rank and file and 8986 horses. Of these, the Royal Artillery employed in the siege and with the field-batteries amounted to 6778 rank and file.

Overleaf: Battle of the Tchernaya. To the left are the Fediukine Heights on which the French allowed the Russians to get two-thirds of the way up the hill before they charged. The attack was a most determined one, notwithstanding that the Russians had been up all night and had had to scramble under fire through a river and a deep canal which can be seen on the right of the picture. French and English cavalry mass down the valley under the Fediukine Heights. In the distance (in the centre) is the conical cliff on which was situated the Russian battery called Bilboquet. The Russian artillery occupied a low ridge of ground on the other side of the Tchernaya. In the distance under Bilboquet are the Russian cavalry of which there were 48 squadrons. The attacking columns were formed behind the undulations of ground which extended from the Mackenzie Ridge. At the rear is the Mamelon where the Sardinian forward post was ousted by the Russians after a most gallant resistance.

was to remain under arms in front of the English camp, in readiness to give support if required. The 3rd Division, under Major-General Sir. W. Eyre, and the 4th Division, under Lieut.-General Sir H. Bentinck, were to be placed in the left attack, to support the right if necessary. The signal of assault was to be given when the French had gained possession of the Malakoff.

From the French Inkermann attack, there were to be three objects of attack, viz., the Malakoff, the Little Redan, and the curtain which connected them together. The left column, to attack the Malakoff, was to consist of General M'Mahon's division, having in reserve the Zouaves of the Garde Impériale and a brigade of General Camou's division, which was to be brought up for that purpose from the Tchernaya. The centre column, to attack the curtain which connected the Malakoff with the Little Redan, was to consist of the division of General La Motterouge; the right column, to attack the Little Redan, was to consist of General Dulac's division, supported by the Chasseurs of the Garde Impériale and a brigade of General d'Aurelle's division. Each column was to be accompanied by 60 sappers of the Corps du Génie, 300 men with scaling ladders, etc., and 50 artillerymen to spike the enemy's guns, or turn them as might be found necessary. The three columns of assault were to be under the direction of General Bosquet; the whole of the remainder of the Garde Impériale were to be placed in the trenches immediately in rear of the Mamelon, ready to advance to give support to General M'Mahon's division on its attack on the Malakoff, as it was determined at any sacrifice to capture this stronghold. There was to be no signal for attack, but the assault was to take place precisely at midday. It was finally settled that the allied batteries should open fire on the morning of September 5th, and the grand assault take place on the 8th. It was also agreed that several ships-of-the-line of the allied fleets should engage the Quarantine Fort, by which means it was hoped that the enemy would be prevented from pouring an enfilading fire against the column of French troops which was to assault the Bastion Centrale, as a portion of the guns on the said fort swept the ground between the French trenches and the works of the town. This was to take place at 12 noon. Such were the arrangements made at the Council of War on the 3rd.

On the morning of the 5th the allied batteries opened with a tremendous roar, and continued firing throughout the day. The batteries of the French left attack were ordered to fire as rapidly as possible, whereas those in the English and French Inkermann attacks were to fire steadily, and reserve all their energies for the day of the assault.*

The enemy appeared completely paralysed by the severe fire poured upon them, and scarcely answered at all. Some said they were only reserving their fire and keeping their artillerymen under cover, and were waiting until the assault should arrive, when every gun would be found serviceable, and their batteries swarming with artillerymen. During the day the enemy made a reconnaissance in the neighbourhood of Tchorgoun, and some little skirmishing went on between their

*The number of guns that opened from the allied batteries on September 5th were as follows: — Old French attack, composed of 49 batteries, containing 332 pieces; French Inkermann attack, composed of 34 batteries, containing 267 pieces. Total, 83 French batteries, containing 599 pieces of ordnance.

English attacks, 32 batteries, containing 204 pieces of ordnance.

Grand total of the Allies, 115 batteries, containing 803 pieces of ordnance.

advanced parties and the Sardinian outposts. The force was consider-able—estimated at 15,000 men. It was probably more with a view of making the Allies fancy that they intended to attack the rear again, in the hope to thus preventing them from bringing up reinforcements from their rear, to assist during the assault on the town.

On the night of the 5th, a large Russian frigate was seen about 9 p.m. to break forth in flame, and was burnt to the water's edge by midnight. During the whole of the 6th and 7th the bombardment continued without intermission, the Russians replying but rarely, and then in the most feeble manner. On the afternoon of the last-named day a Russian line-of-battle ship caught fire, and burnt fiercely all through the following night: the whole harbour and town of Sevastopol were lit up by this great conflagration. Excitement and confidence in the approaching assault were at the highest pitch in the allied camps. The burning of this ship was looked upon as an omen of disaster to the enemy. Since the commencement of the cannonade the enemy had used the bridge across the harbour night and day: thousands of carts passed over from the south to the north side loaded with things, and returned empty for more. The losses of the Russians during these days of the bombardment was something quite prodigious; it averaged from 1000 to 1500 daily.*

*Mortars.				Guns.					Total
13-Inch.	10-Inch.	8-Inch.	5½-Inch.	Lancaster.	68-Pndrs.	32-Pndrs.	10-Inch.	8-Inch.	
34	27	10	20	2	6	61	7	37	204

On the evening of the 7th the final instructions were issued by General Simpson in a long divisional After-Order to his Generals.**

The morning of September 8th broke gloomy enough; throughout the night the weather had been boisterous, and with the return of day this rather increased than otherwise, and the whole face of the plateau was covered with clouds of dust. Moreover, the thermometer had gone down, and the temperature after the late hot weather felt bitterly cold. Soon after 8 a.m. several squadrons of cavalry marched up to the front, and were posted in a line of videttes along the ridge in front of the English camps, to keep back camp-followers and others from collecting in groups

---

* According to the statement as it appeared in the *Invalide Russe*, the Russian losses in Sevastopol, from August 17th to September 7th, were as follows:—August 17th, 1500 men; from the 18th to the 21st, 1000 men daily = 4000 men; and from August 22nd to September 4th, from 500 to 600 men every twenty-four hours, say = 7700 men. Their loss on September 5th, 6th and 7th was 4000; consequently the total number of killed and wounded in the garrison of Sevastopol, from August 17th to September 7th inclusive, was no less than 17,200, *not* including the artillerymen who perished at their guns. This statement is the admission of Prince Gortschakoff, Commander-in-Chief of the Russian army.

** Vide Appendix C.

Overleaf: The blowing up of Fort Nicholas. 50,000 kilos of powder were distributed in 14 mines along the whole length of the building.

on the heights and thus drawing down the fire from the enemy. About the same time a number of gunboats and mortar vessels belonging to the allied fleets opened fire upon the Quarantine Fort from Streletska Bay, where they had been previously placed for that purpose. They continued throughout the day firing with great steadiness and precision, and must have caused the Russians very severe loss. The weather was so boisterous that it was quite impossible for the line-of-battle ships to attempt engaging the sea-defences of Sevastopol. It was not until past 7 a.m (when the allied armies were under arms) that the Light and 2nd Divisions moved down to the trenches and took up the positions assigned to them; this took a very long time, as some of the approaches did not admit of more than two men going abreast in comparative safety. Every man carried with him two days rations cooked, as it was thought possible that we might have to occupy a portion of the town a day or two after carrying the principal works.

About 10.30 a.m. General Simpson and the Headquarters Staff entered the approaches of the left attack, and took up their station in the 2nd parallel to witness the assault. Lieut.-General Sir Harry Jones, commanding the Royal Engineers, was in so weak a state that he was unable to walk. He was still suffering from the effects of the wound he received on June 18th, and which for some time after had seriously injured his health; but being most anxious to be present at the assault, he was carried down to the trenches on a stretcher.

General Pélissier entered the French Inkermann attack, and placed himself in the Mamelon shortly before midday. Up to near that time the fire of artillery had been more rapid and heavier, if possible, than it had ever been before; it then gradually ceased, as had been more or less the custom lately, in consequence of the usual intense heat at that period of the day; and although on this occasion the weather was cold, still it was thought that a partial cessation of the fire would be calculated to lead the enemy into the belief that no assault was to take place. These calculations appear to have been verified, for, at 12 noon precisely, the French rushed out of their most advanced trench in front of the Malakoff, and, in less time than it takes to describe, had reached the ditch. A moment later and the ladders were thrown across, their ends resting on each side of the ditch, thus forming a sort of bridge, and a few planks being then thrown on them made it a good crossing for any number of troops. They rushed on, and, literally within three minutes from the time of starting, the head of the column had entered the Malakoff. The enemy were completely taken by surprise; the few behind the parapet facing the French fired off their muskets, and never attempted to stop the progress of their invaders, but retired behind the traverses, and there began their first attempt to hold this formidable work. But it was now too late; the French came pouring on in immense numbers, and, in a short quarter of an hour, were in possession of the key of Sevastopol.

To give an idea of how completely taken by surprise the Russians were, it may be mentioned that some of the Zouaves (who, as usual, were among the first) penetrated into a bomb-proof chamber, where they found the Russian General commanding the Malakoff at dinner! as well as a great many officers employed in the same agreeable manner, who threw up their hands in despair on seeing the French soldiers.

Immediately the French gained possession, a strong working party of sappers commenced closing the gorge in rear of the Malakoff, and, in digging a trench across it, came upon the wires which were there for the purpose of exploding the mines from the exterior. These were instantly cut, rendering the mines useless.

Simultaneous with the advance on the Malakoff, the divisions of Generals La Motterouge and Dulac rushed forward against their objects of attack, viz. the curtain and the Little Redan next to it. As at the Malakoff, the French troops, from being within 30 yards of the enemy's batteries, arrived up to them in less than a minute's time, and sprang over the parapet despite the resistance which was made to them — for here, although the Russian force was not large, they were not taken by surprise. However, the Russians speedily brought up enormous reinforcements, besides no less than 20 pieces of field-artillery, which opened on the French columns at short range with grape, and caused them enormous loss. In addition to this, all the guns in the Russian batteries on the north side that were within range, and several of the ships and steamers in harbour, opened upon the French as soon as their object became apparent. One French regiment (49th of the Line) was seized with panic and retired to their trenches, from which all the exhortations of their officers would not induce them to return. The rest of the French troops who had penetrated the Little Redan, after the most gallant efforts to hold what they had gained, were compelled to retire to their trenches, thus leaving the column next to them (General La Motterouge's division) exposed to the flank fire of the Little Redan. They were, consequently, unable to continue in possession of that portion of the enemy's works, which they had captured with so much bravery, and were forced to retire. General Bosquet, on seeing this, ordered up two of the batteries of field-artillery which had been placed in reserve. The French had made an admirable arrangement, before the assault, for the passage of gun-carriages. An opening of some 50 yards had been made in all the parapets, so that, if required, troops could be brought down in formation, as well as artillery: these were blinded by gabions, and a certain number of men were placed on each side ready to knock them over when the opening should be required. Down this sort of road the two field-batteries came, and, on arriving close up to the defences of the town, they opened with grape upon the mass of Russian infantry which were collected together. This fire caused the enemy considerable loss, but at the same time almost all the French artillerymen were killed or wounded at their guns.

About 12.10 p.m., General Pélissier, seeing that General M'Mahon's division had gained thorough possession of the Malakoff, ordered the signal (that of the French flag put up in the Mamelon) to be made, and thus acquaint General Simpson with his success. The English Commander-in-Chief, upon seeing this, instantly ordered a flight of four rockets to be fired from close to his position. This was to attract the attention of the commanding officers of the columns of assault. Immediately after General Simpson put up the signal for the advance, which was a square white flag with the red cross of St. George, and directly the English rushed over the parapets and advanced towards the Redan. The ladder and storming parties dashed on in a very gallant manner against the salient of the Redan, under a heavy fire of grape, and the foremost of them got over the ditch, up the parapet, and into the body of the work with wonderful rapidity, especially when it is

Overleaf: The chiefs of the allied Staffs meet the Russian officers to negotiate the terms of the armistice at Tractir.

considered that they had to traverse over 200 yards. But there, poor fellows! they only met with a soldier's death! Despite these difficulties the storming parties still continued to arrive at the salient of the Redan, but numbers of officers and men were killed and wounded on their way towards it. Brigadier-General Shirley, who led the stormers of the Light Division, was severely contused in the face immediately on leaving our trenches, and had to retire; Colonel Handcock and Major Welsford, 97th Regiment, who had important commands, were both struck down — the former mortally wounded and the latter shot dead. Brigadier-General Van Straubenzee and Colonel Unett (19th Regiment) fell also at this time, the latter mortally wounded.

The senior officer who now remained with the stormers was Colonel Windham, who was acting Brigadier, and commanded the 2nd Division column of assault. He behaved throughout in the most gallant and determined manner; on arriving in the Redan he at once saw the difficulties to be overcome. The body of the work was entirely open to the rear, and had only a sort of covered way, or light parapet, across the gorge. Behind this, those of the enemy who had been driven away were standing firing. Large reinforcements had come up, and a mass of Russian infantry was now formed immediately in rear of this parapet. The enemy poured a most galling fire upon the salient angle, where the British troops were for the most part assembled; numbers of the poor fellows were dropping, killed or wounded, every instant. Colonel Windham at once saw that the only thing to be done was to form the men up, and take the parapet at the point of the bayonet; but the difficulty was to get the troops into any sort of formation for that purpose. So many officers had been killed or disabled, that Colonel Windham had to depend to a great extent on his own exertions in collecting together the troops, who were standing up behind the traverses firing at the enemy; but as fast as he got any number of men in formation, they were shot down by the terrible fire poured upon them from the Russians in rear of the parapet. Many officers most brilliantly distinguished themselves by the gallant manner in which they stood out in the open, in order to induce their men to follow; but, among other difficulties, the men one and all believed that the Redan was mined. The English newspapers had done their best to din the fact into their ears ever since the first bombardment. This, doubtless, added to the disinclination to advance; but the real fact of the matter was, that there were not enough men. It could hardly be expected that a mere handful would stand up in the open to be shot at, while others were being got together and formed up. There was no place available for this, except inside the work, and there they were exposed to the terrible fire of the enemy behind the often-mentioned parapet. Colonel Windham despatched no less than three officers to General Codrington, begging him to send up reinforcements *in formation*; but none of these officers ever arrived — they were either killed or wounded.

Colonel Windham, seeing that it was hopeless waiting for reinforcements, determined at last to go himself and beg them of General Codrington. He was more fortunate than his messengers, for he arrived untouched; but before the reinforcement which he was going to bring up got out of our trenches, the few untouched men that were left in the Redan were driven out by the overwhelming mass of Russians which charged down upon them. It was then utterly useless attempting to assault the work again, without regularly reorganizing the columns, and this, from the crowded state of the trenches and from the number of wounded men being carried to the rear, was quite impossible. Accordingly, to the bitter disappointment of the British, the assault on the Redan was obliged to be given up for the time being, and General Simpson arranged with Sir Colin Campbell that the Highland Division should attack on the following morning. He then ordered the whole of the guns that could be brought to bear, to fire upon the Redan, which was accordingly done with frightful loss to the enemy.

The French fared no better than the English in their left attack. Immediately on the signal being given by General Pélissier in the Mamelon (which, like that of the English, was the French flag hung out), the first column to assault (General Levaillant's division) sprang out of their trenches, and advanced with great bravery towards the Bastion Centrale; but they were met by a most overwhelming fire from the enemy's batteries, both of heavy ordnance and small arms, before they had left their trenches a dozen yards. It appeared that the enemy were expecting an assault, and consequently had their batteries manned, and immense numbers of men in reserve. So great was the loss to the French on their first onset, that reserves had immediately to be brought up, but, as in the English attack, the trenches were so crowded with troops and with the wounded being carried to the rear, that it was quite impossible to move them out in anything like formation. Generals Rivet and Breton set noble examples to their men by rushing over the parapets, and calling upon the men to follow, but both were instantly killed, and, seeing this, the troops got disheartened, and nothing would induce them to leave their trenches and face the awful fire to which they would then have been exposed. The confusion now became general; from the frightful number of men that had been wounded, the advanced trenches soon became completely clogged; all the Generals commanding the storming columns had been either killed or wounded, consequently no orders were given, and, after fruitless efforts to cross the ditch and enter the work, the French were finally compelled to retire and give up the assault. All their guns in the left attack then opened on the enemy's defences. General de Salles commenced arrangements for a fresh assault, and in the meantime sent off word to General Pélissier of his failure, but the French Commander-in-Chief, having gained the Malakoff, considered that it would be a useless sacrifice of life attacking anew the Bastion Centrale or the Little Redan.

It was now about 3 p.m., and between that time and nightfall the Russians made repeated attacks upon the Malakoff, but the French were so firmly established in it, that, although the Russians brought up enormous masses of men, and attacked it with a courage amounting almost to ferocity, they were never able even to obtain a temporary footing in the great work they had lost. In fact, the very strength of the Malakoff on every side, and its admirable construction, which gave a flanking fire to each face, prevented the enemy from retaking it. Had the gorge been open, and its rear defences weaker than those in front, it is not improbable that the Russians might have recaptured it with their legions; as it was, all their efforts were utterly useless, and every fresh attack only added to their enormous loss of killed and wounded. After nightfall no further attempt was made.

Overleaf: After long and fierce battles, a meeting of a group of officers of all nations during the armistice discussions.

During the afternoon the French had a considerable loss from an explosion that took place near the Malakoff. It was never ascertained how this occurred, and for some minutes afterwards great apprehensions were felt that it was only preliminary to the Malakoff itself being blown into the air; for, although the French had discovered, shortly after they entered the work, four wires which doubtless were connected with the mines under it, they were still not altogether sure that there might not be other wires which as yet had escaped their observation. These four wires were found out in a curious manner. When the French had captured the Malakoff, and had killed, wounded, or driven out, as they thought, the whole of the garrison, it was discovered that a strong picket of men were still inside the ruins of what had been the celebrated Malakoff Tower, the lower part of which had a passage running round inside, with the exterior wall loopholed. Through these the Russians inside fired upon the French, and killed and wounded several officers and men. As the only entrance was strongly blocked up from the inside, it was very difficult to check this fusillade; but the French engineers got some gabions, and piled them before the loopholes, and then set them on fire. This was to choke the inmates with smoke, and thus compel them to surrender. It instantly had the desired effect; for the Russians came out and gave themselves up as prisoners. The gabions continued to burn fiercely, so much so that the engineer officers became alarmed lest the falling sparks might ignite one of the expense magazines which were placed at intervals in the interior parapet of the work. Orders were therefore given for them to be immediately extinguished; but this was no easy task. The sappers were then ordered to dig a trench and throw up the earth so as to put out the flames; this was done, and, while digging, they discovered two wires, which it was naturally supposed communicated with mines. They were instantly cut, and shortly after two more were discovered. This circumstance saved the Malakoff and its numerous French garrison from utter destruction by the enemy.

Soon after dark several conflagrations burst out in the town, and it became evident that these were not done by accident or from the effects of the fire from the allied batteries, but from deliberate pre-arrangement. About 11 p.m. some Russian magazines, immediately in rear of the Little Redan, blew up, and they appeared to be only preliminary to others of a more formidable nature. About 12 noon, an engineer officer crept quietly up to the Redan, and, entering, found it deserted. This being communicated to Sir Colin Campbell, he directed parties to go in and withdraw as many of our wounded as possible, which was immediately done. Explosions then became frequent, but it was not until 4 a.m on the 9th instant that the first of the magazines blew up. This was the Redan—the report was so great that it shook the earth, and made those who had lain down in the different camps for a short interval to rest, start out of their sleep and rush to the front to ascertain what had happened, but they could only see before them the doomed city a sheet of flame. At 4.45 a.m. another great explosion took place; this was the Bastion du Mât, and it was immediately followed by those of the Garden Batteries.

As morning broke on the burning town, it was found that during the night it had been totally evacuated by the enemy, and Sevastopol at length was in the possession of the Allies. The manner in which the Russians evacuated the town did them immense credit; indeed, it may be looked upon as one of the best-executed movements during the war. Over the floating bridge, within a few days of the fall of the town, immense quantities of ammunition were carried, and during the night of the 8th from 30,000 to 40,000 human beings had passed over it in safety; so nicely timed were the Russian arrangements, that at the first gleam of day on September 9th the bridge was broken up, its different portions disconnected and towed over to the northern shore of the harbour, while the rear column of the Russian garrison could be seen making its way up from the water's edge to the plateau above – a proof of how lately they must have crossed over. The first thing which attracted observation was the absence of the Russian line-of-battle ships; they had been sunk during the night.

The next great incident in this memorable day was the total destruction of Fort Paul, close to the dockyard; it blew up with a terrific roar, which shook the country all round, and, when the smoke had cleared away, nothing remained of the handsomest and best constructed fort in Sevastopol but a huge heap of smouldering ruins. Frequent explosions of small mines and magazines continued to take place in the course of the day, and consequently a cordon of sentries was placed all round Sevastopol, to prevent, as far as possible, the troops and stragglers from entering the town. Nevertheless, numbers managed to evade the sentries, and wandered among the burning ruins, seeking for what little plunder might remain.

The town continued to burn fiercely all through the day and night of the 9th, when, from want of ignitable matter, the fire gradually subsided, and no building in that vast city remained intact except one huge barrack near the Dockyard Creek. It was not until the afternoon of the 10th that the reason for this was discovered, when it appeared that the enemy had used it as their great temporary hospital, before the removal of their wounded to the north side of the harbour. No less than 2000 human beings, the majority shockingly wounded, and many having undergone amputation, had been collected within the walls of this building during the 8th of September, and had been abandoned to their fate on the evacuation of the town by the Russians. It was discovered by a steamer coming across the harbour with a flag of truce, and begging to be allowed to remove their wounded. About 500 of these poor creatures were found alive (these were given over to the Russians), upwards of 1500 were corpses. Who shall describe the torture and agony these unfortunate men must have suffered during the 48 hours they had been lying there? In one immense underground cellar 700 bodies were lying in a state of rapid decomposition. Nothing could exceed the horrors of this charnel-house. Captain Vaughan, of the 90th Regiment, was found amongst the dead and dying, and several English and French soldiers, who must have been glad, poor fellows! to be rescued from such a mass of putrefaction, and to find themselves cared for by friends. In another portion of the building 200 coffins were found, with a corpse in each, ready for burial; they were said to be those of officers who had fallen during the last bombardment. How they could find means or time to encase each body in this manner is inexplicable! Perhaps this last fact speaks better than any other of the frightful losses the enemy must have sustained.

It may be as well here to state the losses on both sides on the memorable September 8th. The following is taken, as regards the Russians, from Prince

Overleaf: Promotions, decorations and rewards were given to the successful Generals of the allied armies following the fall of Sevastopol. In the centre is Lord Stratford distributing the Grand Order of the Bath.

Clem   D. of Newcastle Rose Pelissier Simpson   Ld. Stratford   Barnard
           La Marmora   George Paget   Steele

Colin Campbell   Gen.l Eyre   Sir H Bentinck
                  Sir H Airey
Gen.l Scarlett

Gortschakoff's account, as published in the *Invalide Russe*, but it is generally supposed to be much understated.

	OFFICERS.			MEN.			TOTAL.
	Killed.	Wounded.	Missing.	Killed.	Wounded.	Missing.	
Russian	59	279	24	2,625	6,964	1,739	11,690
French	145	254	10	1,489	4,259	1,400	7,557
English	29	129	1	361	1,914	176	2,610
	233	662	35	4,475	13,137	3,315	21,857

Thus the capture of Sevastopol cost (deducting the missing) between 18,000 and 19,000 killed and wounded men, and these returns, as before mentioned — *certainly* as regards the Russians, and *probably* as regards the French — are understated.

On September 12th, Colonel Windham was appointed English Commandant of Sevastopol, as far as regarded the portion of the town known as the Karabelnaia; at the same time, General Bazaine was appointed French Commandant. The 3rd Regiment (Buffs) and 500 of the Royal Artillery were ordered into the town as the English garrison. They took up their quarters in the great barracks close to the Dockyard, but the enemy kept up such a perpetual shower of shells upon them from the north side, that it was deemed advisable to withdraw the troops for the time being, and simply leave strong pickets in different places near the water's edge. But in the course of a few days the Russians got less aggressive, and did not fire unless they saw numbers of men collected together, or groups of officers standing near the harbour; they appeared chiefly to turn their attention to strengthening their position on the north side, and for this purpose very large bodies of men were employed in erecting new earthworks, and improving those already made.

A commission of officers of the English and French armies was appointed to sit daily to apportion the immense quantities of stores which had fallen into the hands of the Allies by the capture of Sevastopol, such as guns, ammunition, anchors, and naval stores, including an amount of copper sheeting, church bells, etc.

Great was the rejoicing in England on the receipt of the intelligence announcing the fall of Sevastopol, and every place in the United Kingdom, from London to the smallest hamlet, made some demonstration in token of their joy and pleasure. The Queen directed her War Minister to express her approbation of the conduct of the British army during the whole of this memorable siege, and it was communicated to the troops in the Crimea by General Simpson in the General Orders of September 14th.* (footnote see page 263) Promotions, decorations, and rewards were given to the successful Generals of the allied armies. General Pélissier was made a Marshal of France, and General Simpson received the Grand Cross of the Bath. Colonel Windham was made Major-General for his distinguished gallantry at the attack on the Redan, and numerous officers were promoted and decorated.

Thus terminated the ever memorable siege of Sevastopol; in duration, far surpassing any other of modern times; and in material, calling forth resources never dreamt of before.

On September 17th, the Naval Brigade was ordered to rejoin the fleet, their services being no longer required. The important duties they had performed throughout the siege, and the cheerful manner in which they had been rendered, together with the courage and bravery displayed on every occasion during nearly a year of danger and hardship, entitle them to the admiration of their countrymen, and prove that the English Navy has not degenerated during 40 years of peace, and that the naval heroes of Sevastopol are worthy to be classed with those of the Nile and Trafalgar.

A few days after the fall of Sevastopol, the English Commander-in-Chief, for the first time finding it in his power to commence the construction of a high road from Balaklava to the front, had a large body of men employed for that purpose. At first, some 1500 were set apart for this duty, but by the beginning of October that number was increased to 6000 men daily. They laboured in conjunction with the Army Works Corps, under the able direction of its superintendent, Mr. Boyne. It was a work of great toil and difficulty: by the middle of October the number of men employed, including civilians, exceeded 10,000; but in spite of this large force, the main road from Balaklava to the English Headquarters (a distance of about six miles) was not opened until November 10th. It will thus be seen how utterly impossible it would have been to have spared a sufficient number of men for the construction of a road, after the commencement of the siege, previous to the winter of 1854–55, when it took an average number of 8000 men, employed daily for seven weeks, to accomplish this object, when no active operations were going on in the field.

About the middle of September a strong body of French light cavalry, mustering near 2000 horses, together with several battalions of infantry, the whole under the command of General d'Allouville, was transported from Kamiesch to Eupatoria, to aid the 30,000 Turkish troops under the command of Achmet Pasha. On September 24th and 25th, two slight engagements occurred between the allied (French and Turkish) troops and the Russians in the neighbourhood of Lake Sasik, but without any important result. The French cavalry distinguished themselves by a

---

* *Morning General Order, September 14th, 1855.* — The Commander of the Forces has great pleasure in publishing to the troops the following telegraphic message received from the Minister-at-War: —

London, Wednesday.

The Queen has received with deep emotion the welcome intelligence of the fall of Sevastopol, penetrated with profound gratitude to the Almighty, who has vouchsafed this triumph to the allied army.

Her Majesty has commanded me to express to yourself, and through you to her army, the pride with which she regards this fresh instance of their heroism.

The Queen congratulates her troops on the triumphant issue of their protracted siege, and thanks them for the cheerfulness and fortitude with which they have encountered its toils, and the valour which has led to its termination.

The Queen deeply laments that this success is not without its alloy in the heavy losses which have been sustained; and while she rejoices in the victory, Her Majesty deeply sympathises with the noble sufferers in their country's cause.

You will be pleased to congratulate General Pélissier, in Her Majesty's name, upon the brilliant success of the assault on the Malakoff, which proves the irresistible force, as well as the indomitable courage, of our brave allies.

(Signed)   PANMURE.

263

charge on the enemy, in which a Russian Colonel and 50 men were killed, and 150 made prisoners; they also captured a battery of artillery consisting of six pieces of ordnance and 12 artillery waggons, with their horses. The loss of the Allies was but trifling amounting to about 40 casualties.

Early in October Marshall Pélissier applied to the English Commander-in-Chief to reinforce the French cavalry at Eupatoria with a portion of the English. Accordingly, the Light Cavalry Brigade, under the command of Brigadier-General Lord George Paget, consisting of the 6th Dragoon Guards,* 4th and 13th Light Dragoons, and 12th Lancers, and also a troop of horse artillery, were landed at Eupatoria about the middle of October. They were attached to the French cavalry. The services they were called upon to perform were of an arduous though not very hazardous nature; they consisted chiefly in tedious reconnaissances to ascertain the enemy's position and strength, but without ever being regularly engaged, although on more than one occasion a few shots were exchanged. The most important of these was made on October 27th, from Eupatoria, when the troops did not return until the evening of the 29th, after having lost several horses which had died from exhaustion in consequence of the want of water, and having only ascertained the fact that the enemy had erected a few earthworks near the village of Tchobtar, behind which they were posted in considerable force. What rendered this position strong and unassailable by the Allies was, that a marsh extended for some way round the village, which was consequently only approachable at one or two places, and these the Russians had defended by heavy guns of position. The achievements at Eupatoria altogether were not such as could add fresh lustre to the allied arms. They, nevertheless, were of importance, as compelling the enemy to keep a large force to watch Eupatoria, and greatly harass them by obliging them to carry their supplies, which came in through Perekop for the Russian troops in the Crimea, by a road which ran father from the coast than the usual one from that place to Simferopol.

On October 7th, an expedition of French and English set sail from Kamiesch and Kazatch Bays, for the purpose of capturing the Russian fort of Kinburn. The reason for attacking this place was that it commanded the entrance to the estuary into which the rivers Dnieper and Bug empty themselves. Near the mouth of the former is situated the town of Kherson, which is some 60 miles from Kinburn; and at a distance of 25 miles up the last-named river is that of Nicholaieff, the great nursery of the Russian fleet in the Black Sea; for at this place were constructed almost the whole of the enemy's navy which perished in the harbour of Sevastopol. The English troops employed in this expedition consisted of a brigade of the 4th Division under the command of Brigadier-General Hon. A. Spencer, composed of the 17th, 20th, 21st, 57th and 63rd Regiments, besides a force of artillery, engineers, and Royal Marines, amounting altogether to about 5000 men, of whom 1350 were marines belonging to the line-of-battle ships. These were embarked on board the English fleet which comprised six ships of the line, 17 frigates, 16 gun

* The 6th Dragoon Guards (Carabineers) were under orders for India two years previous to the war with Russia, and it was then thought advisable by the Horse Guards to change them into a regiment of light cavalry, which was accordingly done, as regards their dress and accoutrements, though they retained the appellation of Dragoon Guards, which to the uninitiated would signify that they were still heavy cavalry.

and mortar boats, and some dozen transports, the whole being steam-vessels. The French military force was somewhat stronger than the English, and was under the command of General Bazaine. They were embarked on board the French fleet, consisting of several line-of-battle ships and frigates, besides three large floating batteries. In order to mislead the enemy, the expedition anchored off Odessa on the 9th, and there remained within sight of the town a few days; but again leaving it, arrived off Kinburn on October 16th. The following telegraphic despatch, received by the English Commander-in-Chief from Rear-Admiral Sir Edmund Lyons, will in a few words describe the success of the Allies: —

Royal Albert, off the Mouth of the Dnieper
October 17th, 1855.

The three forts on the Kinburn Spit, mounting upwards of 70 guns, and garrisoned by 1300 men under the command of Major-General Kokonovitch, have this day capitulated to the Allied forces.

The day before yesterday a flotilla of gun-vessels forced an entrance into the Dnieper, and the allied troops landed on the Spit to the southward of the forts; thus, by these simultaneous operations, the retreat of the garrison and the arrival of reinforcements were effectually cut off, so that the forsts, being bombarded today by the mortar-vessels, gun-vessels, and French floating-batteries, and being closely commanded by the steam line-of-battle ships and frigates, having only two feet of water under their keels, were soon obliged to surrender.

The casualties in the fleets were very few; but the enemy had 45 killed and 130 wounded.

A steam-squadron, under the orders of Rear-Admirals Stewart and Pellion, lies at anchor in the Dnieper, and commands the entrance of Nicholaieff and Kherson. The forts are occupied by the allied troops. The prisoners will be sent to Constantinople immediately.

The stores found in the fort were considerable: more than 90 dismounted guns, independent of those in battery, were captured, besides upwards of 25,000 missiles and 120,000 cartridges: two rafts of fine timber, were also taken by the English fleet.

On the morning of the 18th, the fort of Otchakoff, on the point of land on the opposite side of the estuary, was blown up by the Russians, the garrison retreating to Nicholaieff. After the occupation of Kinburn by the English and French military force for a few days, a reconnaissance was made by a portion of the troops under General Bazaine. This occupied three days, but, with the exception of burning a few villages and exchanging occasional shots with the Cossacks who hovered round the allied troops, nothing more of importance was effected. On October 27th, Generals Bazaine and Spencer selected the troops which were to form the permanent garrison, the fort being again placed in a good state of repair. Almost all the English troops and a large portion of the French were then re-embarked, and returned to Sevastopol early in November, leaving their comrades and a few ships of war, English and French, to guard the estuary and make preparations for the ensuing winter.

Shortly after the capture of Sevastopol, General Sir James Simpson tendered his resignation to the English Government, but it was some time before it was accepted, chiefly, it is said, in consequence of the difficulty of deciding who should succeed him. However, on November 10th, Sir James Simpson announced to the army that his resignation had been accepted, and that General Sir W. Codrington (who had been promoted to that rank for the purpose) was to be his successor. The next day Sir William Codrington took command of the army.

His advent to power was ushered in by an untoward catastrophe; for on November 13th, but two days after he had assumed the command, the French *parc de siège*, near Inkermann, blew up about three in the afternoon, causing also the explosion of a large quantity of ammunition in the English right siege train, which was contiguous to it. It was never satisfactorily ascertained how the explosion originated, though a French officer of high rank affirmed that some artillerymen were smoking during the removal of barrels of gunpowder in the *parc de siège*. The loss to the Allies in this unfortunate affair was severe, although not so great as might have been expected: the English had 27 killed and 106 wounded, while the French loss amounted to upwards of 240 casualties.

Soon after the occupation of Sevastopol by the Allies, orders were given to the engineer officers of the English and French armies to make arrangements for the total destruction of the remaining Russian forts, docks, barracks, and public buildings in the town. Accordingly a division was made of the principal works between the commanding engineers of the two armies. It was a labour of some months before this undertaking was completed. The principal works destroyed were: —the Great Docks, in the Karabelnaia suburb; blown up piecemeal, the first explosion taking place on December 23rd, 1855, and the final explosion on February 1st, 1856. Fort Nicholas was blown up on February 4th; Fort Alexander on the 11th; the aqueduct (which conveyed the water supply for the docks from the Tchernaya river, near the village of Tchorgoun) on the 12th; and the White Works on the 28th. The Great Barracks were destroyed during the same month.

During the winter the British army was brought into a very high state of discipline. The recruits that were sent out from England, barely trained to fire off their rifles properly, were constantly drilled, and practised both in firing and manoeuvring in the field, so that by the spring a finer body of troops could not have been found in Europe than those who formed the British force under Sir William Codrington's command. Well-fed, well-clothed, and well-sheltered, with no harassing duty to perform, the English soldiers were a great contrast to those of the previous winter; no one would have taken the smart, healthy, clean troops on the plateau of Sevastopol in January, 1856, to have been of the same race and nation as the careworn, overworked, and sickly soldiers guarding the trenches in January, 1855. But it must be remembered that it was to the patient long-suffering, and courageous conduct of these same careworn, hardworked, and sickly soldiers of the winter of 1854–55, that the English army was indebted for the ease and comfort with which they passed the winter of 1855–56.

Such was unfortunately not the case with the French, for disease made dreadful havoc in their army, and death sadly thinned their ranks. The commissariat and medical department, which had been so often extolled during the active operations of the last campaign, and which were being perpetually held up by the English press as models to be imitated by the British Government, all at once appeared in their true light. From the accounts of all who witnessed it, nothing could be worse than the state of the French army during the first quarter of the year 1856. They appear to have been indifferently fed and badly clothed; typhus fever raging at the time among them drove immense numbers into hospital, where their state was truly deplorable. The ambulances were so dreadfully crowded, the medical officers so overworked, that many of their patients were necessarily neglected, added to which there was the greatest want of the most ordinary medicines, and a perfect dearth of medical comforts and even necessities. In the months of January, February, and March, 1856, between 30,000 and 40,000 men of the French army were acknowledged by the authorities to have died of disease, this being over one-fifth of their force in the East.* Yet during the severest weather of the months of December, January, and February, 1854–55, when the English army was suffering its greatest hardships, and its most severe loss from sickness and disease, the deaths *in proportion* were not quite one-tenth of the strength of the British force then in the East. During the war in the East the English loss was as follows: —

	Killed in Action.	Died of their Wounds.	Died of Disease.	Total.
Officers ..	158	51	55	264
Men	1775	1870	15,669	19,314
Total ..	1933	1921	15,724	19,578

It would appear also that 2873 men were discharged from the service in consequence of being incapacitated from disease or wounds; which makes a total loss during the two years of the war (from March 31st, 1854, to March 31st, 1856) of 264 officers and 22,187 men. As regards the Russian losses, it is quite impossible to speak with any accuracy; they have been variously stated at from 500,000 to 800,000 men; and enormous as this number may appear at first sight, the medium is perhaps not far from the truth. The Russian General commanding in Sevastopol, after the peace, admitted that 250,000 of his countrymen were buried in its neighbourhood, and that during the winter of 1854–55 the regiments which arrived from Central Russia, to reinforce the army of the Crimea, lost on the line of march from a third to one half of their number. If this be true, it will testify better than anything to the sacrifice the Russian nation made to the ambition of its Emperor, Nicholas I.

During the first months of the present year (1856), negotiations were commenced between the belligerent powers for arranging a congress to take into consideration the proposals offered to them by Austria, as a basis for terms of peace.** After a

* Vide Appendix E.

** The immediate reason assigned for the Emperor's ready acquiescence in the Austrian proposals, which but a few months before he had summarily rejected, was said to be as follows. During his stay at Nicholaieff, towards the close of the year 1855, he received intelligence from General Lüders that, in consequence of the incessant vertical fire of the Allies from the town of Sevastopol, the northern forts were untenable. Upon this the Emperor determined to visit the north side, and judge for himself as to its capability of holding out longer. He found on his arrival that General Lüders's report was perfectly correct, for, out of the casemates constructed for 15,000 men, there were scarcely any that were not riddled with shot, or honeycombed by the constant volleys of shells thrown from the English and French batteries on the southern side of the harbour. The Russian Emperor, seeing the impracticability of further resistance at this point, sent orders to his Plenipotentiary at Vienna to accept the Austrian proposals as a basis of negotiations for terms of peace with the allied belligerent powers.

considerable delay, it was at length settled that Paris should be the scene of the conference, and that each power should send two representatives. Accordingly, the first meeting of the congress took place at the hotel of the Minister of Foreign Affairs at Paris on February 25th. The representatives commenced by arranging an armistice, which was to expire by March 31st. It was not until two days before that date that the terms of peace were finally agreed to, and they were signed on March 30th, 1856.

Thus ended the war between the Allies—England, France, Turkey, and Sardinia—and Russia: a war which, although short, yet,—from the efforts it has called forth beyond all former parallel and precedent;—from the new light it has thrown upon the attack and defence of fortified places;—from the probable series of weighty political issues it will have effected;—from the amount of brilliant and heroic courage that was displayed;—and, above all, from the circumstance of two ancient rivals fighting side by side (in the cause of justice, against tyranny and oppression), linking thus, at least in honourable partnership, the prominent nations of our globe;—will be handed down to the end of time, as one of the most memorable since its beginning.

APPENDICES

Weekly State of Arm

| | OFFICERS. | | | | SERJEANTS. | | | | | | | TRUMPETERS | | | |
	Field Officers.	Captains.	Subalterns.	Staff.	Present. Under Arms.	Present. Otherwise employed.	Sick. Present.	Sick. Absent.	Command.	Prisoners of War and Missing.	Total.	Present. Under Arms.	Present. Otherwise employed.	Sick. Present.	Sick. Absent.
Mounted Staff.	..	1	2	..	2	..	..	..	1	..	3	..	..	..	..
Cavalry Division	16	29	39	46	125	45	9	14	15	..	208	28	..	1	2
Infantry .	85	246	391	218	1293	165	150	406	134	2	2150	488	2	35	106
Ambulance .	1	1	1	1	. 6	..	..	1	3	..	10	..	..	..	1
ARTILLERY.															
Staff. . . .	7	12	..	5	27	..	..	2	..	..	29	..	..	..	..
Field Batteries .	..	16	25	10	52	..	..	5	..	..	57	11	..	1	1
Siege Train .	..	28	34	4	66	1	3	8	1	..	79	26	..	1	2
Total .	7	56	59	19	145	1	3	13	1	..	163	37	..	2	3
Royal Engineers, Sappers, and Miners	4	9	15	6	19	2	3	4	20	..	48	12	..	..	..

| ORDNANCE. | SIEGE GUNS. | | | | | | | | | FIELD GUNS. | | | | |
	10-inch.	8-inch.	68-pounders.	32-pounders.	24-pounders.	9-pounder Field guns.	13-inch Mortars.	10-inch Mortars.	Total.	9-pounders.	24-pounder Howitzers.	6-pounders.	12-pounder Howitzers.	Total.
	2	15	6	62	24	2	8	14	135	36	18	4	2	60

of March, 1855.

...MMERS.			RANK AND FILE.							HORSES.			
			Present.		Sick.								
Command.	Prisoners of War and Missing.	Total.	Under Arms.	Batmen and otherwise employed.	Present.	Absent.	Command.	Prisoners of War and Missing.	Total.	Present.	Sick.	Command.	Total.
..	..	..	15	1	..	9	12	..	37	18	6	31	55
2	..	33	989	233	140	312	114	1	1,789	315	323	82	720
8	..	639	15,920	1854	3394	9476	1713	64	32,421	..	..	..	..
..	..	1	85	..	4	66	41	..	196	..	..	..	..
										Native Horses.			
..	..	..	..	68	..	..	..	..	68	51	12	..	
..	..	13	1,196	..	175	307	..	3	1,681	749	290		
..	..	29	1,608	6	90	291	..	..	1,995	17	73		
..	..	42	2,804	74	265	598	..	3	3,744	817	375		
2	..	14	406	43	37	76	106	..	668	..	..	..	

GRAND TOTAL.

Cavalry and Infantry.		Ordnance Corps.		Whole Army.	
Officers	1,077	Officers	175	Men	43,318
Serjeants	2,371	Serjeants	211	Horses	1,967
Trumpeters, &c.	673	Drummers	56	Guns	195
Rank and File	34,443	Rank and File	4,412		
Horses	775	Horses	1,192		

| | OFFICERS. | | | | SERJEANTS. | | | | | | | TRUMPETERS | | | |
| | | | | | Present. | | Sick. | | | | | Present. | | Sick. | |
	Field Officers.	Captains.	Subalterns.	Staff.	Under Arms.	Otherwise employed.	Present.	Absent.	Command.	Prisoners of War and Missing.	Total.	Under Arms.	Otherwise employed.	Present.	Absent.
Mounted Staff.	1	1	2	..	2	..	..	..	1	..	3	..	..	..	..
Cavalry Division	21	43	70	·58	211	65	12	10	13	..	311	52	..	4	..
Infantry .	105	317	475	246	1576	204	136	307	99	1	2323	595	4	33	61
Ambulance .	1	1	1	1	2	..	..	..	1	..	3	..	..	..	..
ARTILLERY.															
Staff. . . .	9	15	..	..	38	..	..	2	..	..	40	..	..	..	..
Field Batteries and Ball cartridge Brigade }	..	22	36	15	71	..	..	1	..	..	72	16	..	1	1
Siege Train .	..	38	56	5	80	1	2	8	1	..	92	28	..	..	2
Total .	9	75	92	25	189	1	2	11	1	..	204	44	..	1	3
Royal Engineers, Sappers, and Miners }	3	4	11	5	15	2	6	3	22	..	48	11	1	..	..

| ORDNANCE. | SIEGE GUNS. | | | | | | | | FIELD GUNS. | | | | |
	10-inch.	8-inch.	68-pounders.	32-pounders.	9-pounder Field guns.	13-inch Mortars.	10-inch Mortars.	Total.	9-pounders.	24-pounder Howitzers.	18-pounders.	32-pounder Howitzers.	Total.
	8	46	8	49	2	26	17	156	44	22	4	4	74

of June, 1855.

MMERS.			RANK AND FILE.							HORSES.			
			Present.		Sick.								
Command.	Prisoners of War and Missing.	Total.	Under Arms.	Batmen and otherwise employed.	Present.	Absent.	Command.	Prisoners of War and Missing.	Total.	Present.	Sick.	Command.	Total.
..	..	..	11	1	1	6¹	14	..	33	32	10	12	54
2	..	58	2,138	305	212	92	136	1	2,884	1729	349	122	2200
2	..	695	22,329	2078	2477	6332	992	28	34,236	..	..	..	..
1	..	1	80	..	10	..	38	..	128	..	..	..	..
										Mules.			
..	..	..	..	77	..	..	..	..	77	65	..	..	..
..	..	18	2,370	..	127	158	1	..	2,656	2180	465		..
..	..	30	1,805	6	114	246	..	..	2,171	9	97		..
..	..	48	4,175	83	241	404	1	..	4,904	2254	562		..
2	..	14	315	28	61	48	138	..	590	..	..		..

GRAND TOTAL.

Cavalry and Infantry.		Ordnance Corps.		Whole Army.	
Officers	1,342	Officers	224	Men	48,039
Serjeants	2,640	Serjeants . ..	252	Horses	4,510
Drummers, &c. ..	754	Drummers	62	Mules	562
Rank and File ..	37,271	Rank and File ..	5,494	Guns . . .	230
Horses	2,256	Horses	2,254		
		Mules . ..	562		

APPENDIX C

Divisional After-Order.

September 7th, 1855.

No. 1. The Redan will be assaulted after the French have attacked the Malakoff. The Light and 2nd Divisions will share this important duty, each party respectively the half of each party.

The 2nd Brigade of Light Division, with an equal number from the 2nd Division, will form the first body of attack, each division furnishing—first, a covering party of 100 men, under a field officer; second, a storming party, carrying ladders, of 160 men, under a field officer (these men to be selected for this essential duty will be first to storm after they have placed the ladders); third, a storming party of 500 men, with two field officers; fourth, a working party of 100 men, with a field officer. The support will consist of the remainder of the brigade, to be immediately in the rear.

No. 2. The covering party will consist of 100 rank and file of the Rifle Brigade, 2nd Battalion, under the command of Captain Fyers, and will be formed on the extreme left of the fifth parallel, ready to move out steadily in extended order towards the Redan; their duty being to cover the advance of the ladder party and keep down the fire from the parapets.

No. 3. The first storming party of Light Division will consist of 100 men of the 97th Regiment, under the command of Major Welsford. This party will carry the ladders and be the first to storm; they will be formed in the new boyeau running from the centre of the fifth parallel; they will follow immediately in rear of the covering party; they must be good men and true to their difficult duty, which is to arrive at the ditch of the Redan and place the ladders down it, to turn 20 of them, so as to get up the face of the work, leaving the other 20 ladders for others to come down by.

No. 4. The next storming party will consist of 200 men of the 97th Regiment, under the command of the Lieutenant-Colonel the Hon. H. R. Handcock, and 300 of the 90th Regiment, under the command of Captain R. Grove. This party will be stationed in the fifth parallel, and will assemble in a column of divisions at one place. The Light Division will lead the whole column of attack, which will be formed of divisions of 20 files, and so be told off.

No. 5. The supports, consisting of 750 men of the 19th and 88th Regiments (with part of the 2nd Division) on the left, will be placed as they stand in brigade, in the third parallel, whence they will move into the fifth parallel so soon as the assault is made by those in front of them.

No. 6. The working party of 100 men will be furnished by the 90th Regiment, under Captain Perrin, and be placed in No. 2 and 3 left boyeaus; they will receive afterwards instructions from an officer of the Engineers.

No. 7. The remainder of the Light and 2nd Divisions will form a reserve; Light Division in right boyeau, between third and fourth parallels; 2nd Division in the left boyeau, between the third and fourth parallels.

No. 8. The Highland Division will be formed in that part of the third parallel in communication with the French right attack and middle ravine.

APPENDIX D

Table of English Batteries and Expenditure of Ammunition

| | ARMAMENT. | | | | | | | | | | TOTAL. | EXPENDITURE | |
| | Mortars. | | | | Guns. | | | | | | | Mortars | |
	13-inch.	10-inch.	8-inch.	5½-inch.	Lancaster.	24-pounder.	32-pounder.	8-inch.	10-inch.	68-pounder.		13-inch.	10-inch.
17 Oct. 1854	..	10	..	..	4	30	7	16	..	5	72	..	2,745
9 April, 1855	20	16	..	..	..	20	42	15	4	6	123	5,519	4,922
6 June, 1855	27	17	..	..	..	..	49	46	8	8	155	8,271	5,543
17 June, 1855	30	17	8	..	..	..	49	46	8	8	166	2,286	884
17 Aug. 1855	33	24	7	20	1	..	53	46	8	4	196	5,976	5,267
8 Sept. 1855	34	27	10	20	2	..	61	37	7	6	204	6,677	4,860
											9-pr. field guns.	28,729	24,221
Total number in use during the siege }	35	35	11	20	7	57	140	76	10	7	3	Total.	
Unserviceable from use. }	1	5	..	1	3	29	100	36	1	2	..		
Destroyed by the enemy or by accidents. }	4	2	..	..	..	25	32	25	2	3	1		
Remaining	30	28	11	19	4	3	8	15	7	2	2		
Expended at intermediate times												10,607	13,122
Total expended during the siege												39,336	37,343

	Tons.	cwts.	qrs.	lbs.
Total weight of Shot and Shell expended	9053	14	1	9
,, Powder expended	1239	3	3	26

the several Bombardments of Sevastopol.

| AMMUNITION. | | | | | | | | TOTAL. | ORDNANCE. | |
| Mortars. | | Guns. | | | | | | | Manned by Navy. | Manned by Artillery. |
8-inch.	5¼-inch.	Lancaster.	24-pounder.	32-pounder.	8-inch.	10-inch.	68-pounder.			
..	..	370	7,112	5,711	5,943	..	..	21,881	..	..
..	..	..	8,679	5,539	1,604	640	3730	30,633	49	74
..	..	..	..	5,627	12,300	1142	..	32,883	56	98
..	..	..	..	9,746	6,712	1706	1350	22,684	51	115
..	906	..	..	6,984	6,500	492	145	26,270	55	141
870	314	..	..	9,894	4,111	254	1496	28,476	49	158
870	1220	370	15,791	43,501	37,170	4234	6721	162,827	. . . Total.	
Light balls, 300; carcases, 105—from 17th Aug. to 8th Sept.								405		
From 9-pounders in advanced trenches at intermediate times.								682		
2304	3627	1172	12,713	22,375	20,161	1877	..	88,640		
3174	4847	1542	28,504	65,876	57,331	6111	6721	251,872		

Total issued 300,892

Remaining in Battery 49,425

APPENDIX E

*Extracts from an Article which appeared in the 'Medical Times and Gazette',
on Saturday, June 14th, 1856.*

Mortality in the French army . . . . . . For the truth of the following statements
we have the authority of medical officers both in our own and the French service,
and have permission to name them, if need be. They are not only interesting in
themselves, but additionally so, as the facts have been studiously concealed by the
French Government, and are now made known for the first time in this country.

1. There were 14 French hospitals in the Bosphorus up to the end of March, since
then three others have been added. The following is a copy of an official return of
the patients treated in all the hospitals in January, February, and March, 1856: —

January	13,520
February	21,309
March	18,167

2. During the 10 days ending on the 20th of March, 1009 *patients died*, and
during the following 10 days 948 *patients died* in these hospitals. The number of
sick under treatment, for all diseases, on March 20th, was 11,366, and on the 30th,
9763.

3. The aggregate loss by death from sickness (being from typhus) in the French
hospitals on the Bosphorus exceeded 10,000 during the first quarter of 1856.

The daily mortality in 12 of these hospitals, in January and February, ranged up
to 240.

4. From January 1st to March 17th, when the transport of typhus cases from the
Crimea was discontinued authoritatively, more than 5000 deaths occurred on
board French transports and men-of-war, between the Crimea and the Bosphorus.

5. In the Crimea there were 14 field-hospitals or ambulances during the same
period, each containing from 800 to 1100 sick. The deaths in each varied from 15
to 20 daily. Thus the aggregate loss by death from disease in these hospitals, during
this period, exceeded 19,000, and is believed to have been little under 25,000.

6. It is *known* that more than 34,000 French soldiers of the army of the East died from disease during the months of January, February, and March, 1856. It is *believed* by those able to judge that those deaths exceeded 40,000.

7. 64 French surgeons have died in the Crimea and on the Bosphorus since last November. Of 362 surgeons of all ranks who have served with the French army since its landing in Gallipoli in the autumn of 1854 to April, 1856, 72 have died from typhus alone.

8. On March 15th, 1856, there were, in the officers' hospital at Constantinople, 31 surgeons in different stages of typhus, and only one combatant officer.

9. Of 840 hospital orderlies and attendants employed in the 60 days of January and February, 603 were attacked by typhus when on service. . . . Why should typhus have arisen in the French camp, and not in ours? Why did it spread so awfully after it had originated? . . . The condition of the French soldier in camp sufficiently accounts for the *origin* of the epidemic. He was crowded in tents or huts, imperfectly warmed and insufficiently ventilated, upon ground soddened by the products of animal and vegetable decomposition. He was attenuated by want of sufficient food, affected by scurvy from the *quality* of the food he did receive. The same causes led to like results with us the year before. We removed them, and our army has been ever since in the highest health and efficiency. Our allies continued in our former erroneous path, and lost a fourth of their army in three months. The condition of the ambulances, transports, and hospitals accounts for the rapid *spread* of the epidemic. The French surgeons admit that the condition of the places to which the sick were first sent for treatment was horrible. The huts and tents were overcrowded; the only latrine was a cask. The beds were the lits-de-camp for two persons; the beds and bed clothes were unchanged for several months. When a patient died, no matter of what disease, his bed was occupied by a fresh arrival. There were no trained attendants; the only nurses were soldiers fit for no other duty, and, of course, *unfit* for the office. The duties of nightwatching were added to those of day attendance; patients were therefore unavoidably neglected. Typhus affected *nine-tenths of all the patients who passed through the ambulances*. In all the transports the sick were so over-crowded that the French medical officers, when defending the practice of removing the sick from the Crimea, could only say that it was better to take them on board than to leave them dying on the beach at

Kamiesch. Everyone who has visited the French hospitals on the Bosphorus lately agrees in stating that, with the exception of the officers' hospital, they are over-crowded; that the ill effects of crowding are not diminished by free ventilation; that the patients themselves, their bedding and clothing, and the floors, walls, and windows of the buildings are offensively dirty; that the latrines, etc., are odious: and that the supply of medical officers and their attendants is insufficient. No one who has witnessed the admirable conduct of the French army surgeons can conceal the admiration he feels for the courage, zeal, and self-sacrifice they have shown in the discharge of their duties. But they have been overworked and unsupported. The following is an instance. The Hospital de Pera has beds for 2400 sick, besides officers and attendants. On March 1st last there were only a few unoccupied beds, left so by the deaths of the preceding 24 hours. The medical staff consisted of three first-class and three second-class surgeons and four assistants. According to Imperial ordonnance, there *should have been* 24 qualified surgeons and half this number of clerks and dressers (sous-aides). The chief, Dr. Cambay, had sole charge of 203 beds, assisted only by one aide-major and a civil surgeon, an Italian. The smallest number under the care of one surgeon was 153. During the morning visit on March 1st, from 7 to 9.30 a.m., Dr. Cambay actually dictated the diet and treatment of 196 sick, many of them being acute cases. But the surgeons are not only overworked; their position is such that they cannot enforce obedience to their orders. They are strictly confined to the *art of healing*; in all other matters they are made subordinate to the Intendance. They cannot thin or ventilate a crowded ward, obtain a change of bed or body linen for a patient, or alter the diet, without the permission of the Intendant. . . . Our correspondent writes that the influence of the Intendance prevented the segregation of the fever cases, and thus led to the spread of the disease by contagion.

INDEX